First World War

and Army of Occupation

War Diary

France, Belgium and Germany

36 DIVISION
107 Infantry Brigade
Headquarters
20 October 1915 - 31 March 1919

WO95/2502/1

The Naval & Military Press Ltd
www.nmarchive.com
Published in association with The National Archives

Published by

The Naval & Military Press Ltd

Unit 10 Ridgewood Industrial Park,

Uckfield, East Sussex,

TN22 5QE England

Tel: +44 (0) 1825 749494

www.naval-military-press.com

www.nmarchive.com

This diary has been reprinted in facsimile from the original. Any imperfections are inevitably reproduced and the quality may fall short of modern type and cartographic standards.

Contents

Document type	Place/Title	Date From	Date To
Heading	WO95/2502/1		
Heading	36th Division 107th Infy Bde Bde Headquarters Oct 1915 Mar 1919 1915 Oct-1919 Mar		
Heading	36 Div Attached 4th Division War Diaries 107th Infantry Bde H.Q. 1915 Oct.-1916 Jan		
Heading	107th Inf Bde. 4th Division. 107th Infantry Brigade Headquarters. November 1915		
Heading	Fourth Division Transferred For 36th (Ulster) Div on Nov. 2nd 107th Infantry Brigade I.A Nov. 1915		
War Diary	Trenches	08/11/1915	12/11/1915
War Diary	To Acheux	13/11/1915	18/11/1915
War Diary	Mailly Maillet	23/11/1915	25/11/1915
War Diary	Acheux	26/11/1915	30/11/1915
War Diary	To Trenches (Mailly)	19/11/1915	22/11/1915
Heading	107th Inf Bde 4th Division. 107th Infantry Brigade Headquarters December 1915		
War Diary	Acheux	01/12/1915	01/12/1915
War Diary	Acheux To Trenches At Mailly	02/12/1915	02/12/1915
War Diary	Mailly	03/12/1915	07/12/1915
War Diary	To Acheux	08/12/1915	08/12/1915
War Diary	Acheux	09/12/1915	12/12/1915
War Diary	To Trenches (Mailly)	13/12/1915	13/12/1915
War Diary	Mailly	14/12/1915	16/12/1915
War Diary	To Acheux	17/12/1915	18/12/1915
War Diary	Acheux	19/12/1915	20/12/1915
War Diary	To Trenches (Mailly)	21/12/1915	21/12/1915
War Diary	Mailly	22/12/1915	24/12/1915
War Diary	To Acheux	25/12/1915	28/12/1915
War Diary	To Trenches (Mailly)	29/12/1915	29/12/1915
War Diary	Trenches At Mailly	30/12/1915	31/12/1915
Heading	107 Inf Bde. 4th Division. This Bde Rejoined 36th Division 7.2.1916 107th Infantry Brigade Headquarters. January 1916		
Heading	4th Div Rejoined 36 Div 7.2.16 107th Inf BDe Vol 3 Jan 16		
War Diary	Trenches At Mailly	01/01/1916	05/01/1916
War Diary	Mailly	05/01/1916	31/01/1916
Heading	36th Division Oct. & Nov. 15 Transferred To IVth Div. Nov. 4th Rejoining XXXVIth Feb. 7th 107th Inf Bde Vol I		
War Diary	Vignacourt	20/10/1915	21/10/1915
War Diary	To St. Leger	22/10/1915	25/10/1915
War Diary	To Canaples	26/10/1915	01/11/1915
War Diary	On The March	02/11/1915	02/11/1915
War Diary	To Acheux	03/11/1915	06/11/1915
War Diary	To Trenches (Mailly)	07/11/1915	07/11/1915
War Diary	Mailly	01/02/1916	26/02/1916
War Diary	Acheux	27/02/1916	29/02/1916
War Diary	Harponville	01/05/1916	08/05/1916
War Diary	To Martinsart	09/05/1916	31/05/1916

War Diary	Acheux	01/03/1916	02/03/1916
War Diary	Mailly	03/03/1916	30/03/1916
War Diary	Mailly To Puchevillers	30/03/1916	30/03/1916
War Diary	Puchevillers	31/03/1916	19/04/1916
War Diary	Harponville	20/04/1916	30/04/1916
Heading	36th Division. B.H.Q. 107th Infantry Brigade June 1916		
War Diary	Martinsart	01/06/1916	22/06/1916
War Diary	To Varennes	23/06/1916	27/06/1916
War Diary	Forceville	28/06/1916	29/06/1916
Heading	36th Division. B.H.Q. 107th Infantry Brigade July 1916		
War Diary	Thiepval Wood	01/07/1916	03/07/1916
War Diary	Martinsart	03/07/1916	03/07/1916
War Diary	Harponville	04/07/1916	04/07/1916
War Diary	Rubempre	05/07/1916	09/07/1916
War Diary	Bernaville	10/07/1916	10/07/1916
War Diary	Wardrecques	11/07/1916	12/07/1916
War Diary	La Panne	13/07/1916	19/07/1916
War Diary	Volkeringkove	20/07/1916	20/07/1916
War Diary	Wormhoudt	21/07/1916	21/07/1916
War Diary	St Marie Cappel	22/07/1916	22/07/1916
War Diary	Steenwerck	23/07/1916	27/07/1916
War Diary	Bailleul	28/07/1916	30/07/1916
War Diary	Trenches	31/07/1916	29/10/1916
Miscellaneous	Report On Raid By 10th R. Irish Rifles.		
War Diary	Trenches E Of Wulverghem	30/09/1916	30/09/1916
War Diary	Trenches	01/10/1916	13/11/1916
War Diary	Wulverghem Sector	14/11/1916	30/11/1916
Miscellaneous	Headquarters. 36th Division "G"	02/01/1917	02/01/1917
War Diary	Wulverghem Sector	01/12/1916	04/12/1916
War Diary	Wulverghem	05/12/1916	09/12/1916
War Diary	Wulverghem Sector	10/12/1916	07/01/1917
War Diary	Wulverghem	08/01/1917	16/01/1917
War Diary	Wulverghem Sector	17/01/1917	27/01/1917
War Diary	Bailleul	28/01/1917	25/02/1917
War Diary	English Fm.	26/02/1917	26/02/1917
War Diary	Douve Sector	27/02/1917	28/02/1917
Miscellaneous	Roll Of Officer Casualties Of 107th Infantry Brigade During Month Of June 1917		
War Diary	Douve Sector	01/03/1917	14/03/1917
War Diary	Spanbroek Sector	15/03/1917	24/03/1917
Map	Second Army Barrage Map June, 1917		
Miscellaneous	Enemy Attitude During The Tour. Appendix 16	28/06/1917	28/06/1917
Miscellaneous	Plan Of Attack And Account Of Operations Which Took Place On 7th June 1917 Appendix V	07/06/1917	07/06/1917
Miscellaneous	Statement Of Casualties Which Occurred In 107th Infantry Brigade During Month Of June 1917 Appendix XVI		
War Diary	Spanbroek Sector	25/03/1917	07/04/1917
War Diary	Dranoutre	08/04/1917	14/04/1917
War Diary	Hazebrouck	15/04/1917	15/04/1917
War Diary	Arques	16/04/1917	16/04/1917
War Diary	Westbecourt	17/04/1917	19/04/1917
War Diary	Boisdinghem	20/04/1917	30/04/1917
War Diary	Hazebrouck	01/05/1917	01/05/1917
War Diary	Meteren	02/05/1917	13/05/1917

War Diary	Dranoutre	14/05/1917	31/05/1917
War Diary	S.5.d.60.70 Dranoutre	01/06/1917	01/06/1917
War Diary	Berthen Area	02/06/1917	05/06/1917
War Diary	Dranoutre S.5.d.60.70	06/06/1917	06/06/1917
War Diary	In The Line	07/06/1917	07/06/1917
War Diary	M.26.B.4.1	08/06/1917	08/06/1917
War Diary	S.5.d.6.7.	09/06/1917	09/06/1917
War Diary	S.4.d.10.10	10/06/1917	16/06/1917
War Diary	S.4.d.1.1.	17/06/1917	19/06/1917
War Diary	In The Line Regent Dugouts	19/06/1917	28/06/1917
War Diary	Duttersteene	29/06/1917	04/07/1917
War Diary	Caestre	05/07/1917	05/07/1917
War Diary	Rennescure	06/07/1917	06/07/1917
War Diary	Westbecourt	07/07/1917	19/07/1917
War Diary	Esquerdes	20/07/1917	25/07/1917
War Diary	Looge-Hoek	26/07/1917	30/07/1917
War Diary	Watou No. 3 Area	31/07/1917	31/07/1917
War Diary	Watou Area	01/08/1917	01/08/1917
War Diary	Should raid Aug. 2nd C.Falls	08/08/1917	08/08/1917
War Diary	Wieltje	03/08/1917	08/08/1917
War Diary	Brandhoek	08/08/1917	12/08/1917
War Diary	Wieltje	13/08/1917	14/08/1917
War Diary	Brandhoek	15/08/1917	15/08/1917
War Diary	Mill Cotts	16/08/1917	16/08/1917
War Diary	Vlamertinghe	18/08/1917	18/08/1917
War Diary	Looge Hoek	19/08/1917	22/08/1917
War Diary	Barastre	23/08/1917	26/08/1917
War Diary	Neuville	27/08/1917	27/08/1917
War Diary	Metz	28/08/1917	31/08/1917
Miscellaneous	Report On Operations From 2nd To 18th August, 1917. Appendix XXXI	18/08/1917	18/08/1917
Map	Revised Map "A" To Accompany 36th Div. G.S.5/21/3		
Map	Frezenberg		
Miscellaneous	Appendix XIX		
War Diary	Metz	01/10/1917	19/11/1917
War Diary	Lechelle	19/11/1917	20/11/1917
War Diary	Havrincourt	20/11/1917	21/11/1917
War Diary	W Of Graincourt	21/11/1917	26/11/1917
War Diary	Hermies	27/11/1917	27/11/1917
War Diary	Barastre	27/11/1917	28/11/1917
War Diary	Berneville	29/11/1917	30/11/1917
War Diary	Courcelles-Le-Comte	30/11/1917	01/12/1917
War Diary	Beaulencourt	02/12/1917	02/12/1917
War Diary	Ytres	03/12/1917	04/12/1917
War Diary	Metz-En-Couture	05/12/1917	09/12/1917
War Diary	S. Of Marcoing (in Old Hindenburg Front Line)	09/12/1917	14/12/1917
War Diary	S. Of Marcoing	14/12/1917	14/12/1917
War Diary	Metzen Couture	15/12/1917	15/12/1917
War Diary	Manancourt	15/12/1917	17/12/1917
War Diary	Ivergny	17/12/1917	27/12/1917
War Diary	Corbie	28/12/1917	07/01/1918
War Diary	Rosieres	08/01/1918	09/01/1918
War Diary	Voyennes	10/01/1918	10/01/1918
War Diary	Estouilly	11/01/1918	12/01/1918
War Diary	L'Epine De Dallon. A.3.d.70.20	13/01/1918	13/01/1918
War Diary	L'Epine De Dallon.	14/01/1918	10/02/1918

War Diary	Hamel Lock	10/02/1918	15/02/1918
War Diary	Dury	16/02/1918	20/02/1918
War Diary	Gd. Seraucourt	22/02/1918	28/02/1918
War Diary	Grand Seraucourt	01/03/1918	31/03/1918
Heading	36th Division. B.H.Q. 107th Infantry Brigade March 1918		
Miscellaneous	Narrative Of Operations Commending 21st March, 1918 Appendix VI	21/03/1918	21/03/1918
Operation(al) Order(s)	107th Infantry Brigade Order No. 221 Appendix I	03/03/1918	03/03/1918
Operation(al) Order(s)	107th Infantry Brigade Order No. 222 Appendix II	04/03/1918	04/03/1918
Operation(al) Order(s)	107th Infantry Brigade Order No. 223 Appendix III	12/03/1918	12/03/1918
Operation(al) Order(s)	107th Infantry Brigade Order No. 224 Appendix IV	20/03/1918	20/03/1918
Miscellaneous	107th Brigade No. S.614 Appendix V		
Miscellaneous	107th Infantry Brigade Defence Scheme	01/03/1918	01/03/1918
Miscellaneous	Artillery Arrangements Appendix IV		
Miscellaneous	Battle Stragglers' Posts Appendix "P"		
Heading	36th Division. B.H.Q. 107th Infantry Brigade April 1918		
War Diary	Feuquieres	01/04/1918	03/04/1918
War Diary	Hospital Fm	05/04/1918	05/04/1918
War Diary	Alberta	07/04/1918	12/04/1918
War Diary	Ref Sheet 28 C.25.b.1.2.	13/04/1918	18/04/1918
War Diary	(Gloucester Terrace, Canal Bank East)	19/04/1918	20/04/1918
War Diary	C.25.d.2.5. (Canal Bank West)	21/04/1918	27/04/1918
War Diary	Canal Bank West.	28/04/1918	30/04/1918
Operation(al) Order(s)	107th Infantry Brigade Order, No. 225. App I	03/04/1918	03/04/1918
Miscellaneous	Addendum No. 1 To 107th Inf. Brigade Order No. 226. App II	05/04/1918	05/04/1918
Operation(al) Order(s)	107th Infantry Brigade Order No. 226		
Miscellaneous	Table "A"		
Operation(al) Order(s)	107th Infantry Brigade Order No. 227. App III	05/04/1918	05/04/1918
Miscellaneous	Table "A"		
Operation(al) Order(s)	107th Infantry Brigade Order No. 226. App IV	09/04/1918	09/04/1918
Operation(al) Order(s)	107th Infantry Brigade Order No. 229. App V	11/04/1918	11/04/1918
Miscellaneous	Table "A" To Accompany 107th Infantry Brigade Order No. 229		
Miscellaneous	Copies To:		
Miscellaneous	Warning Order	11/04/1918	11/04/1918
Operation(al) Order(s)	107th Infantry Brigade Order No. 230. App VI	14/04/1918	14/04/1918
Operation(al) Order(s)	107th Infantry Brigade Order No. 231 Appendix VII	15/04/1918	15/04/1918
Operation(al) Order(s)	107th Infantry Brigade Order No. 232. Appendix VIII	17/04/1918	17/04/1918
Miscellaneous	Addendum No. 2 To 107th Infy. Bde. Order No. 232. Appendix VIII	17/04/1918	17/04/1918
Miscellaneous	107th Infantry Brigade, Defence Scheme. Appendix IX	17/04/1918	17/04/1918
Operation(al) Order(s)	107th Infantry Brigade Order No. 233. Appendix X	18/04/1918	18/04/1918
Operation(al) Order(s)	107th Infantry Brigade Order No. 234. Appendix XI	19/04/1918	19/04/1918
Miscellaneous	Appendix XII	21/04/1918	21/04/1918
Miscellaneous	107th Infantry Brigade Defence Scheme	21/04/1918	21/04/1918
Miscellaneous	107th Infantry Brigade Defence Scheme		
Operation(al) Order(s)	107th Infantry Brigade Order No. 236. Appendix XIII	21/04/1918	21/04/1918
Operation(al) Order(s)	107th Infantry Brigade Order No. 237. Appendix XIV	22/04/1918	22/04/1918
Operation(al) Order(s) Diagram etc	107th Infantry Brigade Order No. 237. Appendix XV	24/04/1918	24/04/1918
Operation(al) Order(s)	107th Infantry Brigade No. 240. Appendix XVI	26/04/1918	26/04/1918
Miscellaneous	Headquarters, 36th Division 'G'	21/05/1918	21/05/1918

Miscellaneous	107th Infantry Brigade. Narrative Of Operations During Month Of April, 1918		
War Diary	Canal Bank West	01/05/1918	13/05/1918
War Diary	Canal Bank	14/05/1918	18/05/1918
War Diary	A.22.B.5.5	19/05/1918	29/05/1918
War Diary	Canal Bank	30/05/1918	05/06/1918
War Diary	F.25.d. Janter Biezen	06/06/1918	12/06/1918
War Diary	Proven	13/06/1918	20/06/1918
War Diary	Tunnellers Camp	21/06/1918	29/06/1918
Operation(al) Order(s)	107th Infantry Brigade Order No. 249. Appendix I	01/06/1918	01/06/1918
War Diary	Tunnelling Camp	30/06/1918	30/06/1918
War Diary	Tunnellers Camp.	01/07/1918	02/07/1918
War Diary	St. Marie Cappel	03/07/1918	07/07/1918
War Diary	Sh. 27. R.33.b.5.1.	08/07/1918	14/07/1918
War Diary	Piebrouck	15/07/1918	31/07/1918
War Diary	Piebrouck. (Sh. 27. R.27.a.10.95)	01/08/1918	21/08/1918
War Diary	Piebrouck	21/08/1918	27/08/1918
War Diary	St. Marie Cappel	28/08/1918	31/08/1918
War Diary	Budget Copse (Mont Noir)	31/08/1918	01/09/1918
War Diary	St. Jans Cappel Chateau (M.32.a.00.20)	02/09/1918	02/09/1918
War Diary	S.18.a.50.65.	03/09/1918	05/09/1918
War Diary	T.19.b.90.90.	06/09/1918	15/09/1918
War Diary	Mont Des Cats.	16/09/1918	18/09/1918
War Diary	P.24.a.70.40.	19/09/1918	20/09/1918
War Diary	Esquelbecq	21/09/1918	26/09/1918
War Diary	Tunnelling Camp.	27/09/1918	27/09/1918
War Diary	'P' Camp.	28/09/1918	28/09/1918
War Diary	White Chateau	29/09/1918	29/09/1918
War Diary	Westhoek	30/09/1918	30/09/1918
War Diary	Terhand	01/10/1918	07/10/1918
War Diary	J.11.d.10.20.	08/10/1918	08/10/1918
War Diary	Polygonne Butt.	09/10/1918	13/10/1918
War Diary	Guinness Farm.	14/10/1918	14/10/1918
War Diary	Ashmore Farm.	14/10/1918	16/10/1918
War Diary	G.14.c.60.20. L.3.b.45.75.	16/10/1918	18/10/1918
War Diary	B.13.a.20.40.	19/10/1918	19/10/1918
War Diary	B.17.cent.	20/10/1918	20/10/1918
War Diary	C.20.c.30.40.	20/10/1918	24/10/1918
War Diary	C.20.a.40.30.	25/10/1918	26/10/1918
War Diary	Lendelede	27/10/1918	27/10/1918
War Diary	N.29.c.10.80.	28/10/1918	31/10/1918
Miscellaneous	Narrative Of Operations Carried Out By The 107th Inf. Bde. 28.9.1918 To 28.10.1918.	08/11/1918	08/11/1918
War Diary	Belleghem	01/11/1918	01/11/1918
War Diary	Reckem	02/11/1918	03/11/1918
War Diary	Mouscron	04/11/1918	31/03/1919

WO95/2502/1

36TH DIVISION

107TH INFY BDE

BDE HEADQUARTERS

OCT 1915 ~~&~~

~~FEB 1916~~-MAR 1919

1915 OCT - 1919 MAR

230 2

36 DIV

ATTACHED. 4th Division

War Diaries

104th Infantry Bde. H. Q.

~~November 1st 1915 to January~~

~~1915 - 16~~

1915 OCT ~~Nov~~ — 1916 JAN

107th Inf Bde.

4th Division.

This Bde was transfered from 36th Div on Nov 2nd 1915.

107th INFANTRY BRIGADE HEADQUARTERS.

N O V E M B E R   1 9 1 5

FOURTH DIVISION.

transferred from 36th (Ulster) Divn on Nov. 2nd.

107th INFANTRY BRIGADE.

I.A Nov. 1915

107th Infantry Brigade

Army Form C. 2118.

Instructions regarding War Diaries and Intelligence Summaries are contained in F. S. Regs., Part II. and the Staff Manual respectively. Title pages will be prepared in manuscript.

WAR DIARY
or
INTELLIGENCE SUMMARY.
(Erase heading not required.)

Place	Date	Hour	Summary of Events and Information	Remarks and references to Appendices
	November			
			relieved by 10th Infy Bde.	
Trenches	8th		In trenches in Left Sector of 4th Divisional Line	
-"-	9th			
-"-	10th			
-"-	11th			
-"-	12th			
To ACHEUX	13th		107th Bde was relieved by 10th Infy Bde + retired into Divisional Reserve as follows:- R Irish Fusks MAILLY. 10th R.I.R. FORCEVILLE 9th R.I.R. VARENNES 1st Rifle Bde ACHEUX 2nd Monmouths BEAUSSART.	
	14th		In Divisional Reserve.	
	15th			
	16th			
	17th			
	18th			
	[illegible]			

107th Infantry Brigade

Army Form C. 2118.

Instructions regarding War Diaries and Intelligence Summaries are contained in F. S. Regs., Part II. and the Staff Manual respectively. Title pages will be prepared in manuscript.

WAR DIARY
or
INTELLIGENCE SUMMARY.
(Erase heading not required.)

Place	Date	Hour	Summary of Events and Information	Remarks and references to Appendices
	November	1915		
MAILLY MAILLET	23rd		In trenches of Left Sector of 4th Divl line (vide attached trench maps) – Battns distributed as follows:– Right Sector (56-62) 9th R.I.R. Right Centre (63-74) 1st R Irish Fusrs. Left Centre (75-85) 10th R.I.R. Left (86-95) 1st Rifle Bde. 2nd Monmouths in Brigade Reserve at MAILLY. Captain M.F. DAY Kings Own Yorkshire Light Infantry took over the duties of Brigade Major 107th Infy Bde vice Major J.A. NIXON Royal Lancaster Regt.	[initials]
—"—	24th		In trenches – at 8 am the Enemy shelled the REDAN and AUCHONVILLERS with field guns.	
—"—	25th		In trenches.	
ACHEUX	26th		The Brigade was relieved by 10th Infy Bde at 6 P.m. & retired into Divisional Reserve as follows:– 9th RIR ACHEUX. 10th RIR VARENNES. R Irish Fusil. in FORCEVILLE. 1st Rifle Bde MAILLY. 2nd Monmouths Beaussart. Bde H.Q. ACHEUX.	
—"—	27th		In Divisional Reserve. } 500 men from Battns at Forceville & Varennes employed daily at work on Corps Line. 300 men of Beaussart & Mailly Battns employed on Divl second line. Remainder daily drills & route marches & musketry.	[initials]
—"—	28th		—"—	
—"—	29th		—"—	
—"—	30th		—"—	

T2134. Wt. W708—776. 500000. 4/15. Sir J. C. & S.

107th Infty Brigade

Army Form C. 2118.

Instructions regarding War Diaries and Intelligence Summaries are contained in F. S. Regs., Part II. and the Staff Manual respectively. Title pages will be prepared in manuscript.

WAR DIARY
or
INTELLIGENCE SUMMARY.
(Erase heading not required.)

Place	Date	Hour	Summary of Events and Information	Remarks and references to Appendices
	November			
To Trenches (MAILLY)	19th		The 107th Infty Bde Relieved 10th Infty Bde in the Left Sector of 4th Divisional Line.	
— " —	20th		In Trenches	
— " —	21st		In Trenches	
— " —	22nd		In Trenches	

T2134. Wt. W708—776. 500000. 4/15. Sir J. C. & S.

107th Inf Bde

4th Division.

107th INFANTRY BRIGADE HEADQUARTERS

D E C E M B E R   1 9 1 5

107th Infty Brigade

Army Form C. 2118.

Instructions regarding War Diaries and Intelligence Summaries are contained in F. S. Regs., Part II. and the Staff Manual respectively. Title pages will be prepared in manuscript.

WAR DIARY
or
INTELLIGENCE SUMMARY.
(Erase heading not required.)

Place	Date	Hour	Summary of Events and Information	Remarks and references to Appendices
	December 1915			
ACHEUX	1st		In Divl. Reserve. At 10 am. Officers of the Brigade attended a lecture at 4th Divl HQ. on use of gas Helmets.	[initials]
ACHEUX to Trenches at MAILLY	2nd		107th Infty Bde relieved 10th Infty Bde in the Trenches at 6 P.m. Distribution of Battns the same as last tour. Owing to the very wet state of the trenches Battns found great difficulty in taking over. Several men having to be dug out of the mud. 2 Coys of 11th S Lancs Pioneers attached to Brigade for instruction & placed in Reserve at MAILLY.	[initials]
MAILLY	3rd		In Trenches. Our Artillery Bombarded the German lines at 10 am. doing considerable damage. Very little retaliation. 1 Coy 11th S Lancs sent into trenches with 1st Rifle Bde & one Coy to R Irish Fusiliers.	[initials]
MAILLY	4th		In Trenches. } Trenches in very wet state & Communication Trenches mostly flooded & impassable. Our Bombing Patrols have been very active in raiding the Enemy Trenches. Very little retaliation by Germans.	[initials]
—"—	5th		—"—	
—"—	6th		—"—	
—"—	7th		—"—	
To ACHEUX	8th		Relieved by 10th Infty Bde & retired into Divisional Reserve as follows:- 10th RIR. ACHEUX. Irish Fusiliers Varennes. Rifle Bde Forceville. 9th RIR. Mailly. 2nd Monmouths Beaussart. Bde HQ. ACHEUX.	[initials]

T2134. Wt. W708—776. 500000. 4/15. Sir J. C. & S.

107th Infty Bde

Army Form C. 2118.

Instructions regarding War Diaries and Intelligence Summaries are contained in F. S. Regs., Part II. and the Staff Manual respectively. Title pages will be prepared in manuscript.

WAR DIARY
or
INTELLIGENCE SUMMARY.
(Erase heading not required.)

Place	Date	Hour	Summary of Events and Information	Remarks and references to Appendices
	Dec:			
ACHEUX	9th		In Divisional Reserve. Large working Parties at work daily on 2nd Divl Line + on Corps Line near VARENNES.	
	10th			[initials]
	11th			
	12th			
To Trenches (MAILLY)	13th		Relieved 10th Infty Bde in Trenches in left sector of Divisional Line. Same distribution as last tour.	
MAILLY	14th		In Trenches. Artillery Bombardment of German Trenches at 10 a.m. in which 94th Trench Mortar Batty co-operated. Much damage done + no retaliation by Enemy.	[initials]
—"—	15th		In Trenches.	
—"—	16th		—"—	
To ACHEUX	17th		Relieved by 10th Infty Bde + retired into Divisional Reserve. ~~[illegible]~~. The 107th Bde was reformed into its original composition the 8th + 15th R.I.R. replacing the Rifle Bde + R Irish Fusilrs who returned to the 11th + 10th Brigades respectively.	[initials]
	18th		In Divl Reserve.	

T2134. Wt. W708—776. 500000. 4/15. Sir J. C. & S.

107th Inf Bde

Instructions regarding War Diaries and Intelligence Summaries are contained in F. S. Regs., Part II. and the Staff Manual respectively. Title pages will be prepared in manuscript.

WAR DIARY
or
INTELLIGENCE SUMMARY.
(Erase heading not required.)

Army Form C. 2118.

Place	Date	Hour	Summary of Events and Information	Remarks and references to Appendices
	Dec.			
ACHEUX	19th		In Divisional Reserve } usual working Parties on Corps & Divl line supplied	B.E.
—"—	20		—"— } daily. Drilles - Route marches carried out by Battns.	
To Trenches (MAILLY)	21st		107th Bde relieved 10th Bde in left Sector at 6 P.m. The Brigade Machine Gun Company having been formed, under command of Capt Woodgate E Lancashire Regt, went in the line for the first time, the Battns taking in their Lewis Guns.	B.E.
MAILLY	22nd		In Trenches. }	B.E.
	23rd		—"—	
	24th		—"—	
To ACHEUX	25th		Relieved by 10th Infantry Bde & returned to Divisional Reserve at 6 P.m. Distribution. 8th R.I.R. Varennes. 9th R.I.R. FORCEVILLE. 10th R.I.R. ACHEUX 15th R.I.R. MAILLY. 2nd Monmouths MAILLY. Bde M.G. Coy Forceville. Bde H.Q. ACHEUX.	B.E.
	26th		} In Divisional Reserve. When the Brigade found the usual working Parties & carried out usual Training.	B.E.
	27th			
	28th			

T2134. Wt. W708—776. 500000. 4/15. Sir J. C. & S.

107th Infty Bde

Army Form C. 2118.

Instructions regarding War Diaries and Intelligence Summaries are contained in F. S. Regs., Part II. and the Staff Manual respectively. Title pages will be prepared in manuscript.

WAR DIARY
or
INTELLIGENCE SUMMARY.
(Erase heading not required.)

Place	Date	Hour	Summary of Events and Information	Remarks and references to Appendices
	December			
To Trenches (MAILLY)	29th		Conference of Commanding Officers at Bde H.Q. 10 a.m. The Brigade relieved 108th Infty Bde in Divisional Left Sector at 6 P.m. Distribution of Battns as usual.	[illegible]
Trenches at MAILLY	30th		Usual artillery duel in which our artillery had superiority. Otherwise everything very quiet. Col Baird + Col Gordon Clark of 60th Div attached for instruction.	[illegible]
— " —	31st		Trenches at MAILLY.	

[illegible]
Bde Major
107th Infty Bde

1/1/16

T2134. Wt. W708—776. 500000. 4/15. Sir J. C. & S.

107th Inf Bde.

4th Division.

This Bde rejoined
36th Division 7. 2. 1916

107th INFANTRY BRIGADE HEADQUARTERS.

J A N U A R Y   1 9 1 6

4th Div

~~36th Div.~~

Rejoined 36 Div 7.2.16.

107th Inf: Bde:
Vol: 3

Jan '16.

107th Infantry Brigade

Army Form C. 2118.

Instructions regarding War Diaries and Intelligence Summaries are contained in F. S. Regs., Part II. and the Staff Manual respectively. Title pages will be prepared in manuscript.

WAR DIARY
or
~~INTELLIGENCE SUMMARY.~~
(Erase heading not required.)

Place	Date	Hour	Summary of Events and Information	Remarks and references to Appendices
	January 1916			
Trenches at MAILLY	1st		The ~~[illegible]~~ 4th Divisional Left Sector was divided up into 2 Subsectors, the Right to be held permanently by 107th Infy Bde & the Left by 10th Infy Bde the dividing line between the two Brigades being the SERRE ROAD. To carry out this the adjustment the 2nd Dublin Fusiliers (10th Bde) relieved 15th R.I.R. in old Left Sector & the 1st R. Irish Fusiliers relieved 10th R.I.R. in old Left Centre Sector. Brigade H.Q. moving to new H.Q. in MAILLY the 10th Infy Bde retaining the old Bde H.Q.	
—"—	2nd		Trenches at MAILLY. Colonels Baird, Gordon Clark ceased to be attached to the Brigade.	
—"—	3rd		10th R.I.R. relieved 8th R.I.R. in Right Sector & 15th R.I.R. relieved ~~[illegible]~~ 9th R.I.R. in Left Sector.	
—"—	4th		The Enemy heavily Bombarded HAMEL and neighbouring trenches in 11th Infy Bde area on our immediate right. About 4000 shells (5.9, 4.2 & field guns) were fired. The enemy [illegible] at rapid rifle & Machine Gun fire but did not attempt to attack or leave their trenches. Our Artillery put a barrage of fire in front of our line and also shelled BEAUCOURT and ST PIERRE DIVION.	
—"—	5th		In retaliation for the German bombardment of the 4th our Heavy & Field Artillery Bombarded BEAUCOURT & ST PIERRE DIVION and neighbouring trenches. The	

T2134. Wt. W708—776. 500000. 4/15. Sir J. C. & S.

107th Infantry Brigade

Army Form C. 2118.

Instructions regarding War Diaries and Intelligence Summaries are contained in F. S. Regs., Part II. and the Staff Manual respectively. Title pages will be prepared in manuscript.

WAR DIARY
or
INTELLIGENCE SUMMARY.
(Erase heading not required.)

Place	Date	Hour	Summary of Events and Information	Remarks and references to Appendices
January MAILLY	5th		The Enemy in return again shelled HAMEL and MESNIL & the artillery duel continued during most of the day.	[initials]
—"—	6th		Trenches near MAILLY.	
—"—	7th		Brigade relief. 8th R.I.R. relieved 10th R.I.R. in right sector and 9th R.I.R. relieved 15th R.I.R. in left sector. 10th R.I.R. withdrew to MAILLY & 15th R.I.R. to Divl Reserve at VARENNES.	[initials]
—"—	8th		Trenches near MAILLY	
—"—	9th		—"—	
—"—	10th		—"— The Commander-in-Chief visited Brigade H.Q. at 3 pm and Representatives of an Irish recruiting Commission also visited the various Battalions. The Final of the Lambton Cup was played between the 10th R.I.R. & 7th Argyll & Sutherland H'rs (10th Infy Bde). Result was a draw — 1 Goal all after extra Time.	[initials]
—"—	11th		Brigade relief 10th R.I.R. relieved 8th R.I.R. in Right Sector and 15th R.I.R. relieved 9th R.I.R. in left sector. 8th R.I.R. to MAILLY & ~~[struck out]~~ 9th R.I.R. to VARENNES.	[initials]
—"—	12th		Trenches. Enemy very active with trench Mortars & Rifle Grenades in REDAN	

T2134. Wt. W708—776. 500000. 4/15. Sir J. C. & S.

107th Infy Brigade

Army Form C. 2118.

Instructions regarding War Diaries and Intelligence Summaries are contained in F. S. Regs., Part II. and the Staff Manual respectively. Title pages will be prepared in manuscript.

WAR DIARY
or
INTELLIGENCE SUMMARY.

(Erase heading not required.)

Place	Date	Hour	Summary of Events and Information	Remarks and references to Appendices
	January			
MAILLY	13th		Trenches at MAILLY. Brigadier ordered home to receive his C.M.G.	
— " —	14th		— " — Our artillery Bombarded German Trenches opposite REDAN. All troops in REDAN being withdrawn to MAXIM STREET.	
— " —	15th		H.Q. and 2 Coys of 2nd West Riding Regt arrived at 1 P.m. being attached to 107th Infy Bde for work. 8th R.I.R. relieved 10th R.I.R. in right sector and 9th R.I.R. relieved 15th R.I.R. in left — 15th withdrew to VARENNES & 10th to MAILLY.	
— " —	16th		Trenches at MAILLY.	
— " —	17th		— " — Quiet Day. A very successful operation in advancing the right portion of our front line about 100 yards on a front of 550 yards was carried out by 8th & 10th R.I.R. (orders for same attached). The object of this advance was to occupy an important ridge to our front & deny it to the Germans who if they occupied it could enfilade the Tenderloin. The Trench was dug & wired without a hitch & with the loss of only 3 men. 7th Argylls beat 10th R.I.R. in final of [illegible] football cup 1-0.	
— " —	18th		Trenches at Mailly. Enemy artillery active. Owing to shelling & Trench Mortaring by enemy the 8th R.I.R. withdrew their Batt. H.Q. to AUCHONVILLERS.	
— " —	19th		Brigadier returned from London. 10th R.I.R. relieved 8th R.I.R. on right & 15th R.I.R. relieved 9th R.I.R. on left. 8th R.I.R. withdrew to VARENNES and 9th R.I.R. to MAILLY. A German Patrol attempted to Bomb the Crater in front of REDAN but failed.	

107th Infy Bde

~~Army~~ Form C. 2118.

Instructions regarding War Diaries and Intelligence Summaries are contained in F. S. Regs., Part II. and the Staff Manual respectively. Title pages will be prepared in manuscript.

WAR DIARY
or
INTELLIGENCE SUMMARY.
(Erase heading not required.)

Place	Date	Hour	Summary of Events and Information	Remarks and references to Appendices
	January			
MAILLY	20th		Trenches at MAILLY. The Germans made a strong raid on the CRATER throwing in bombs & killing our Post there. They took one man away & then retired. Owing to faulty communication with artillery a good chance of cutting them off was lost.	
— " —	21st		Trenches at MAILLY.	
— " —	22nd		— " —	
— " —	23rd		— " — . 8th R.I.R. relieved 10th R.I.R. in Right Sector and 9th R.I.R. relieved 15th R.I.R. in left sector. 10th R.I.R. withdrew to VARENNES and 15th to MAILLY.	
— " —	24th		Trenches at MAILLY. All quiet on our front but heavy bombardment on our left in 48th Division Section at 2 am.	
— " —	25th		Trenches at MAILLY. The Primate of Ireland Archbishop J.B. Crozier and Sir James Stronge arrived at VARENNES at 3 P.m. & visited 10th R.I.R. They then came on to MAILLY & visited 15th R.I.R. holding a Service for them in the Salle de Réunion at 6 P.m. They dined & spent the night with Brigade Head quarters.	
— " —	26th		Brigadier conducted the Primate and Sir J Stronge round the trenches visiting the O.C. 9th R.I.R. and 8th R.I.R. at their Battn. H.Qrs. They returned to lunch at Brigade H.Q. & afterwards proceeded to visit Albert & then returned to 36th Divn	

T2134. Wt. W708—776. 500000. 4/15. Sir J. C. & S.

107th Infty Bde

Army Form C. 2118.

Instructions regarding War Diaries and Intelligence Summaries are contained in F. S. Regs., Part II. and the Staff Manual respectively. Title pages will be prepared in manuscript.

WAR DIARY
or
INTELLIGENCE SUMMARY.
(Erase heading not required.)

Place	Date	Hour	Summary of Events and Information	Remarks and references to Appendices
	Jany			
MAILLY	27th		Trenches at MAILLY. Quiet Day. at 7.45 P.m. the Gas Alarm was given but further South & did not affect us. 10th RIR relieved 8th RIR and 15th relieved 9th. 8th RIR to MAILLY – 9th RIR to YARENNES.	
–"–	28th		Another Gas alarm from CARNOY at 7 am.	
–"–	29th		The Divisional Commander delivered a farewell address to 2nd Monmouths at 12 Noon.	
–"–	30th		2nd Monmouths left 107th Bde for Lines of Communication, marching from MAILLY at 9.30 am.	
–"–	31st		Trenches at MAILLY. 8th RIR relieved 10th RIR in right Sector and 9th RIR relieved 15th RIR in left Sector. 10th RIR withdrew to MAILLY and 15th RIR to YARENNES.	

[signature]
Bde Major
107th Infty Bde

3/2/16

T2134. Wt. W708–776. 500000. 4/15. Sir J. C. & S.

36th Division.

107th Inf: Bde:
Vol: I

121
7795

Oct. [& Nov.] 15.

Transferred to IVth Divn Nov. 4th, rejoining XXXVIth on Feb. 7th

107th Infantry Brigade

Army Form C. 2118.

Instructions regarding War Diaries and Intelligence Summaries are contained in F. S. Regs., Part II. and the Staff Manual respectively. Title pages will be prepared in manuscript.

WAR DIARY
or
INTELLIGENCE SUMMARY.
(Erase heading not required.)

Place	Date	Hour	Summary of Events and Information	Remarks and references to Appendices
	October 1915			
Vignacourt	20th		Br Genl W.M. Withycombe C.M.G. took over command of 107th Infy Bde from Br Genl G.H.H. Couchman	[illegible]
–"–	21st		Divisional Field day –	[illegible]
To St Leger	22nd		The 107th Bde moved to St Leger the Battns being distributed as follows:– 8th & 9th & Bde HQ at St Leger – 10th R.I.R. at Bertrancourt 15th R.I.R. at Pernois and Halloy. 1/1 London RFA at CANAPLES.	[illegible]
	23rd		Brigade Training	
	24th		—"—	
	25th		—"—	
To CANAPLES	26th		Bde HQ moved to CANAPLES. The remainder of the Brigade did not move.	
	27th		94 Trench Mortar Batty joined 107th Infy Bde.	
	28th		Brigade Training	[illegible]
	29th		—"—	
	30th		—"—	
	31st		—"—	

T2134. Wt. W708–776. 500000. 4/15. Sir J. C. & S.

107th Infantry Brigade

Instructions regarding War Diaries and Intelligence Summaries are contained in F. S. Regs., Part II. and the Staff Manual respectively. Title pages will be prepared in manuscript.

WAR DIARY
or
INTELLIGENCE SUMMARY.
(Erase heading not required.)

Army Form C. 2118.

Place	Date	Hour	Summary of Events and Information	Remarks and references to Appendices
	November			
CANAPLES	1st		at Canaples Brigade Training.	
On the march.	2nd		The 107th Bde marched to join the 4th Division & halted for the night at HERISSART and PUCHEVILLERS.	
To ACHEUX	3rd		Joined 4th Division. The 8th R.I.R. were detached to 10th Infy Bde & the 15th R.I.R. to 11th Infy Bde. The 1st Rifle Bde & 1st Royal Irish Fusiliers & 2nd Monmouths joined 107th Infy Bde. The 107th Bde from this date was composed as follows:- 1st Rifle Bde (at VARENNES) 1st R Irish Fusiliers (at ACHEUX) 2nd Monmouths (at MAILLY MAILLET) 9th R.I.R. (at FORCEVILLE) 10th R.I.R. (at BEAUSSART). Bde H.Q. (at ACHEUX)	
ACHEUX	4th		Training.	
– " –	5th			
– " –	6th			
To Trenches (MAILLY)	7th		The Army Commander (Genl Allenby) presented French Decorations to men in 3rd Army the R Irish Fusiliers parading for the occasion. The 107th Bde moved into the Left Sector of 4th Divisional Line –	

Instructions regarding War Diaries and Intelligence Summaries are contained in F. S. Regs., Part II. and the Staff Manual respectively. Title pages will be prepared in manuscript.

WAR DIARY
or
INTELLIGENCE SUMMARY.
(Erase heading not required.)

107th BHQ. 36.

Army Form C. 2118.

2 Feby 1916

Place	Date	Hour	Summary of Events and Information	Remarks and references to Appendices
	February 1916			
MAILLY	1st		Trenches at MAILLY. Conference of Brigade Majors at 4th Divl. H.Q. at ACHEUX at 3 P.m. at which it was notified that 107th Infy Bde would return to 36th Divn which was coming up to relieve 4th Divn in the line, taking over only the right & Centre Brigade sectors from 4th Divn who would leave one Brigade in Sector on our left.	[initials] [initials]
—"—	2nd		Genl Lambton (G.O.C. 4th Divn) presented football medals to 10th R.I.R. for having been 2nd in Lambton Cup.	
—"—	3rd		Trenches at MAILLY. 2nd West Ridings ~~[illegible]~~ ceased to be attached to 107th Infy Bde, rejoining 12th Infy Bde.	[initials]
—"—	4th		Trenches at MAILLY. 10th R.I.R. relieved 8th R.I.R. in right Sector & 15th R.I.R. relieved 9th R.I.R. in left Sector. 8th & 9th R.I.R. withdrew into Brigade reserve in MAILLY	[initials]
—"—	5th		Trenches in MAILLY. Enemy artillery activity.	
—"—	6th		Trenches in MAILLY. 12th Infy Bde relieved 10th Infy Bde on our left & 108th Infy Bde relieved 11th Infy Bde on our right.	
—"— X	7th		Trenches at MAILLY. 36th Division took over command of the line from 4th Divn at 12 noon and 107th Infy Bde rejoined 36th Division.	[initials]

T2134. Wt. W708—776. 500000. 4/15. Sir J. C. & S.

Instructions regarding War Diaries and Intelligence Summaries are contained in F. S. Regs., Part II. and the Staff Manual respectively. Title pages will be prepared in manuscript.

WAR DIARY
or
INTELLIGENCE SUMMARY.
(Erase heading not required.)

Army Form C. 2118.

Place	Date	Hour	Summary of Events and Information	Remarks and references to Appendices
	July			
MAILLY	8th		Trenches at MAILLY. 8th R.I.R. relieved 10th R.I.R. in right Sector and 9th R.I.R. relieved 15th R.I.R. in left Sector. 10th & 15th R.I.R. withdrew to Brigade reserve in MAILLY.	[illegible]
—"—	9th		Gen'l Nugent (Divl Commander) inspected 8th & 9th R.I.R. on Parade in Mailly at 10 am.	[illegible]
—"—	10th		Trenches at MAILLY.	
—"—	11th		—"— Divisional Commander went round Billets of 10th & 15th R.I.R.	[illegible]
—"—	12th		—"— 11th R Innis Fus (109th Inf Bde) attached to 107th Inf Bde. The Brigade took over Trenches 51 to 55 from 108th Infy Bde & the 11th R Innis Fus occupied this extra portion of our line. Brigade relief. 10th R.I.R. relieved 8th R.I.R. and 15th R.I.R. relieved 9th R.I.R. 8th R.I.R. withdrew to Mailly & 9th R.I.R. sent 2 Coys to MAILLY & 2 Coys to FORCEVILLE. Details of Battns of 109th Infy Bde came into trenches with 10th & 15th R.I.R. for instruction in trench warfare.	
—"—	13th		Trenches at Mailly.	
—"—	14th		—"— Auchonvillers shelled.	
—"—	15th		—"—	

T2134. Wt. W708—776. 500000. 4/15. Sir J. C. & S.

Instructions regarding War Diaries and Intelligence Summaries are contained in F. S. Regs., Part II. and the Staff Manual respectively. Title pages will be prepared in manuscript.

WAR DIARY
or
INTELLIGENCE SUMMARY.
(Erase heading not required.)

Army Form C. 2118.

Place	Date	Hour	Summary of Events and Information	Remarks and references to Appendices
	February			
MAILLY	16th		Trenches at MAILLY – Brigade Relief – 8th R.I.R. relieved 10th R.I.R. + 9th R.I.R. relieved 15th R.I.R. The 11th R Innis Fus. carried out their own relief in Right Sector. On relief 10th R.I.R. + 2 Coys 15th R.I.R. withdrew to MAILLY + 2 Coys 15th R.I.R. + 2 Coys 11th R Innis Fusrs withdrew to Forceville. The 1/5th Sherwood Foresters arrived in MAILLY + were attached to 107th Inf Bde for work. The following is now the constitution of 107th Inf Bde:– 8th R.I.R. – 9th R.I.R. – 10th R.I.R. – 15th R.I.R. – 11th R Innis Fus. – 1/5 Sherwood Foresters. Bde M.G. Coy – 107th Trench Mortar Batty – 94th Trench Mortar Batty + 9th R Innis Fusrs (attached for work only). Auchonvillers was heavily shelled just before reliefs commenced (about 6 P.m.) Capt Woodgate D.S.O. the O.C. Bde M.G. Coy being seriously wounded.	B2
MAILLY	17th		Trenches at MAILLY. Our artillery heavily bombarded the German trenches opposite the Redan. Our troops in the Redan being withdrawn during the bombardment which lasted from 10 am to 11.30 am.	
MAILLY	18th		Trenches at MAILLY –	
MAILLY	19th		— " — – at 6 P.m. the enemy opened an intense bombardment	

T2134. Wt. W708—776. 500000. 4/15. Sir J. C. & S.

Instructions regarding War Diaries and Intelligence Summaries are contained in F. S. Regs., Part II. and the Staff Manual respectively. Title pages will be prepared in manuscript.

WAR DIARY
or
INTELLIGENCE SUMMARY.
(Erase heading not required.)

Army Form C. 2118.

Place	Date	Hour	Summary of Events and Information	Remarks and references to Appendices
MAILLY	Feb 19th		of the REDAN & also of the trenches on our left held by 12th Inf Bde. At about 6.25 P.m. the enemy lifted his fire in the Centre onto Vallade Corner and MOUNTJOY AVENUE forming a Barrage there. Any attempt of his to raid the REDAN however was frustrated by the quick action of our Artillery (4th Div.) supporting us & also by the action of the troops in the REDAN (9th R.I.R.) who lined the parapets as soon as the Barrage lifted & opened Rapid Rifle & Lewis Gun fire. The Bombardment ceased at about 7.30 P.m. after which all was quiet. On our left in 12th Bde area a party of Germans succeeded in entering our trenches but were immediately driven out again by a Counter attack leaving some dead behind.	FPC
—"—	20th		Trenches at MAILLY. Brigade relief. 10th R.I.R. relieved 8th R.I.R. and 15th R.I.R. relieved 9th R.I.R. The 11th R Innis Fus's carried out their own relief. On relief 9th R.I.R. withdrew to BEAUSSART. 8th R.I.R. to FORCEVILLE & 2 Coys of 11th R Innis Fus's to MAILLY	FPC
—"—	21st		Trenches at MAILLY. Quiet day. Commenced to Snow.	FPC

T2134. Wt. W708—776. 500000. 4/15. Sir J. C. & S.

Army Form C. 2118.

Instructions regarding War Diaries and Intelligence Summaries are contained in F. S. Regs., Part II. and the Staff Manual respectively. Title pages will be prepared in manuscript.

WAR DIARY
or
INTELLIGENCE SUMMARY.
(Erase heading not required.)

Place	Date	Hour	Summary of Events and Information	Remarks and references to Appendices
	Feby			
MAILLY	22nd		Trench at MAILLY – Snowing –	
"	23rd		" "	[initials]
"	24th		" – Heavy snow + frost – 109th Infy Bde relieved 107th Infy Bde in the line. The command of the line passing to B.G. Comdg 109th Bde at 12.30 am. The 8th R.I.R. attached to 109th Bde relieved 11th R. Innis Fusrs in right sector. The 9th R. Innis Fusrs relieved 10th R.I.R. in centre sector & 10th R. Innis Fusrs relieved 15th R.I.R. in left sector. On relief 15th R.I.R. withdrew to Acheux + 10th R.I.R. to YARENNES. The 9th R.I.R. being attached to 109th Infy Bde for work. The 5th Sherwood Foresters + 110th Trench Mortar Batty were transferred to 109th Infy Bde.	[initials] [initials]
"	25th		Brigade H.Q. should have moved to ACHEUX but owing to hard frost + heavy snow wagons were unable to move.	
"	26th		MAILLY to ACHEUX. Snow.	
ACHEUX	27th		At ACHEUX – snow.	[initials]
"	28th		At ACHEUX – Snow	
"	29th		" – Thaw. 15th R.I.R. marched from ACHEUX to Mailly + were placed at disposal of 109th Infy Bde for work.	

T2134. Wt. W708–776. 500000. 4/15. Sir J. C. & S.

Instructions regarding War Diaries and Intelligence Summaries are contained in F. S. Regs., Part II. and the Staff Manual respectively. Title pages will be prepared in manuscript.

WAR DIARY
or
INTELLIGENCE SUMMARY.
(Erase heading not required.)

Army Form C. 2118.

Place	Date	Hour	Summary of Events and Information	Remarks and references to Appendices
	May			
Harponville	1st		Brigade Training over Dummy Trenches near Clairfaye	
—"—	2nd		—"—	
—"—	3rd		Brigade Field day near CLAIREFAYE.	
—"—	4th		Brigade Training	
—"—	5th		—"—	
—"—	6th		—"—	
—"—	7th		15th R.I.R. marched from VARENNES to Forceville (2 Coys + H.Q. + Hédauville (2 Coys))	
			Brigade Field day for remaining 3 Battns.	
—"—	8th		8th R.I.R. marched from LEALVILLERS to MARTINSART Wood at 10 am.	
			10th —"— —"— —"— to MARTINSART at 2 P.m.	
			9th —"— —"— FORCEVILLE to MARTINSART Wood at 6.30 P.m.	
To MARTINSART	9th		Relieved 109th Infy Bde in MARTINSART at 3 P.m. Bde M Gun Coy moved from VARENNES to MARTINSART.	
Martinsart	10th		All Battns finding 530 men for work per day.	
—"—	11th		—"—	
—"—	12		—"—	

Instructions regarding War Diaries and Intelligence Summaries are contained in F. S. Regs., Part II. and the Staff Manual respectively. Title pages will be prepared in manuscript.

WAR DIARY
or
INTELLIGENCE SUMMARY.
(*Erase heading not required.*)

Army Form C. 2118.

Place	Date	Hour	Summary of Events and Information	Remarks and references to Appendices
Martinsart	13th		Battns all finding 520 men for work per day.	
"	14		———"——— (14th–29th)	
"	15			
"	16			
"	17			
"	18			
"	19			
"	20			
"	21			
"	22			
"	23			
"	24			
"	25			
"	26			
"	27			
"	28			
"	29			

T2134. Wt. W708—776. 500000. 4/15. Sir J. C. & S.

Instructions regarding War Diaries and Intelligence Summaries are contained in F. S. Regs., Part II. and the Staff Manual respectively. Title pages will be prepared in manuscript.

WAR DIARY
or
INTELLIGENCE SUMMARY.
(Erase heading not required.)

Army Form C. 2118.

Place	Date	Hour	Summary of Events and Information	Remarks and references to Appendices
Martinsart	30		107th Bde relieved 108th Bde in the Front line. 9th R.I.R. relieved 13th R.I.R. in Thiepval Subsector and 10th R.I.R. relieved 12th R.I.R. in HAMEL Subsector. 8th R.I.R. in Martinsart (2 Coys + H.Q.) and THIEPVAL WOOD (2 Coys). 15th R.I.R. remained in Forceville + HEDAUVILLE.	[initials]
"	31		In trenches. Quiet Day.	

3/6/16

[signature] Major
Bde Major
107th Inf Bde

T2134. Wt. W708—776. 500000. 4/15. Sir J. C. & S.

Instructions regarding War Diaries and Intelligence Summaries are contained in F. S. Regs., Part II. and the Staff Manual respectively. Title pages will be prepared in manuscript.

WAR DIARY *or* INTELLIGENCE SUMMARY.

(Erase heading not required.)

Army Form C. 2118.

Place	Date	Hour	Summary of Events and Information	Remarks and references to Appendices
	March 1st			
ACHEUX.	1st		At ACHEUX. Thaw set in.	
—"—	2nd		—"— Orders to relieve 109th Infy Bde in the line on night of 3rd/4th.	
MAILLY	3rd		Brigade moved to MAILLY and relieved 109th Infy Bde in Left Sector of Divisional Line. 10th R.I.R. took over Centre Sector and 15th R.I.R. the Left Sector. The 8th R.I.R. remaining in Right Sector & returning to 107th Bde. The 9th R.I.R. ~~[illegible]~~ remained in MAILLY in Brigade Reserve. Relief completed at 12.30 am. at which hour the Br-Gen took over command of the line from B.G.C 109th Bde.	[initials]
MAILLY	4th		In trenches at Mailly. Heavy fall of Snow.	
—"—	5th		—"— Heavy Snow. A Battn of 108th Infy Bde on our right took over Trenches 51 to 55 from 8th R.I.R. the latter retiring into Brigade Reserve in MAILLY.	[initials]
—"—	6th		Trenches at MAILLY. At 8.30 P.m. the Germans opened a heavy bombardment of our trenches from 60 to 65 & also shelled TENDERLOIN and ROMAN ROAD. Bombardment lasted 20 minutes. Damage slight & casualties light	[initials]

T2134. Wt. W708—776. 500000. 4/15. Sir J. C. & S.

Instructions regarding War Diaries and Intelligence Summaries are contained in F. S. Regs., Part II. and the Staff Manual respectively. Title pages will be prepared in manuscript.

WAR DIARY
or
INTELLIGENCE SUMMARY.
(Erase heading not required.)

Army Form C. 2118.

Place	Date	Hour	Summary of Events and Information	Remarks and references to Appendices
MAILLY	7th		Trenches at MAILLY – Snow & Frost – Brigade relief. 8th R.I.R. relieved 10th R.I.R. in right sector and 9th R.I.R. relieved 15th R.I.R. in left Sector. On relief 10th R.I.R. withdrew to MAILLY and 15th R.I.R. to BEAUSSART – The 4th & 5th Dukes arrived in MAILLY (147th Infy Bde 49th Divn) to assist us in mining fatigues.	[initials]
"	8th		Trenches. Snow & Frost.	
"	9th		"	
"	10th		"	
"	11th		Trenches. Brigade relief. 10th R.I.R. relieved 8th R.I.R. in right Sector and 15th R.I.R. relieved 9th R.I.R. in left Sector. 8th R.I.R. withdrew to MAILLY and 9th R.I.R. to BEAUSSART.	[initials]
"	12th			
"	13th			
"	14th		Trenches at MAILLY	
"	15th		Brigade relief. 8th R.I.R. relieved 10th R.I.R. in right Sector and 9th R.I.R. relieved 15th R.I.R. in left Sector. 10th R.I.R. withdrew to MAILLY and 15th R.I.R. to BEAUSSART	[initials]
[illegible]	[struck out]			

T2134. Wt. W708—776. 500000. 4/15. Sir J. C. & S.

Army Form C. 2118.

Instructions regarding War Diaries and Intelligence Summaries are contained in F. S. Regs., Part II. and the Staff Manual respectively. Title pages will be prepared in manuscript.

WAR DIARY
or
INTELLIGENCE SUMMARY.
(Erase heading not required.)

Place	Date	Hour	Summary of Events and Information	Remarks and references to Appendices
	March			
MAILLY	16th		Trenches at MAILLY – TENDERLOIN heavily shelled.	
"	17th		"	
"	18th		" – At 2 am. the Germans heavily bombarded Redan Tenderloin – Roman Road. Sucherie. + Auchonvillers – Also the outskirts of MAILLY. No attack made.	
"	19th		Trenches at MAILLY.	
"	20th		Trenches at MAILLY.	
"	21st		" Brigade relief 10th RIR relieved 8th RIR in Right Sector + 15th RIR relieved 9th RIR in left Sector. On relief 8th RIR withdrew to MAILLY + 9th RIR to Beaussart.	
"	22		Trenches.	
"	23		" – 10 Offrs + 40 NCOs of 15th W Yorks + similar number of 16th W. Yorks (31st Div 8th Corps) arrived for instruction in the trenches	
"	24		Trenches at MAILLY – 6 inches of snow on the ground.	
"	25		"	
"	26		"	

T2134. Wt. W708–776. 500000. 4/15. Sir J. C. & S.

Instructions regarding War Diaries and Intelligence Summaries are contained in F. S. Regs., Part II. and the Staff Manual respectively. Title pages will be prepared in manuscript.

WAR DIARY
or
INTELLIGENCE SUMMARY.
(Erase heading not required.)

Army Form C. 2118.

Place	Date	Hour	Summary of Events and Information	Remarks and references to Appendices
	March			
MAILLY	27		Trenches at MAILLY – Brigade relief – 8th R.I.R. relieved 10th R.I.R. in Right Sector and 10th R.I.R. relieved 15th R.I.R. in left sector. 10th R.I.R. withdrew to MAILLY and 15th R.I.R. to BEAUSSART.	[initials]
–"–	28		Trenches at MAILLY – 93rd Infty Bde (31st Divn, 8th Corps) commenced to take over from 107th Infty Bde – 15th West Yorks arrived in MAILLY at 9 P.M. & relieved 10th R.I.R. who withdrew to LEALVILLERS and 18th Durham L.I. arrived at BEAUSSART at 9.30 P.M. & relieved 15th R.I.R. who withdrew to VARENNES. The 13th York & Lancs (94th Bde) arrived in MAILLY vice 4th & 5th West Ridings for work on Mines.	[initials]
–"–	29		H.Q. 93rd Infty Bde arrived in MAILLY. The 15th West Yorks relieved 8th R.I.R. in right Sector and 18th Durham L.I. relieved 9th R.I.R. in left Sector. On relief 8th R.I.R. withdrew to MAILLY & 9th R.I.R. to Beaussart.	
–"– to PUCHEVILLERS	30		The 16th West Yorks Regt relieved 8th R.I.R. in MAILLY and 18th West Yorks relieved 9th R.I.R. in Beaussart at 6.15 P.M. On relief 8th & 9th R.I.R. withdrew to PUCHEVILLERS where they arrived at 10.30 P.M. This completed the relief of 107th Infty Bde & Bde H.Q. moved to PUCHEVILLERS at 6 P.M. The 107th Bde M.Gun Coy remained in the line with 93rd Infty Bde	[initials]
PUCHEVILLERS	31		At PUCHEVILLERS. All Battns finding large working Parties on new CANDAS–ACHEUX Railway.	[initials]

T2134. Wt. W708–776. 500000. 4/15. Sir J. C. & S.

Instructions regarding War Diaries and Intelligence Summaries are contained in F. S. Regs., Part II. and the Staff Manual respectively. Title pages will be prepared in manuscript.

WAR DIARY
or
INTELLIGENCE SUMMARY. XXXVI
(*Erase heading not required.*)

Army Form C. 2118. Vol 6

107th Infty Brigade

Place	Date	Hour	Summary of Events and Information	Remarks and references to Appendices
	APRIL			
PUCHEVILLERS	1st		Distribution of Brigade as follows:- Bde H.Q. 8th R.I.R. + 9th R.I.R. at PUCHEVILLERS 10th R.I.R. LEALVILLERS – 15th R.I.R. VARENNES. Bde M.Gun Coy in Trenches attached to 93rd Infty Bde – 107/1 T.M. Batty. Trenches with 93rd Bde.	
—"—	2nd		Working Parties found by all Battns: remainder of men Training.	
"	3rd		——— " ———	
"	4th		——— " ———	
"	5th		The Brigade Machine Gun Coy moved from the Trenches to PUCHEVILLERS.	
"	6th		The 107/1 T.M. Batty moved from Trenches to VARENNES.	
"	7th		Working Parties + Training	
"	8th		——— " ———	
"	9th		——— " ———	
"	10th		——— " ———	
"	11th		——— " ———	
"	12th		——— " ———	
"	13th		——— " ———	

T2134. Wt. W708—776. 500000. 4/15. Sir J. C. & S.

Instructions regarding War Diaries and Intelligence Summaries are contained in F. S. Regs., Part II. and the Staff Manual respectively. Title pages will be prepared in manuscript.

WAR DIARY
or
INTELLIGENCE SUMMARY.
(Erase heading not required.)

Army Form C. 2118.

107th Infty Brigade

Place	Date	Hour	Summary of Events and Information	Remarks and references to Appendices
	April			
PUCHEVILLERS	14th		Working Parties & Training	[initials]
	15		— " — 107/2 T.M. Batty joined Brigade –	
	16		— " —	[initials]
	17		— " —	
	18		— " —	
	19		— " —	
HARPONVILLE	20		Brigade Headquarters closed at Puchevillers at 5 P.m. & opened at Harponville at same hour – The 9th R.I.R. moved from Puchevillers to Forceville at 10 am and the Brigade Machine Gun Coy from Puchevillers to Varennes at 10.30 am.	[initials]
"	21		at Harponville	
"	22		— " —	
"	23		— " — – 8th R.I.R. moved from Puchevillers to Léalvillers	[initials]
"	24		— " — } Brigade Training in area near Clairfaye –	
"	25		— " — }	[initials]
	26			
"	27		— " — }	
	28			
"	29		— " — }	
"	30			

[signature] Capt
Bde Major
107th Inf Bde

4/5/16

T2134. Wt. W708—776. 500000. 4/15. Sir J. C. & S.

36th Division.

B.H.Q.

107th INFANTRY BRIGADE.

JUNE 1 9 1 6 :

107th Inf Bde

Instructions regarding War Diaries and Intelligence Summaries are contained in F. S. Regs., Part II. and the Staff Manual respectively. Title pages will be prepared in manuscript.

107/36

WAR DIARY
or
INTELLIGENCE SUMMARY.
(Erase heading not required.)

XXXVI

Army Form C. 2118.

Vol 8 June

Place	Date	Hour	Summary of Events and Information	Remarks and references to Appendices
	June			
MARTINSART	1st		Trenches in HAMEL and THIEPVAL Sectors. 15th R.I.R. relieved 9th R.I.F. in Mesnil	[initials]
"	2nd		Trenches in HAMEL and THIEPVAL Sectors.	
"	3rd		Everything very quiet.	
"	4th			
"	5th			
"	6th		Trenches. 8th R.I.R. relieved 9th R.I.R. in THIEPVAL WOOD and 15th R.I.R. relieved 10th R.I.R. in HAMEL sector. 9th R.I.R. withdrew to MARTINSART leaving 2 Coys in THIEPVAL WOOD. 10th R.I.R. withdrew to MESNIL.	[initials]
"	7th		Trenches THIEPVAL + Hamel sectors	
"	8th		"	
"	9th		"	
"	10th		at 11.30 P.M. the enemy opened a violent Bombardment round WILLIAM REDAN in HAMEL sector held by 15th R.I.R. This lasted till 12.50 a.m. when the Germans attempted to raid our trenches but failed completely. A few succeeded in getting in but were immediately turned out leaving some dead behind. The 15th R.I.R. & 8th R.I.R. had casualties from the bombardment + the trenches were badly knocked about in both subsectors.	[initials]

107th Bde

Army Form C. 2118.

Instructions regarding War Diaries and Intelligence Summaries are contained in F. S. Regs., Part II. and the Staff Manual respectively. Title pages will be prepared in manuscript.

WAR DIARY
or
INTELLIGENCE SUMMARY.
(Erase heading not required.)

Place	Date	Hour	Summary of Events and Information	Remarks and references to Appendices
MARTINSART	11		} Trenches.	
	12		}	
	13		— " — . 9th R.I.R. relieved 8th R.I.R. in THIEPVAL WOOD and 10th R.I.R. relieved 15th R.I.R. in HAMEL Sector. On Relief 8th R.I.R. withdrew to MARTINSART leaving 2 Coys in THIEPVAL WOOD and 15th R.I.R. withdrew to MESNIL	
	14		Trenches.	
	15		Trenches.	
	16		Trenches. 12th R.I.R. (108 Bde) relieved 15th R.I.R. in MESNIL & 15th R.I.R. withdrew to AVELUY WOOD.	
	17		}	
	18		} In Trenches.	
	19		}	
	20		}	
	21		}	
	22		}	

107th Inf Bde

WAR DIARY
or
INTELLIGENCE SUMMARY.
(Erase heading not required.)

Army Form C. 2118.

Instructions regarding War Diaries and Intelligence Summaries are contained in F. S. Regs., Part II. and the Staff Manual respectively. Title pages will be prepared in manuscript.

Place	Date	Hour	Summary of Events and Information	Remarks and references to Appendices
TO VARENNES	23		Brigade H.Q. moved back to VARENNES. The 9th & 10th R.I.R. withdrew to LEALVILLERS and 8th & 15th to VARENNES being relieved in the trenches by 108th Bde in HAMEL Subsector and 109th Bde in THIEPVAL WOOD Subsector. The Brigade M. Gun Coy put 4 guns into Positions in HAMEL Sector + 4 guns in Positions in THIEPVAL Sector its H.Q. being in AVELUY WOOD. 107 T.M. Batty in AVELUY WOOD.	
VARENNES	24		Our Bombardment commenced at 9 am.	
VARENNES	25		Brigade field day over dummy trenches near CLAIRFAYE. Bombardment in full blast all day.	
"	26		Bombardment (3rd Day)	
"	27		Bombardment (4th Day) – 9th & 10th R.I.R. moved up from Lealvillers to FORCEVILLE & 8th & 15th from VARENNES to Hedauville. Bde H.Q. from VARENNES to Forceville.	
Forceville	28		Final day of bombardment. Brigade all ready to move up to assembly positions but at last moment order was cancelled & the 9th & 10th R.I.R. withdrew again to Lealvillers the remainder of the Brigade remaining where it was.	
"	29		Bombardment continued incessantly. Brigade did not move.	

T2134. Wt. W708–776. 500000. 4/15. Sir J. C. & S.

36th Division.

B. H. Q.

107th INFANTRY BRIGADE

JULY 1916

107th Inf Bde

July 1916

Army Form C. 2118.

WAR DIARY
or
INTELLIGENCE SUMMARY.
(Erase heading not required.)

Instructions regarding War Diaries and Intelligence Summaries are contained in F. S. Regs., Part II. and the Staff Manual respectively. Title pages will be prepared in manuscript.

Place	Date	Hour	Summary of Events and Information	Remarks and references to Appendices
	July 1st		Commencement of the Battle of the SOMME.	
THIEPVAL Wood.	1st	4 am.	Brigade distributed as follows:- Bde H.Q. in S.W. Corner of THIEPVAL WOOD. 8th R.I.R. } in assembly trenches in N Portion of AVELUY WOOD. 9th R.I.R. } —"— 10th R.I.R. } —"— 15th R.I.R. in assembly trenches in W Portion of THIEPVAL WOOD under orders of B.G.C. 108th Inf Bde. Bde M.Gun Coy. 4 Guns in front Trenches in THIEPVAL WOOD. 4 Guns —"— HAMEL SECTOR. 2 Guns attached to each Battn. under O.C. Battn. 107 T.M. Batty 2 Guns attached to 8th 9th & 10th R.I.R. 6 Guns in N Portion of AVELUY WOOD. Dispositions for attack are briefly as follows:- (Ref. Trench Maps 57 d SE 1+2 Parts of 1:10,000) (X Corps map 1:20,000.) The 4th Army will take the offensive along its whole front on July 1st. The 36th Div will attack on both sides of the ANCRE with 32nd Div on its Right + 29th Div on its left. Right boundary a line drawn from NE Corner of THIEPVAL WOOD to R 21 C 2.6. Left Boundary a line drawn from Point of MARY REDAN to R 7 C 20. Thence to River at R13 a 45 thence along the River to R 8 C 4.6 thence along the Railway. Objectives. Left of ANCRE. German D line from D8 to D 12 (both inclusive) Right of ANCRE. The triangle of trenches enclosed between left of attack, the ANCRE + BEAUCOURT STATION.	

T2134. Wt. W708—776. 500000. 4/15. Sir J. C. & S.

Instructions regarding War Diaries and Intelligence Summaries are contained in F. S. Regs., Part II. and the Staff Manual respectively. Title pages will be prepared in manuscript.

WAR DIARY
or
INTELLIGENCE SUMMARY.
(Erase heading not required.)

Army Form C. 2118.

Place	Date	Hour	Summary of Events and Information	Remarks and references to Appendices
(Continued)	1st		Subdivision of Front for Purposes of attack.	
			Right Section. Right Boundary to a line drawn from our trenches at Q 24 1/2 - S of C 9 to R 21 A 10.90	
			Right Centre Section. Left of Right Section to a line drawn from N corner of THIEPVAL WOOD through B 19 C 11 to D 11 (all inclusive)	
			Left Centre Section. Left of Right Centre Section to River ANCRE	
			Left Section. From ANCRE to left boundary of Divl attack.	
			Allotment of Troops. Right Section. 109 Infy Bde.	
			Right Centre Section. Two Battns 108 Infy Bde and 1 Battn 107 Bde (15 R.I.R.)	
			Left Centre Section. Not being directly attacked.	
			Left Section. Two Battns 108 Bde.	
			Divl Reserve. 107 Bde (less 15 R.I.R.) to pass through C line after capture & assault D line.	
			3 Field Coys R.E.	
			16 (P) R.I.R.	

T2134. Wt. W708—776. 500000. 4/15. Sir J. C. & S.

Instructions regarding War Diaries and Intelligence Summaries are contained in F. S. Regs., Part II. and the Staff Manual respectively. Title pages will be prepared in manuscript.

WAR DIARY
or
INTELLIGENCE SUMMARY.
(Erase heading not required.)

Army Form C. 2118.

Place	Date	Hour	Summary of Events and Information	Remarks and references to Appendices
(Contd)			Plan of attack. 109 Infy Bde are ordered to assault the German A & B lines & to press on & take the C line from C 8 to C 9 & hold this line. Two Battns 108 Bde and 15th R.I.R. to assault A & B lines & advance to C line & hold C 9 C 10 C 11. Two Battns 108 Bde to occupy BEAUCOURT STATION & trenches near it. 107 Infy Bde To assault D line from D 8 to D 9, by passing through 108th & 109th Bdes at C line, & extend to the left to D 11. For this operation the following dispositions were made:- 10th R.I.R. on right. 9th R.I.R. on left & 8th R.I.R. in Support. The 10th R.I.R. to attack with their right on D 8 & 9th R.I.R. with their left on D 9. After the Capture of the position the 9th R.I.R. were to extend as far as D 10 & the 10th R.I.R. as far as D 9. The 8th R.I.R. were to occupy & hold from D 10 to D 11. The 4 Machine Guns in HAMEL subsector were to Support the attack on THIEPVAL side of the ANCRE & the 4 M Guns in Thiepval Wood Subsector were to Support the attack N of the ANCRE.	

T2134. Wt. W708—776. 500000. 4/15. Sir J. C. & S.

Instructions regarding War Diaries and Intelligence Summaries are contained in F. S. Regs., Part II. and the Staff Manual respectively. Title pages will be prepared in manuscript.

WAR DIARY
or
INTELLIGENCE SUMMARY.
(Erase heading not required.)

Army Form C. 2118.

Place	Date	Hour	Summary of Events and Information	Remarks and references to Appendices
			ZERO 7.30 am. Intense Bombardment started at 6.25 am.	
	1st	5 am	The 8th 9th & 10th R.I.R (in this order) moved from assembly Trenches AVELUY WOOD marching at 15 minutes interval across the ANCRE & lay down in the Slopes of SPEYSIDE being in position there at 6.15 a.m, i.e. 10 minutes before the intense bombardment started. In this march Battalions had practically no casualties – (Reported to Divn).	
		6.25 am	Intense Bombardment started and enemy shelled the Marsh. SPEYSIDE and scattered H.E. and Shrapnel about in THIEPVAL WOOD. Shelling of SPEYSIDE caused some casualties especially to 8th R.I.R. (about 40) but protection was good.	
		6.45 am	Reported from Bde O.P. that Germans were barraging SUNKEN ROAD.	
		6.50 am	Reported from Bde O.P. the enemy were heavily shelling Q34 d 8.1	
		7.20 am	108th Bde out in No Mans Land (O.P.)	
		7.20 am	109th Bde out in No Mans Land (O.P.)	
		7.30 am	ZERO. Battalions moved from SPEYSIDE (in order 10th – 9th – 8th) up through THIEPVAL WOOD, and deployed for attack on clearing wood and advanced in rear of 109th Bde. 10th R.I.R on right, 9th R.I.R on left, and 8th R.I.R in support. Col H.C. Bernard killed near ROSS CASTLE, leading 10th R.I.R. into action	

T2134. Wt. W708—776. 500000. 4/15. Sir J. C. & S.

Army Form C. 2118.

Instructions regarding War Diaries and Intelligence Summaries are contained in F. S. Regs., Part II. and the Staff Manual respectively. Title pages will be prepared in manuscript.

WAR DIARY
or
INTELLIGENCE SUMMARY.
(Erase heading not required.)

Place	Date	Hour	Summary of Events and Information	Remarks and references to Appendices
	10th	7.45 am	Thick smoke - unable to observe. (O.P.)	
		8 am	109th Bde at B15 (O.P.)	
		8.02 am	Consolidating B.15 Casualties appear few (O.P.)	
		8.10 am	Platoon appears to be retiring near B15 other troops advancing (O.P.)	
		8.15 am	Platoon advancing again (O.P.)	
		8.22 am	Fresh Battalion advancing from THIEPVAL WOOD probably 8th R.I.R (O.P.)	
		8.25 am	15th R.I.R. report by runners that their right Coy had reached A line at 7.50 and Coy on its left at 7.45 am.	
		8.28.	9th R.I.R. report by runner "Batt launched to attack 8.5 am. Batt H.Q R 25 a 15.55. Casualties trifling.	
		8.29 am	12 men retiring from A 13. Rest advancing well. Shrapnel bursting all round them.	
		8.30 am	Report from 109 Bde. All going well. Our support Batts in A line. No news of B line yet.	
		8.39 am	Two parties of prisoners seen coming in from A13.	
		8.45 am	Message by runner from Capt Gaffikin 9th R.I.R. that C line had been easily reached at 8.18 am and that our barrage was short.	

T2134. Wt. W708—776. 500000. 4/15. Sir J. C. & S.

Instructions regarding War Diaries and Intelligence Summaries are contained in F. S. Regs., Part II. and the Staff Manual respectively. Title pages will be prepared in manuscript.

WAR DIARY
or
INTELLIGENCE SUMMARY.
(Erase heading not required.)

Army Form C. 2118.

Place	Date	Hour	Summary of Events and Information	Remarks and references to Appendices
	1st	8.50am	About 40 prisoners coming in from direction of Crucifix (O.P.)	
		8.51am	About 18 prisoners coming in from A.18.	
		8.55am	Our troops advancing over skyline between C9 & C11 and large number of men at Crucifix (O.P.)	
		9.5am	9th R.I.R report their left Coy past CLONES (B.17) attack somewhat mixed up with 108 Inf Bde but going on well.	
		9.10am	15th R.I.R. report left Coy at B line. Casualties heavy	
		9.15am	Batch of prisoners coming in from Crucifix (O.P)	
			9th R.I.R report their left Coy at C line mixed up with 109th Bde but reorganizing	
			15th R.I.R report one Coy passed B line and going forward well.	
		9.20am	9th R.I.R report considerable enemy M. Gun activity from THIEPVAL. Still causing many casualties. (Divn)	
		9.27am	Attack on right of ANCRE (our left) appears to be held up and enemy are still holding their front line (O.P.) (To Div)	
		9.50am	Message from 11th R. Innis Fus (109th Bde) saying that 9th R.I.R were in C line with practically no casualties.	

Instructions regarding War Diaries and Intelligence Summaries are contained in F. S. Regs., Part II. and the Staff Manual respectively. Title pages will be prepared in manuscript.

WAR DIARY
or
INTELLIGENCE SUMMARY.
(Erase heading not required.)

Army Form C. 2118.

Place	Date	Hour	Summary of Events and Information	Remarks and references to Appendices
	1st	10.am	message from 8th R.I.R that enemy are running into our lines in considerable numbers with hands up. (To Div).	
		10.30am	Message again sent to Division that 2 guns near THIEPVAL CHATEAU are still doing considerable damage. (This information received from 9th & 10th R.I.R.)	
		10.40am	15th R.I.R. report that prisoners identified in C. line belong to 12th, 99th, 8th & 479th Rgts. also that heavy rifle fire from our right flank was damaging.	
		11.am	Divn notified that 32nd Div are making a fresh attack on THIEPVAL and that if the line was not already taken it was not to be attacked but 107th Bde was to assist 109th Bde to consolidate and hold C line	
			9th R.I.R report 109th Bde digging in on C line and 107th Bde passing thro'	
			9th R.I.R. report that their C Coy got into C line at 9.50. am. without much loss	
			8th R.I.R report units of 107th and 108th Bde between C & D lines and Germans surrendering from D line.	
		11.40am	9th R.I.R. report their right Coy in position N of Crucifix 9.30.am.	
		12 noon	Message received from 109th Bde to effect that 11th 13th and 15th R.I.R (108th Bde) require reinforcements	

T2134. Wt. W708—776. 500000. 4/15. Sir J. C. & S.

Army Form C. 2118.

Instructions regarding War Diaries and Intelligence Summaries are contained in F. S. Regs., Part II. and the Staff Manual respectively. Title pages will be prepared in manuscript.

WAR DIARY
or
INTELLIGENCE SUMMARY.
(Erase heading not required.)

Place	Date	Hour	Summary of Events and Information	Remarks and references to Appendices
	1st.	12 noon	message received from O.C. 107th T.M. Btty. that they could not advance out of right of THIEPVAL WOOD owing to M. Gun fire from THIEPVAL.	
			message received from 9th R.I.R. that Batts were in front of C line somewhat mixed up	
			message from Lieut Sinclair 9th R.I.R. that 8th and 9th R.I.R had passed through C line and were waiting for the barrage to lift off D line	
			message from Capt Gaffiken 9th R.I.R. sent at 10.47. a.m. he was holding C line near Strabane C 10 and that 8th R.I.R. were near B16. DUNGANNON	
		12.20pm	Message from 13th R.I.R. asking for carrying party at once (Twenty Bde carriers sent)	
		1.15pm	40 Germans seen between A.19 and river (O.P.) (artillery notified)	
		1.30pm	message from 8th R.I.R. that their A Coy is consolidating C9 but cannot get touch with 10th R.I.R. and that reinforcements are urgently required.	
		1.45pm	Message sent to Div to say that messages from the captured C line indicate that troops are very exhausted and that reinforcements are required and that unless THIEPVAL VILLAGE is taken our line will be difficult to hold	

Army Form C. 2118.

Instructions regarding War Diaries and Intelligence Summaries are contained in F. S. Regs., Part II. and the Staff Manual respectively. Title pages will be prepared in manuscript.

WAR DIARY
or
INTELLIGENCE SUMMARY.
(Erase heading not required.)

Place	Date	Hour	Summary of Events and Information	Remarks and references to Appendices
	1st.	1-40 pm	Message from 9th R.I.R. quotes message timed 10.42 am. from Maj Gaffikin to say that he has tried to get in front of C line at C9 OMAGH but held up by M. Gun fire from left front, and reporting D line strongly held	
		1-55 pm	Germans at A19 shelled and bombed back towards River ANCRE. (To Div)	
		2. pm	Lieut McClinton 10th R.I.R. reports that C line is only thinly held and that the troops there are ~~being~~ having a rough time.	
			9th R.I.R. report that their left Coy has diverged to its left towards C10 (STRABANE)	
		2-15 pm	Message from 8th R.I.R. that their A Coy has had to fall back to line B15 – B14 Crucifix owing to heavy casualties from shell fire.	
			Party of prisoners being brought in to THIEPVAL WOOD (O.P.)	
		2-25 pm	9th R.I.R. report Trench Mortar active from THIEPVAL. (To Div)	
		2.30 pm	Germans are between A19 & A21, and our bombers are working down towards them (O.P.)	
		2-45 pm	M. Gun in trench between A19 & B19 (Div asked for this to be shelled)	

T2134. Wt. W708—776. 500000. 4/15. Sir J. C. & S.

Army Form C. 2118.

Instructions regarding War Diaries and Intelligence Summaries are contained in F. S. Regs., Part II. and the Staff Manual respectively. Title pages will be prepared in manuscript.

WAR DIARY
or
INTELLIGENCE SUMMARY.
(Erase heading not required.)

Place	Date	Hour	Summary of Events and Information	Remarks and references to Appendices
	1st	2.50pm	Message from Div saying that R.31 & R 32 will be bombarded till 2-45 pm and that 32nd Div will then attack THIEPVAL again	
		2.33pm	Message from Lieut Liptaft that he is holding a post in B line and has a Lewis gun there and that 11th R.I.R. (108th Bde) have similar post on his left. Bombs - SAA - and reinforcements urgently required (passed to 108th Bde)	
		3.35pm	Message from 9th R.I.R that Germans are shelling our front line with heavies and also their own old front line and that a M. Gun is firing from Right bank of river as well as from THIEPVAL	
		3.40pm	Message from Div that enemy front and support line trenches from R25 c 8.3 to R25 b 1.2 will be bombarded intensely from 3.30 to 4 pm when 49th Div will attack THIEPVAL in co-operation with a Batt of 32nd Div moving on it from the north.	
		4pm	Yellow flag flying at C11 ENNISKILLEN. Party retiring to right of it. Party retiring on B18 - (O.P.)	
		4.5pm	The party seen retiring from B18 is now in NEB (O.P.)	

T2134. Wt. W708—776. 500000. 4/15. Sir J. C. & S.

Instructions regarding War Diaries and Intelligence Summaries are contained in F. S. Regs., Part II. and the Staff Manual respectively. Title pages will be prepared in manuscript.

WAR DIARY
or
INTELLIGENCE SUMMARY.
(Erase heading not required.)

Army Form C. 2118.

Place	Date	Hour	Summary of Events and Information	Remarks and references to Appendices
	1st	4-5pm	message from Division that 107th Bde is if necessary to reinforce troops holding C line and FORT SCHWABEN if necessary D line not now its objective. Two Coys to be sent to left of C line to close road from Grandcourt and reinforce 13th R.I.R. One Coy with Bombers to be sent to left 108th Bde Zone in A & B trenches if 108th Bde requires assistance there. (answered that 107th Bde is already merged into the 108th & 109th Bdes in the holding of C line and FORT SCHWABEN	
		4-15pm	Enemy in B line from B17 to B19 - (O.P.)	
		4-20	message sent to B.G. 146 Bde asking him to give assistance to 109 & 107 who are being driven back.	
			message to Div notifying that 146 Bde had been asked for help as fresh reinforcements were required at once.	
			answer from 146 Brigade that 2 Batts were attacking THIEPVAL. one holding line and one in reserve.	
		4-30pm	message from Div that 146 Bde is placed at disposal of 107th Bde and that 2 Batts are to be pushed forward at once to make good the A & B lines. that	

T2134. Wt. W708—776. 500000. 4/15. Sir J. C. & S.

Army Form C. 2118.

Instructions regarding War Diaries and Intelligence Summaries are contained in F. S. Regs., Part II. and the Staff Manual respectively. Title pages will be prepared in manuscript.

WAR DIARY
or
INTELLIGENCE SUMMARY.
(Erase heading not required.)

Place	Date	Hour	Summary of Events and Information	Remarks and references to Appendices
	1st.	4.20pm	the troops of 107 + 109 Bdes now reported retreating must be rallied by C.O's, and that the ground we now hold must not be given up.	
		4.40pm	Message sent to B.G. 146 Bde ordering him to send forward at once 2 Batts to make good the A + B lines between B14 + B17 and between A13 + A16. to regain lost ground and that 146 Bde is at our disposal but that 2 Batts should be enough as aeroplanes flying very low report very few Hostile troops engaged in counter attack. Our troops retiring must be rallied and sent forward again. SCHWABEN REDOUBT must be reoccupied and held at all costs.	
		5. pm	Message sent to 146 Bde that in accordance with Div instructions FORT SCHWABEN must be retaken and held at all costs	
			The 2 Batts 146 Bde now holding the THIEPVAL WOOD sector will advance at once and occupy and hold the line from C8 to C11 and send 2 Coys to form a defensive flank from A19 to B19.	
		5.30pm	Message to Gen Withycombe from Gen Nugent telling him to counter attack with all available troops of 49th Div placed under his orders. Rally the men falling back and see they go forward again. SCHWABEN must be held at all	

Army Form C. 2118.

Instructions regarding War Diaries and Intelligence Summaries are contained in F. S. Regs., Part II. and the Staff Manual respectively. Title pages will be prepared in manuscript.

WAR DIARY
or
INTELLIGENCE SUMMARY.
(Erase heading not required.)

Place	Date	Hour	Summary of Events and Information	Remarks and references to Appendices
	1st.	5.30	costs. A defensive flank East of ST. PIERRE DIVION to be formed to protect left of A & B lines	
		4.38pm	A number of Germans at B19 working up the trench (O.P.)	
		4.49	A number of Germans still occupying trench A19 to A21 (O.P.)	
		4.57	Some more prisoners brought in (O.P.)	
		5.40pm	36th Div letter G.X. 48 forwarded to 146 Bde also asking B. Gen 146 Bde to reinforce us at FORT SCHWABEN in accordance with my previous order issued at 5 pm as soon as possible, also stating that from reports received it would be now possible owing to a lull to proceed. Troops therefore should be sent to their objectives as quickly as possible. THIEPVAL is not being attacked this evening	
		8.55pm	Answer to above from O.C 146 Bde to say that he had given orders at 7.52 pm for this movement and that they are now being carried out.	
		7.05	Message from Div confirming the fact that 146 Bde was placed at our disposal.	
		7pm	Message sent to all Batts to say that 2 Batts 146 Bde would reinforce troops of 107 & 109 Bdes holding C line.	

T2134. Wt. W708—776. 500000. 4/15. Sir J. C. & S.

Army Form C. 2118.

Instructions regarding War Diaries and Intelligence Summaries are contained in F. S. Regs., Part II. and the Staff Manual respectively. Title pages will be prepared in manuscript.

WAR DIARY
or
INTELLIGENCE SUMMARY.
(*Erase heading not required.*)

Place	Date	Hour	Summary of Events and Information	Remarks and references to Appendices
	1st	7.30pm	Division notified that 1½ Batts 146 Bde had left for line C8 – C11 at 7-18 pm and 2 Coys for A19 - B19 also that 16th (P) R.I.R. have reported and have been sent to dig two communicating trenches from THIEPVAL WOOD to A line also that 4th Y&L are holding our front line and that 148th Bde M. Gun Coy have reported.	
		4-55pm	another party of prisoners being brought in from CRUCIFIX. (O.P.)	
		6. pm	Message from 8th R.I.R. that line being held is as follows:- B13. B14. B16. B17. B18 C11 with defensive flank on left Strong point constructed at R13d 3.6 with 2 Vickers guns also bombing party with Lewis Gun on extreme left flank. Also that Capt McCallum and Capt Curtin who sent report cannot estimate casualties which are heavy, and that bombs are urgently required.	
			Copy of order issued by O.C. 9th R.I.R. that no troops are to retire from C line	
			O.C 9th R I R reports that 70 men 108th Bde who were retiring had been sent back and that Lt Finlay had to fire on them.	
			O.C 9th R.I.R. sends message to say that Lt Harding just back from front reports that retirement alluded to is the 108th Bde from B line (Omagh) mixed up with German fugitives and that Maj Woods has gone to stop them and	

Instructions regarding War Diaries and Intelligence Summaries are contained in F. S. Regs., Part II. and the Staff Manual respectively. Title pages will be prepared in manuscript.

WAR DIARY
or
INTELLIGENCE SUMMARY.
(Erase heading not required.)

Army Form C. 2118.

Place	Date	Hour	Summary of Events and Information	Remarks and references to Appendices
	1st		turn them back.	
		6.5 pm	Following report received from Maj Gaffikin 9th R.I.R timed 3.37 pm:- Right of our line is practically CRUCIFIX. We do not hold it, as a M Gun keeps us out of it but we have the road to it blocked and a Lewis gun on it. There are 2 Lewis guns and 2 Vickers guns at the corner. We hold B14 B15 B17 B18 and C11 and there are about 300 men in and around C9 (Omagh)	
			The 10th are not here at all. There are about 60 of 9th about 120 of 8th. Most of Gin Coy. Smyth, McCauley, Campbell, Hamilton, are here	
			We advanced too soon for our artillery, and in some places the barrage came back, and nearly all our casualties were from that. There was no fight in the Bosch. We are in considerable difficulty. CLONES is so enfiladed by M Gun fire from the left N of the ANCRE. We are also getting quite a bad time from our right, and are sniping very sharply. It is impossible to do any work on top & we have practically no consolidation material. 6 balls of wire and no stakes. I do not think we shall be able to hold out tonight if attacked, as we can be taken from front to rear unless THIEPVAL falls	

Army Form C. 2118.

Instructions regarding War Diaries and Intelligence Summaries are contained in F. S. Regs., Part II. and the Staff Manual respectively. Title pages will be prepared in manuscript.

WAR DIARY
or
INTELLIGENCE SUMMARY.
(Erase heading not required.)

Place	Date	Hour	Summary of Events and Information	Remarks and references to Appendices
	1st		and the men are very exhausted, and both Lewis Guns and M Guns are short of Amm. We are short of bombs. Could you send us water tonight. Roughly position is that we are hanging on by our eyebrows to the SW sides of the Parallelogram and Coy in the E front of it. The men are not fit to attack again. We have food enough. There are 2 good dug outs in B line. If it had not been for barrage we could have taken D line sitting. The wire was sufficiently cut	
		6.30	Report from Maj Gaffiken 9th R I R that a trench is dug and is being deepened for right defensive flank	
		6.45p	Following report from 8th R.I.R timed 6 pm:- Can find no foundation for rumour of front troops retiring. About 20 men were seen coming back in 108th Bde area. They appeared to have some Germans with them. They may have been an escort + ammunition party. I believe this party was fired on from our front line but cannot ascertain who by. The Sergeant Maj of my rear Coy reports that his coy is in the German front line and have blocked their flank. He says the other Coys are in the 3rd line mixed up with other units. Our casualties have been extremely heavy. He reports not having seen an officer for 2 hours. I believe Lt McClinton	

T2134. Wt. W708—776. 500000. 4/15. Sir J. C. & S.

Instructions regarding War Diaries and Intelligence Summaries are contained in F. S. Regs., Part II. and the Staff Manual respectively. Title pages will be prepared in manuscript.

WAR DIARY
or
INTELLIGENCE SUMMARY.
(Erase heading not required.)

Army Form C. 2118.

Place	Date	Hour	Summary of Events and Information	Remarks and references to Appendices
	1st		a very excellent officer is there still. The Sergt Maj came back for ammunition for his Coy, and Lewis guns, and has returned. I have no further information up to date.	
		7pm	Following message from 8th R. I R. timed 6.43 p.m. Am in line C10 C11 with Lt Coote, CSM Hall & 50 men with 1 Lewis gun. I have only about 12 of D Coy here. So far as can be observed none of our Bde has been able to enter D line. NB This message was actually written at 12.30 p.m. but only reached Bde HQ at 6.35 pm.	
		7.50	Report from 2/Lt Bennett 10th R I R. Have been in German B line 160x N of CRUCIFIX. Party consists of 2 Sergts 5 men occupied trench about 10.30 a.m.	
		8.15pm	Div wires as follows :- (timed 7.55 pm) 4th Y & L 148 Bde from AVELUY WOOD is ordered up to report to you also 148th Bde M. G. Coy.	
		8pm	Following message received from 9th R. I. R. 'A carrying party of ours going forward with S.A.A. etc has just been turned back for some unknown reason by 109th Bde. We have sent the party forward again with	

Instructions regarding War Diaries and Intelligence Summaries are contained in F. S. Regs., Part II. and the Staff Manual respectively. Title pages will be prepared in manuscript.

WAR DIARY
or
INTELLIGENCE SUMMARY.
(Erase heading not required.)

Army Form C. 2118.

Place	Date	Hour	Summary of Events and Information	Remarks and references to Appendices
	1st		a written order to proceed.	
		8.45pm	Message received from Div that 3 Coys Pioneers and 2 Coys RE of 49th Div are placed at disposal of 36th Div They will all proceed to PAISLEY AVENUE reporting to 107th Bde. N.B. When these units arrived they were deposited in slit trenches in Thiepval Wood to await orders. The Os C remaining at Bde HQ	
		10pm	Message from O.C 9th R Ir Rif to say that troops of 146th Bde are now up in front line and that the Germans had started a bombing attack but were being held.	
		(?)	Message from Lt Lipstaff 15th R.I.R. (no time given) Unless reinforcements with supplies of bombs and ammn come up very shortly I cannot hold A2 line any longer since I have nobody on my right flank and enemy occupies trench on our left.	
		10.30pm	Message from Lt Madden 16th (P) R.I.R. who was sent up to dig a CT from ELGIN AVENUE to the NEB Fear Germans are in A+B lines Men streaming back Can you send help or artillery support.	
		11pm	Following message received from Brig Gen comdg 146th Bde:–	

T2134. Wt. W708—776. 500000. 4/15. Sir J. C. & S.

Instructions regarding War Diaries and Intelligence Summaries are contained in F. S. Regs., Part II. and the Staff Manual respectively. Title pages will be prepared in manuscript.

WAR DIARY
or
INTELLIGENCE SUMMARY.
(Erase heading not required.)

Army Form C. 2118.

Place	Date	Hour	Summary of Events and Information	Remarks and references to Appendices
	1st		Regret to say Batt sent to C8 & C11 has turned back on account of shelling & M. G. fire. Have sent them up again and will organize two more Coys to go up. Have also ordered up Section of M. Guns and to A19 & B19 also".	
		(?)	Message (untimed) from 109 Bde to say that 10th R. Ins Fus report over 100 men of 49th Div are holding German B line opposite ELGIN AVENUE.	
		11-3 pm	Following message received from O. C 9th R/R "Counter attacked 10.5 pm am told Bosch is getting into his original front line. Cannot say how many men were left but counter attack came in great force. (NB about this hour the Bde major came in with similar report.	
		(?)	Message received from Lt Eyde (?) TMSO. 36 Div reporting that considerable numbers of infantry were retiring from German trenches. When questioned they reported that the Germans were attacking from both flanks and that they had been ordered to retire.	
		11-pm	NB. At about 11 pm as the situation seemed somewhat obscure and it was still doubtful whether all our troops had really retired from C & B lines. If so whether they had been ordered to retire. I sent	

T2134. Wt. W708—776. 500000. 4/15. Sir J. C. & S.

Instructions regarding War Diaries and Intelligence Summaries are contained in F. S. Regs., Part II. and the Staff Manual respectively. Title pages will be prepared in manuscript.

WAR DIARY
or
INTELLIGENCE SUMMARY.
(Erase heading not required.)

Army Form C. 2118.

Place	Date	Hour	Summary of Events and Information	Remarks and references to Appendices
	1st		my Bde Major up to the front to try and clear the situation up. From his report after interviewing various commanding Officers and other Officers just back from C line it seemed fairly obvious that none of our troops were now in the parallelogram or in the German A line of the right Section. Men of all units of 107th + 109th Bde, and of 146th Bde were wounded in the front line and Service trench of Thiepval Wood, + the slit trenches were crowded with wounded. The enemy were shelling the whole wood heavily with HE + Shrapnel and gas shells. As far as could be ascertained Maj Peacock who was the senior officer in the parallelogram + Capt Montgomery next senior officer there, had come to the conclusion that their position was now untenable, and that with both flanks in the air the enemy still holding THIEPVAL VILLAGE and their original position across the river ANCRE + ST PIERRE DIVION and counter-attacking him on all sides, he gave the order to retire to avoid being surrounded	

Instructions regarding War Diaries and Intelligence Summaries are contained in F. S. Regs., Part II. and the Staff Manual respectively. Title pages will be prepared in manuscript.

WAR DIARY
or
INTELLIGENCE SUMMARY.
(Erase heading not required.)

Army Form C. 2118.

Place	Date	Hour	Summary of Events and Information	Remarks and references to Appendices
	July ~~2nd~~ 1st	11-pm	The Officer of 109th Bde who originally got to C8 (LISNASKEA) stated that he could not hold it owing to fire from his right and right rear and the same applied to B13 (CRUCIFIX) owing to fire from THIEPVAL VILLAGE. In fact every officer interviewed had the same story, that with the enemy holding THIEPVAL and the trenches to the east of it, and also holding high ground on right of the ANCRE the position in the PARALELLOGRAM was impossible. NB the gist of above report was given on the telephone to the Div.	
			At about this time I rang up the 108th Bde on the telephone to ask if they could give me any instruction as to the situation, and was informed that as far as could be ascertained our troops had retired from the A & B lines in their section (Right Centre)	
			At about 11.30 pm I was informed on the telephone by Div that one ~~Batt~~ (4th YORK & LANC REGT.) of 148th Inf Bde was being sent up to me, and that I was to collect the remnants of 107th & 109th Bde now back in THIEPVAL WOOD and organize an attack (using the 4th Y&L supported by remnants of 107th & 109th Bde to retake the PARALELLOGRAM (FORT SCHWABAN).	
			Shortly afterwards I was informed on the telephone by Div, that instead of using troops of 107th & 109th Bdes to support this attack I would get 2 more Batts of 148th Bde (I.E. 4th & 5th KOYLI) and to attack FORT SCHWABAN with these three Batts	
			The 4th Y&L then arrived, and I sent them to assembly trenches to be ready to attack when required.	

Army Form C. 2118.

Instructions regarding War Diaries and Intelligence Summaries are contained in F. S. Regs., Part II. and the Staff Manual respectively. Title pages will be prepared in manuscript.

WAR DIARY
or
INTELLIGENCE SUMMARY.
(*Erase heading not required.*)

Place	Date	Hour	Summary of Events and Information	Remarks and references to Appendices
	~~1st July~~ 2nd	MIDNIGHT 12	At 12 MN I recived a message from the B.G.C. 146th Bde to the effect that the 4th & 5th K.O.Y.L.I. would leave AVELUY WOOD at 12.15 am & 12.45 am respectively and march to join me. At 1 am these Batts had not yet arrived, and I was faced with the following situation:- (1) It was doubtful whether it would be possible to start the attack before daylight, in which case the advance would be swept by enfilade M.G. fire from THIEPVAL (which I was informed would not be attacked that night) and THIEPVAL WOOD was being so heavily shelled and trench mortared that troops moving up over the open through the WOOD were bound to suffer before deploying to the attack. (2) If the attack did start before dawn it was doubtful whether they could have kept their direction in the dark not having previously reconnoitered the ground by daylight. (3) If they did keep their direction and re-occupied FORT SCHWABAN they would the next day be in the same untenable position that the 36th Div had been in the day before. I was so strongly of opinion from all reports I had received that until THIEPVAL VILLAGE was taken it would be impossible to hold FORT SCHWABAN - I had a final consultation with the B.G.C. 109th Bde who entirely agreed with me, and I advised that this attack should not take place.	

1577 Wt. W10791/1773 500,000 1/15 D. D. & L. A.D.S.S./Forms/C. 2118.

Army Form C. 2118.

WAR DIARY
or
INTELLIGENCE SUMMARY.
(*Erase heading not required.*)

Instructions regarding War Diaries and Intelligence Summaries are contained in F. S. Regs., Part II. and the Staff Manual respectively. Title pages will be prepared in manuscript.

Place	Date	Hour	Summary of Events and Information	Remarks and references to Appendices
	~~1st~~ 2nd	1. am	I was informed on the telephone shortly afterwards that the matter had been referred to the X th Corps, and that being on the spot and in the best position to judge I could make my own decision I consequently cancelled this attack and sent the 4th & 5th K.O.Y.L.I. back to AVELUY WOOD, keeping the 4th Y & L near GORDON CASTLE and the 148th Bde M. Gun Coy in slit trenches just in rear.	
		1-5 am	Message from O.C 107th Bde M. Gun Coy to say he had met men of 107th, 108th & 109th Bdes coming in to the front line of THIEPVAL WOOD from "no mans land", saying that they had been ordered to retire from their positions in the German line. He shortly afterwards saw Major Peacock 9th Royal Innis Fus who confirmed this.	
		2-15	Following message received from B.G.C 146th Bde "After my last message. The Batt & a half did go up towards C8 & C11. I have heard nothing of them since Reports from my companies sent to A19 & B19 state that all our people on that flank have fallen back to German front line about A16 & A17. I reinforced these companies and heard nothing further. The remainder of my Brigade has been placed under 32nd Div." I was now faced with the problem of holding the THIEPVAL WOOD subsector. Daylight was approaching and there was a congestion of troops of all Batts of 107th 108th & 109th Bdes also of two Batts of 146th Bde all mixed up in the front position of the wood each under their respective commanding officers. I accordingly sent the 3 Corps pioneers	

1577 Wt. W10791/1773 500,000 1/15 D. D. & L. A.D.S.S./Forms/C. 2118.

Army Form C. 2118.

WAR DIARY
or
INTELLIGENCE SUMMARY.
(Erase heading not required.)

Instructions regarding War Diaries and Intelligence Summaries are contained in F. S. Regs., Part II. and the Staff Manual respectively. Title pages will be prepared in manuscript.

Place	Date	Hour	Summary of Events and Information	Remarks and references to Appendices
	2nd	2.15a	and 2 Field Companies of 49th Division back to AVELUY WOOD to clear the congestion in the rear portion of THIEPVAL WOOD and ordered the O.C 4th Y&L to take over the line putting 3 Coys in the firing line an 1 in support. I ordered the B G C 146th Bde to collect his Batts and place them in the slit trenches between ELGIN AVE and the River, and to act as support to the left section of the line and the troops of 36th Div all under command of Col Ricardo 9th R. Innis Fus to occupy the slit trenches between Elgin Ave and Enniskillen Ave in support to the left section of the line. All available men I could collect were utilized in clearing wounded under 110 Field Ambulance.	
		3.13a	Following message received from B. G. C. 146th Bde "I do not know where my Batts are. I have only 1 Coy available which is already up in our front line N end of ELGIN AVE. It appears to be true that everybody has retired from A line to our front trench N of THIEPVAL WOOD. No news from C8. Have you?"	
		335	Following message received from O.C 16th R. I Rif (P) "Our troops in enemy A line have fallen back on our front line. There appears to be very little hope of building the communicating trenches across no mans land tonight".	

1577 Wt. W10791/1773 500,000 1/15 D. D. & L. A.D.S.S./Forms/C. 2118

Army Form C. 2118.

Instructions regarding War Diaries and Intelligence Summaries are contained in F. S. Regs., Part II. and the Staff Manual respectively. Title pages will be prepared in manuscript.

WAR DIARY
or
INTELLIGENCE SUMMARY.

(Erase heading not required.)

Place	Date	Hour	Summary of Events and Information	Remarks and references to Appendices
	2nd	6.15	Message received from O.C 9th R.I.R. to say that 3 men of 11th R.I.R. report that A line is unoccupied.	

1577 Wt. W10791/1773 500,000 1/15 D. D. & L. A.D.S.S./Forms/C. 2118.

Instructions regarding War Diaries and Intelligence Summaries are contained in F. S. Regs., Part II. and the Staff Manual respectively. Title pages will be prepared in manuscript.

WAR DIARY
or
INTELLIGENCE SUMMARY.
(Erase heading not required.)

Army Form C. 2118.

Place	Date	Hour	Summary of Events and Information	Remarks and references to Appendices
	2nd	7. a.m	Bde O P reported that there were some of our men (about 20 or 30) still in A line between A18 & A19. They appeared to be wandering about the trenches and that parties of Germans seemed to be doing the same between A19 & A21 and A19 and B19.	
			This was evidently confirmed from various other O.P's to the Div. with the result that at 10 26 am I received the following message from the Div timed 10-6 a.m.	
		10.26	"The detachments of our men now in the German A & B lines must be supported and reinforcements sent. Bombs and SAA to be sent up to them and the position they hold to be consolidated and the flanks strongly held by blocking parties. Report as soon as possible boundaries held by us"	
		11-a.m	In accordance with above I issued the following order:-	
			"It has been ascertained that parties of our men were still in the German trenches between A19 & A15	
			Lieut Colonel F P. Crozier Comdg 9th R. I Rif will organize an operation to reinforce these men and to occupy and consolidate the lines A15. A17. A19.	
			For this purpose all available officers & men of 8-9-10 & 15th R. I Rif will be placed at the disposal of Lt Col Crozier forthwith and the operation will be carried out as soon as possible.	

Army Form C. 2118.

Instructions regarding War Diaries and Intelligence Summaries are contained in F. S. Regs., Part II. and the Staff Manual respectively. Title pages will be prepared in manuscript.

WAR DIARY
or
INTELLIGENCE SUMMARY.
(Erase heading not required.)

Place	Date	Hour	Summary of Events and Information	Remarks and references to Appendices
	2nd	11 a.m	Parties will be detailed for the blocking of all communication trenches to the front. after the position is occupied the O.C. 107th Bde M Gun Coy will send up 4 guns to be placed at the disposal of Lt. Col Crozier. A carrying party will also be sent up with grenades and S.A.A. The artillery will barrage N of A19 and S of A15 and B line E of these two points Lt. Col Crozier will detail a selected officer whose sole duty it will be to report exactly what position we hold in A line. Lt. Col Crozier will notify Brigade the hour at which he will be ready to start. Special care must be taken to indicate our position to the O.P. on MESNIL RIDGE by flags or flares. On receipt of these instructions Lt. Col. Crozier issued the following orders "It has now been ascertained that parties of our men are still holding on in the German trenches between A19 & A15 with the object of occupying these trenches A force as under will leave GORDON CASTLE at 1 pm in the order named 10th R.I.R. 60 men 9th do 100 do 8th do 100 do 15th do. 100 do Having been drawn up in no mans land N of ELGIN AVENUE in lines of columns of Platoons in fours the Right of 10th R I R will march on A15 thence to C T running into trench between A16 & A17. The	

1577 Wt. W10791/1773 500,000 1/15 D. D. & L. A.D.S.S./Forms/C. 2118.

Army Form C. 2118.

WAR DIARY
or
INTELLIGENCE SUMMARY.
(Erase heading not required.)

Instructions regarding War Diaries and Intelligence Summaries are contained in F. S. Regs., Part II. and the Staff Manual respectively. Title pages will be prepared in manuscript.

Place	Date	Hour	Summary of Events and Information	Remarks and references to Appendices
	2nd	11-am	9th R.I.R. will march in line with 10th R.I.R. the 8th R.I.R. will follow 10th R.I.R. and 15th R.I.R. will follow 9th R.I.R.	
			The whole will move forward in succession in artillery formation on whistle which will be taken up by every one in possesion of a whistle.	
			10th R.I.R. will consolidate A15 the 9th R.I.R. will consolidate A17 & A19 and the trench between them. The 8th R.I.R. will consolidate A18 and the trench E of it joining up with 10th R.I.R. who will consolidate A15 to NW	
			The 15th R.I.R. will consolidate from A18 exclusive to 300x W of this point.	
			The 10th R.I.R. will block the German fire trench to the E of A15 and the fire trench to the W of A16	
			The 9th R.I.R. will block the trenches running N & NW from A19.	
			The 15th R.I.R. will block the trench W of the 300x point referred to above.	
			Picks and shovels will be carried by every man, and all work will be taken in hand immediately. All positions will have to be consolidated before being handed over.	
			The artillery will barrage N of A19 and S of A15 and also B line E of these 2 points.	
			9th and 10th R.I.R. will arrange telephone communication from German trenches to our fire trench.	
			Machine Guns Separate orders will be issued to O C Bde M. Gun Coy. All ranks will carry water bottles filled and remaining portion of days ration	
			Batt HQ will be at A18.	
			C C Hine Lt & Adjt. 9th R.I.R.	

1577 Wt. W10791/1773 500,000 1/15 D. D. & L. A.D.S.S./Forms/C. 2118.

Instructions regarding War Diaries and Intelligence Summaries are contained in F. S. Regs., Part II. and the Staff Manual respectively. Title pages will be prepared in manuscript.

WAR DIARY
or
INTELLIGENCE SUMMARY.
(Erase heading not required.)

Army Form C. 2118.

Place	Date	Hour	Summary of Events and Information	Remarks and references to Appendices
	2nd		Reference above orders, the advance was afterwards postponed until 2 p.m	
			Lt Col Crozier had intended to lead the advance himself, but I stopped him and Maj P J WOODS 9th R.I.R took his place.	
			At 2.15 p.m the artillery barrage started and the lines advanced according to orders each line in succession entering the German A line. The 15th R.I.R. unluckily ran into some German shells at the top of ELGIN AVENUE on the way up and lost a lot of men, otherwise the lines were all across before the Germans realised what had happened. Almost immediately afterwards however they started to shell our front line in THIEPVAL WOOD heavily and also put a barrage on the SUNKEN ROAD in No mans land	
			At about 2.30 p.m the sections of the Bde M. Gun Coy ran the gauntlet of this and entered A line with the loss of only 3 men.	
		3 pm	Message as follows received from Lt Hogg 15th R.I.R. I am hit and about done. O'Connor hit badly Crawford lost no men. Very few of 15th with me only about 20 left of my party. Am doing my best tell Col Crozier	
		3-10	Message from Col Crozier observer states Bosch barrage between our line & German line. Heavy shelling in Speyside.	
		3-15	Message from Maj Woods. All are now in position as per O.O. We are working hard on consolidation. We have taken about 40 casualties per Battn	
			Send my signallers I cannot find ours. At A18 I have put a yellow flag where it can be seen from O.P.	

1577 Wt. W10791/1773 500,000 1/15 D. D. & L. A.D.S.S./Forms/C. 2118

Instructions regarding War Diaries and Intelligence Summaries are contained in F. S. Regs., Part II. and the Staff Manual respectively. Title pages will be prepared in manuscript.

WAR DIARY
or
INTELLIGENCE SUMMARY.
(Erase heading not required.)

Army Form C. 2118.

Place	Date	Hour	Summary of Events and Information	Remarks and references to Appendices
	2nd	3-15	Have seen nothing but dead in these trenches 330 pm	
		3.37	Message from Lt G W Garner. 9th R I R all across without casualties as far as I could see. Germans shelling THIEPVAL WOOD but not their own line	
		3.55	Message from Capt J E Sugden 10th R.I.R. "10th R.I.R. are now in German A line. No casualties. Germans not shelling own line"	
			Message from Lt McClinton, 10th R.I.R. timed 3.45 p.m. I think our shelling ought to be ordered to cease. Germans are retaliating on our lines causing numerous casualties.	
			N.B. On receipt of above I asked the artillery Liason Officer to stop our artillery which he did gradually.	
		4 pm	Message from Lt Col Crozier timed 3.50 pm "Phone is not working Lt Garner is at top of Elgin Ave, and will assist in forwarding messages From what I can hear barrage on nomans land is still on. In this case parties may not be able to get through. Sandbags short wire and stakes will be required to-night Gaps can be left in wire to pass through."	
		4-40	Message from Maj Woods (4-10 pm) At 4-3 pm I obtained communication with artillery F.O.O. and asked for barrage on B line between B 14 & River as Headly reported enemy concentrated there.	
			At about this hour I sent a party of 40 men of 16th (P) R I R up with bombs & SAA from Bde HQ. This party under Lieut	

Instructions regarding War Diaries and Intelligence Summaries are contained in F. S. Regs., Part II. and the Staff Manual respectively. Title pages will be prepared in manuscript.

WAR DIARY
or
INTELLIGENCE SUMMARY.
(Erase heading not required.)

Army Form C. 2118.

Place	Date	Hour	Summary of Events and Information	Remarks and references to Appendices
	2nd	4.55	Dawson crossed in a very gallant manner through the barrage and delivered their stores successfully.	
		5 pm	Message from Maj Woods timed 4.30 pm. "40 W Yorks are reported by an intelligent man as being down on extreme left. I am getting them up in touch with my left 16th R.I.R are in on right of 9th R.I.R enemy has been putting H.E and shrapnel on this line and now has a M. Gun from THIEPVAL in action Signallers have arrived on right but wire is cut. I am making arrangements for messages by F.O.O wire Repeated by visual F.O.O wire cut. Message from Maj Woods timed 4.40 pm Bosch throwing Glass bombs are on right of 10th R.I.R. About this hour I sent a second party of 16th (P) R.I.R across with bombs and SAA they crossed successfully but had casualties in doing so I also sent a party of 30 men of 122 F.C.R.E attached to me up with consolidating material but they were unable to cross owing to barrage & remained near Elgin Ave.	
		5.45	Message from Maj Woods timed 4.55 pm 40 W. Yorks on left were found. I have brought them up to my left Cannot find 8th Officer No report from them.	

1577 Wt. W10791/1773 500,000 1/15 D. D. & L. A.D.S.S./Forms/C. 2118.

Instructions regarding War Diaries and Intelligence Summaries are contained in F. S. Regs., Part II. and the Staff Manual respectively. Title pages will be prepared in manuscript.

WAR DIARY
or
INTELLIGENCE SUMMARY.
(Erase heading not required.)

Army Form C. 2118.

Place	Date	Hour	Summary of Events and Information	Remarks and references to Appendices
	2nd	5.45 pm	Message from O C 8th R. I. Rif 5.35 pm "Following report from our Batt in A line "Suffering heavily Bombing attack on our right. One officer just returned wounded reports Germans closing up on A line with a view to attack.	
		6 pm	Message from Lt McClinton 10th R. I. R timed 5.20 pm "Sergt Lammey retd wounded reports consolidation going on ahead. Threats of bomb attack from Right.	
			Following message received from Maj Woods timed 6.30 pm "Corpl Sanders C Coy 7th W. Yorks is with me. His men are fairly played out but full of fight. 30 men and 12 wounded which will require a stretcher party tonight. The trenches in vicinity of A19 are impracticable to work on in daylight so am establishing posts when nothing better can be done.	
			x I received your two messages and will carry them out. We have had a bombing attack on the right and are being considerably annoyed from net work of trenches at A14. Capt McCallum has been to see me. He reports having communicated with Bde O. P. by mirror. A15 A18 A17 almost consolidated. Trenches coming on well. Bosch is too interested in us. No Blighty yet nor expected.	
			x. These two messages referred to were:- (a) Telling Maj Woods to work up CT to B19 and then down towards ST. PIERRE DIVION (b) To send me a report showing exactly the positions held by our troops	

1577 Wt. W10791/1773 500,000 1/15 D. D. & L. A.D.S.S./Forms/C. 2118.

Instructions regarding War Diaries and Intelligence Summaries are contained in F. S. Regs., Part II. and the Staff Manual respectively. Title pages will be prepared in manuscript.

WAR DIARY
or
INTELLIGENCE SUMMARY.
(Erase heading not required.)

Army Form C. 2118.

Place	Date	Hour	Summary of Events and Information	Remarks and references to Appendices
	2nd		message from Maj Woods timed 6.39 pm "Casualties 13th R.I.R about 50 including 2/Lt Wilson killed. 10th RIR 10 killed and wounded 9th R.I.R 30 killed and wounded. 8th RIR 17 killed and wounded including 2 officers.	
			Please send me grenades, red flares and Water. Also some Very lights. Carriers have not reported but are in working in trenches. 2/Lt Martin M.G. Coy wounded.	
			message from Maj Woods timed 7.40 pm "Have posted 30 men and Lewis Gun at A19 similar in A17 and A16 a vickers gun is at A15 and a Lewis gun and 30 men near A18. I am treating this latter as reserve. Its been great Staff work making the guns fit in, but its worked out all right. Every thing is lovely. I intend to take this gun and any men I can get to establish B19 working up trenches (commn) from A16 & A17. The reconnaissance towards St PIERRE DIVION will commence at 8 pm	
			message (?) received In reply ^line^ from 50x SE of A16 to 50x NW of A19. Depth varying from 100x to 200x in accordance with Bosch front line & support line. Men required to hold this line as it is now 300. 5 Lewis Guns. Am doing my best. I dont understand about flares to be fired immediately, but am doing so from each flank at 8 pm.	
			message from 8th R.I.R timed 7.46 pm. "We have practically consolidated, and are standing to now expecting an enemy patrol but up to the present no sign of it. Found 5 men (various Batts) in a dug out. They say the Germans visited them this	

1577 Wt. W10791/1773 500,000 1/15 D. D. & L. A.D.S.S./Forms/C. 2118.

Instructions regarding War Diaries and Intelligence Summaries are contained in F. S. Regs., Part II. and the Staff Manual respectively. Title pages will be prepared in manuscript.

WAR DIARY
or
INTELLIGENCE SUMMARY.
(*Erase heading not required.*)

Army Form C. 2118.

Place	Date	Hour	Summary of Events and Information	Remarks and references to Appendices
	2nd		morning, and took all our men prisoners who could walk (about 9) will require stretcher bearers to bring these men in. Am sending back a map herewith found in a dugout. Water urgently required. Casualties about 30."	
			On receipt of above I sent a party of 131 F.C. RE under Lt Fawcett up with water tins. As Lt Fawcetts party had been at work continually throughout the day in helping the Field Ambulance in carrying wounded, I told him to hand the water over to the officer i/c the party of 132 F.C., R.E. which I had originally sent up with R.E. material, but had failed to get across. This he did but the party of 132 F.C. RE apparently still were unable to cross. The officer i/c came in and told me this, and also that his men were done, so I told him to take them away.	
			At about 7 pm Two Batts of 148th Bde arrived also Bde HQ on their arrival I told the B.G. Comdg 146th Bde that he could move his Batts away which he did and the 4th & 5th K.O.Y.L.I. (148th Bde) took their places in the Assembly trenches in the wood. I had previously given the B.G.C. 109th Bde permission to move his Bde back (about 2 p.m.)	
			Apparently at about this hour the 49th Div assumed command from 36th Div, because at 8.30 pm the B.G.C. 148th Bde received the following messages from the 49th Div:–	
			(1) Time 8.13 p.m.	
			"Artillery observer reports German helmets seen moving along	

1577 Wt. W10791/1773 500,000 1/15 D. D. & L. A.D.S.S./Forms/C. 2118.

Instructions regarding War Diaries and Intelligence Summaries are contained in F. S. Regs., Part II. and the Staff Manual respectively. Title pages will be prepared in manuscript.

WAR DIARY
or
INTELLIGENCE SUMMARY.
(Erase heading not required.)

Army Form C. 2118.

Place	Date	Hour	Summary of Events and Information	Remarks and references to Appendices
	3rd	am 6.50	Have just arrived. Two guns sent over yesterday got there without casualties. One was placed on the Left flank and the other on the Right. The right gun was bombed by German party 2/Lt Martin being killed and the gun knocked out. This team reported at SPEYSIDE at 2.30 am. One Sergt with six men have not reported yet, but were seen in trenches two hours before I left.	
		10.40	Following message sent to me by Lt Col Crozier. "Relief complete have handed over to 4th Y & L to Maj Woods satisfaction. Maj Woods is back and the whole of surviving party. Casualties approximately 200	
		1.15	O C 10th RIR sent following message. "One of my Lewis Gun Sergts has just come in with his team and reports to me that all our men are relieved and on their way back. Two officers are bringing the remainder in in small parties. I think this information is reliable and good. I will let you know as soon as Lt Bennett comes in with his report.	
			During the operations on 2nd July in the German A line round A15 to A19 the following German prisoners were captured and brought back by the party when relieved:- 1 officer (wounded) 7 soldiers (wounded) 6 do (unwounded)	
			At 11 pm on 2nd July the BGC 148 Bde took over command of operations and I withdraw to Martinsart.	

1577 Wt. W10791/1773 500,000 1/15 D. D. & L. A.D.S.S./Forms/C. 2118.

Instructions regarding War Diaries and Intelligence Summaries are contained in F. S. Regs., Part II. and the Staff Manual respectively. Title pages will be prepared in manuscript.

WAR DIARY
or
INTELLIGENCE SUMMARY.
(Erase heading not required.)

Army Form C. 2118.

Place	Date	Hour	Summary of Events and Information	Remarks and references to Appendices
	3rd		I have since received the following report from 2/Lt Harding 9th R.I.R. giving an account of his experiences in A line 2nd July. "At about 3 pm a man of 8th R.I. Rif reported to me that he had found some men of the W Yorks down on my left, so I went down and took them up to join our party. Cpl Sanders was in charge and he had 33 men with him. He told me that the night before he had repulsed a German bombing party, killing 3 men, and said that he had rescued 3 wounded men of 8th R.I. Rif whom the Germans had taken. At about 5 pm the Germans started a bombing attack on our Right near A15. This was beaten off by 8th R.I.R. and 10th R.I.R. During this attack 7 wounded Germans gave themselves up. At about 8 pm the enemy started a bombing attack at A19 down the CT from B line. This was repulsed and the trench was then blocked. After this Lt Healy (since killed) 9th R.I.R took a party and worked up the trench to B line and took 6 wounded Germans prisoner, all of 99th Reserve Inf Rgt. This party penetrated to B line near B19 and tried to work towards ST PIERRE DIVION but were unable to get very far as the trenches were flattened out so they returned to A19 and helped to consolidate it.	

1577 Wt. W10791/1773 500,000 1/15 D. D. & L. A.D.S.S./Forms/C. 2118

Instructions regarding War Diaries and Intelligence Summaries are contained in F. S. Regs., Part II. and the Staff Manual respectively. Title pages will be prepared in manuscript.

WAR DIARY
or
INTELLIGENCE SUMMARY.
(Erase heading not required.)

Army Form C. 2118.

Place	Date	Hour	Summary of Events and Information	Remarks and references to Appendices
	July			
Martinsart	3rd		Remnants of the Brigade under Lt Col F.P. CROZIER 9th R.I.R. were relieved from German A Line by 4th York & Lancaster Regt and returned to MARTINSART where the Brigade assembled – MARTINSART was shelled from 6 P.M. to 8 P.M. 4 officers of 10th R.I.R. being knocked out.	
HARPONVILLE	4th		The Brigade marched to HARPONVILLE at 9 am.	
RUBEMPRE	5		The G.O.C. addressed the Brigade which was drawn up near HARPONVILLE Church at 10.30 am. & congratulated them on the work they had done on July 1st & 2nd. At 12 noon sudden orders were received to move to RUBEMPRE at 3 P.M. which the Brigade did by March Route.	
Rubempré	6		Re organizing at Rubempré.	
– " –	7		– " – . Orders to be ready to move at 1 hours notice	
– " –	8		– " – – " –	
– " –	9		– " – – " –	
BERNAVILLE	10		Brigade marched from Rubempré at 6.30 am. to BERNAVILLE (14 miles) getting in at 11.15 am.	
WARDREQUES	11		Brigade H.Q. marched from BERNAVILLE at 5 am. to AUXI LE CHATEAU & entrained there at 11.15 am. for THIENNES where we arrived at 3.30 P.M. & marched to WARDRECQUES (10m)	

Instructions regarding War Diaries and Intelligence Summaries are contained in F. S. Regs., Part II. and the Staff Manual respectively. Title pages will be prepared in manuscript.

WAR DIARY
or
INTELLIGENCE SUMMARY.
(Erase heading not required.)

Army Form C. 2118.

Place	Date	Hour	Summary of Events and Information	Remarks and references to Appendices
	July			
	11		The 8th 9th 10th & 15th R.I.R. with Bde M Gun Coy & 107 T.M. Batty followed by same route at 3 hours interval entraining at AUXI LE CHATEAU and detraining at THIENNES & marching to WARDRECQUES. The 15th R.I.R. the last Batt to arrive did not reach WARDRECQUES till 10 am, 12th July	R.
WARDRECQUES	12		at WARDRECQUES.	
LA PANNE	13		Brigade marched at 7 am. From WARDRECQUES via ARQUES - St OMER - TILQUES to Billeting area round BAYENGHEM. (13 miles). Battns distributed as follows:-	
			8th R.I.R. BAYENGHEM - OUEST MONT - EST MONT.	
			9th R.I.R. BAYENGHEM. LA COMMUNE - LE COMMUNAL.	
			10th R.I.R. NORTLEULINGHEM.	R.
			15th R.I.R. WESTROVE - MONNECOVE.	
			107 Bde M.Gun Coy. WESTROVE.	
			107 T.M. Batty. NORTLEULINGHEM.	
			Brigade H.Q. LA PANNE.	
— " —	14		} Battns reorganizing & Training. New Drafts arrived.	
	15		}	R.

T2134. Wt. W708—776. 500000. 4/15. Sir J. C. & S.

Instructions regarding War Diaries and Intelligence Summaries are contained in F. S. Regs., Part II. and the Staff Manual respectively. Title pages will be prepared in manuscript.

Army Form C. 2118.

WAR DIARY
or
INTELLIGENCE SUMMARY.
(Erase heading not required.)

Place	Date	Hour	Summary of Events and Information	Remarks and references to Appendices
	July			
LA PANNE.	16		LA Panne Area. All units engaged in training.	
	17			
	18			
	19			
VOLKERING-KOVE.	20		Brigade marched from LAPANNE area at 9 a.m. to VOLKERINGKOVE area. 9th & 15th R.I.R. billeted in BOLLEZEELE. 8th R.I.R. in MERKEGHEM. 10th R.I.R. M Gun Coy. T.M. Batty and Bde H.Q. in VOLKERINGKOVE.	
WORMHOUDT	21		Brigade marched at 9 a.m. from VOLKERINGKOVE area to WORMHOUDT.	
St MARIE CAPPEL	22		Brigade marched at 8 a.m. from WORMHOUDT to ST MARIE CAPPEL and HONNEGHEM via CASSEL. 8th 9th 10th & 15th R.I.R. billeted at HONNEGHEM and Bde H.Q. M gun Coy and T.M. Batty at ST MARIE Cappel.	
STEENWERCK	23		Brigade marched at 9 a.m. to STEENWERCK (15 miles).	
STEENWERCK	24		at STEENWERCK.	
	25			
	26			
	27		8th R.I.R. and 10th R.I.R. moved to KORTEPYP Camp relieving 9th & 10th R. Innis Fus's (109 Bde)	

1577 Wt. W10791/1773 500,000 1/15 D. D. & L. A.D.S.S./Forms/C. 2118.

Instructions regarding War Diaries and Intelligence Summaries are contained in F. S. Regs., Part II. and the Staff Manual respectively. Title pages will be prepared in manuscript.

WAR DIARY
or
INTELLIGENCE SUMMARY.
(Erase heading not required.)

Army Form C. 2118.

Place	Date	Hour	Summary of Events and Information	Remarks and references to Appendices
BAILLEUL	28		Brigade H.Q. moved to BAILLEUL. The 9th R.I.R. & 15th R.I.R. moved to RED LODGE (T 18 d 5.2) & relieved 11th R. Innis Fusrs & 14th R.I.R. (109 Bde). 9th R.I.R. & 15th R.I.R. placed tactically under 109 Bde & 108 Bde respectively. The M Gun Coy & T.M. Batty marched to KORTEPYP Camp.	B2
—"—	29		Bailleul.	
—"—	30		—"—	
Trenches	31		Relieved 108th Infy Bde in trenches from RIVER DOUVE to WULVERGHEM MESSINES ROAD. 109 Bde on our right & 149 Bde of 50th Div on our left.	B2

2/8/16

[signature] Major
Bde Major
107th Infy Bde

1577 Wt. W10791/1773 500,000 1/15 D. D. & L. A.D.S.S./Forms/C. 2118

Instructions regarding War Diaries and Intelligence Summaries are contained in F. S. Regs., Part II. and the Staff Manual respectively. Title pages will be prepared in manuscript.

WAR DIARY
or
INTELLIGENCE SUMMARY.
(Erase heading not required.)

Army Form C. 2118.

107 Infy Bde Vol 10

Place	Date	Hour	Summary of Events and Information	Remarks and references to Appendices
Trenches	August 1st		In Trenches near WULVERGHEM - Brigade Right on River DOUVE + left across WULVERGHEM-MESSINES Road to Junction of C2/C3 Trenches. all four Battns in the line. The 9th & 10th R.I.R. were formed into 1 Composite Battn under Lt Col F.P. Crozier Comdg 9th R.I.R. & held the right of the line. 15th R.I.R. in Centre + 8th R.I.R. on left. 109 Bde on our right + 149 Bde (50 Divn) on our left.	DR
—"—	2nd 3rd		} Trenches - Quiet -	DR
—"—	4th		13th R.I.R. 108 Bde relieved 9th R.I.R. on right + 9th R.I.R. withdrew to KORTEPYP CAMP.	
—"—	5th		The Brigade side slipped to its left. The 9th R.I.R. relieved 7th N.F. (149 Bde) holding from junction of Trenches C2/C3 to DURHAM ROAD. The 10th & 15th R.I.R. were relieved by Battns of 108 Bde & withdrew into Bde Reserve. The 15th to KORTEPYP Camp + 10th To farms on NEUVE EGLISE-WULVERGHEM Road (in close support). The 8th R.I.R. remained in this sector which became the Right subsector extended of the left. Bde H.Q. moved from T21 d 4.1 to T21 d 4.9.	DR
—"—	6th		Trenches	
—"—	7th		Trenches	
—"—	8th		Trenches - Brigade relief - 15th R.I.R. relieved 8th R.I.R. in Right Subsector + 10th R.I.R. relieved 9th R.I.R. in left Subsector. 8th withdrew to KORTEPYP Camp + 9th R.I.R. in to close support in Farms on Neuve Eglise-Wulverghem Road.	DR

1577 Wt. W10791/1773 500,000 1/15 D. D. & L. A.D.S.S./Forms/C. 2118.

Instructions regarding War Diaries and Intelligence Summaries are contained in F. S. Regs., Part II. and the Staff Manual respectively. Title pages will be prepared in manuscript.

WAR DIARY
or
INTELLIGENCE SUMMARY.
(Erase heading not required.)

Army Form C. 2118.

107 Infy Bde

Place	Date	Hour	Summary of Events and Information	Remarks and references to Appendices
Trenches	9th		In Trenches –	
"	10th		— " —	
	11th		— " —	
	12th		— " —	
"	13th		— " —	
	14th		— " —	
	15th		— " — } Things generally quiet except for about 1 hour each evening when both sides show Trench Mortar and artillery activity –	[initials]
"	16th		— " — Brigade relief – 8th R.I.R. relieved 15th R.I.R. in Right Subsector & 9th R.I.R. relieved 10th R.I.R. in Left Subsector – 10th R.I.R. withdrew to KORTEPYP and 15th R.I.R. to close Support –	[initials]
	17th		— " —	
	18th		— " —	
	19th		— " —	
"	20th		— " —	
	21st		— " —	
	22nd		— " —	
	23rd		— " —	
	24th		— " — Brigade Relief – 15th R.I.R. relieved 8th R.I.R. in Right Subsector and 10th R.I.R. relieved 9th R.I.R. in Left Subsector – 8th R.I.R. withdrew to close Support and 9th R.I.R. to KORTEPYP Camp –	[initials]
"	25th		— " —	
	26th		— " —	

Instructions regarding War Diaries and Intelligence Summaries are contained in F. S. Regs., Part II. and the Staff Manual respectively. Title pages will be prepared in manuscript.

WAR DIARY
or
INTELLIGENCE SUMMARY.
(Erase heading not required.)

Army Form C. 2118.

Place	Date	Hour	Summary of Events and Information	Remarks and references to Appendices
Trenches	September 1st		U1a41 to N36 @ 98. Brigade relief – 8th R.I.R. relieved 15th R.I.R. in Right Sector and 9th R.I.R. relieved 10th R.I.R. in left sector – 10th R.I.R. withdrew to close Support and 15th R.I.R. to Divl Reserve at KORTEPYP Camp –	[illegible]
"	2nd			
"	3rd			
"	4th			
"	5th		107 T.M. Batty bombarded the enemy front line from 5.30 to 6 P.M. –	
"	6th		107 T.M. Batty fired 193 Rounds in the afternoon with excellent effect – and later on 150 Rounds. Enemy retaliation feeble –	[illegible]
"	7th		107 T.M. Batty Co-operated in our artillery Bombardment in the afternoon with good effect –	[illegible]
"	8th		Our artillery bombarded the enemy Communications throughout the night. and 107 T.M. Batty bombarded the German line at 8.30 a.m.	
"	9th		Brigade relief. 15th R.I.R. relieved 8th R.I.R. in Right Subsector and 10th R.I.R. relieved 9th R.I.R. in Right Subsector – 8th R.I.R. withdrew to Divl Reserve at KORTEPYP and 9th R.I.R. to Brigade reserve at LYLO Farm.	

1577 Wt. W10791/1773 500,000 1/15 D. D. & L. A.D.S.S./Forms/C. 2118.

Instructions regarding War Diaries and Intelligence Summaries are contained in F. S. Regs., Part II. and the Staff Manual respectively. Title pages will be prepared in manuscript.

WAR DIARY
or
INTELLIGENCE SUMMARY.
(Erase heading not required.)

Army Form C. 2118.

107 Infty Bde

Place	Date	Hour	Summary of Events and Information	Remarks and references to Appendices
Trenches	27		Trenches U 1 a 4.1 to N 36 c 98.	
	28		— " —	
	29		— " —	
	30		— " —	
	31		at 1.30 a.m. our artillery Bombarded the enemy's trenches for half an hour – the Germans retaliated on our Front line + Communication without much effect.	[initials]

[signature] Bde Major
107 Infty Bde

1/9/16

1577 Wt. W10791/1773 500,000 1/15 D. D. & L. A.D.S.S./Forms/C. 2118.

Army Form C. 2118.

Instructions regarding War Diaries and Intelligence Summaries are contained in F. S. Regs., Part II. and the Staff Manual respectively. Title pages will be prepared in manuscript.

WAR DIARY
or
INTELLIGENCE SUMMARY.
(Erase heading not required.)

Place	Date	Hour	Summary of Events and Information	Remarks and references to Appendices
Trenches	10th		Trenches –	
	11th		– " – 107 T.M. Batty registered during the day on enemy line at N 36 d 27 + fired 90 rounds during the night on this point for special reasons connected with coming raid by 9th R.I.R.	[initials]
	12		107 T.M. Batty fired throughout the night on N 36 d 27.	
	13		———— " ————	
	14		———— " ————	
	15		at 8.15 P.M. the 9th R.I.R. carried out a successful raid into the Enemy Trenches at N 36 d 2078 – Bringing back one Prisoner of 121st Infty Regt for identification purposes. The following is the report of Lieut E.J.F. Holland 9th R.I.R. who was in command of the Raiding Party:–	
			I have to report that I carried out a raid into the German trenches at N. 36. d. 20.78.	
			The party under me consisted of 2nd Lieut C.O. Crawford, 2nd Lieut R.R. Kane, and 41 other ranks.	

1577 Wt. W10791/1773 500,000 1/15 D. D. & L. A.D.S.S./Forms/C. 2118.

Army Form C. 21

Instructions regarding War Diaries and Intelligence Summaries are contained in F. S. Regs., Part II. and the Staff Manual respectively. Title pages will be prepared in manuscript.

WAR DIARY
or
INTELLIGENCE SUMMARY.

(Erase heading not required.)

Place	Date	Hour	Summary of Events and Information	Remarks and references to Appendices
Trenches	15		Our own trench D.2, bay 20, was left at 8.19 p.m. No Man's Land was speedily crossed, by crawling with occasional halts when Very Lights were sent up by the Germans. A Gap was found, as expected, in the enemy's wire. 2nd Lieut. Crawford led the party and as he and the leading four reached the German parapet six Germans were seen by them. 2nd Lieut Crawford dropped two of these men with his revolver and fell on a third man, who was eventually brought in a prisoner. The remainder of this German party ran away and then started to throw bombs from the right. There were also some pistol shots from the same direction. 2nd Lieut Kane on entering the trench, turned as ordered to the left and after havinggone about twenty paces came upon a double sentry post. One of these men was killed by him with a revolver; the other made off. The rifle and pack of the man who was killed and the pack of the man who made off were brought in. The right and left parties worked round as ordered. After about five minutes bombing became general. 2nd Lieut Crawford heard Germans in their dug-outs near Point "D" (see sketch) and threw bags of ammonal into three dug-outs. At point "F" (see sketch) 2nd Lieut Kane threw smoke bombs into two small dug-outs and heard loud noises coming from the dug-outs in question. As no	

1577 Wt. W10791/1773 500,000 1/15 D. D. & L. A.D.S.S./Forms/C. 2118.

Army Form C. 2118.

Instructions regarding War Diaries and Intelligence Summaries are contained in F. S. Regs., Part II. and the Staff Manual respectively. Title pages will be prepared in manuscript.

WAR DIARY
or
INTELLIGENCE SUMMARY.
(Erase heading not required.)

Place	Date	Hour	Summary of Events and Information	Remarks and references to Appendices
Trenches	16		Germans came up he threw a bag of ammonal into one dug-out. He concluded that the Germans had been asleep and could not find their way out in the dark.	
			Whilst he was trying to direct ammonal bombs to be thrown down the other dug outs he was heavily bombed from "G."	
			It was reported to me after the party had been in the German lines 14 (fourteen) minutes that the prisoner had been lodged in our lines, and as enemy bombing appeared to be increasing I came to the conclusion that it was time to withdraw the party, so word was passed along to withdraw.	
			Rifleman Kidd was ordered to proceed to Point "C" at the outset. He is a very lengthly thrower and during the time the party was in the trenches he kept back hostile bombing attacks from the right flank and only left his post after I had called out to him from "A" that the party was clear, when he came back to our lines with me.	
			I saw the bodies of three Germans, apparently dead, who had been accounted for by Rifleman Kidd between "A" and "C". The dug-outs are reported to me as not very deep, the majority being not more than four feet below the level of the floor of the trench.	
			No machine Gun emplacements were encountered.	
			The trenches are slightly deeper than ours, boarded on the bottom. Work is in progress on them.	
			Machine gun fire was opened during the re-crossing of No Man's Land but it was high.	
			No barrage was put down by the enemy.	
			2nd Lieut Kane and Rifleman Campbell cut two sets of telephone	

Instructions regarding War Diaries and Intelligence Summaries are contained in F. S. Regs., Part II. and the Staff Manual respectively. Title pages will be prepared in manuscript.

WAR DIARY
or
INTELLIGENCE SUMMARY.
(Erase heading not required.)

Army Form C. 2118.

Place	Date	Hour	Summary of Events and Information	Remarks and references to Appendices
Trenches	15		wires, each set being in a cluster.	
			2nd Lieut. Crawford and Riflemen Kelly and Ronan were wounded in the German trenches but continued to do useful work.	
			15-9-16. (Sgd) E. J. F. Holland, 2nd Lieut. 9th R. Ir. Rifles	
–"–	16		Combined Bombardment of Enemy Trenches with artillery + Trench Mortars from 10.30 a.m. to 12.30 p.m. & from 3 p.m. to 5 p.m. Retaliation feeble –	[illegible]
–"–	17		at 1 a.m. our artillery + Trench Mortars bombarded the enemy's trenches & at 9 a.m. Enemy artillery bombarded ours – No damage except that they burst a gas cylinder & the wind being West got the benefit of it themselves. Several of them ran out of their trenches & were caught in the open by our Lewis Guns – Brigade relief – 8th Relieved 15th in Right Subsector + 9th relieved 10th R. Ir. R. in Left Subsector. 15th withdrew into Brigade Reserve + 10th to Divl Reserve at Kortepyp –	[illegible]
–"–	18th		Enemy artillery active also Trench Mortars – one of the latter killing 4 & wounding 9 – all 9th R.I.R.	[illegible]
–"–	19th		Our Trench Mortar Batty did good work firing 80 rounds –	
–"–	20th		Quiet Day	

Instructions regarding War Diaries and Intelligence Summaries are contained in F. S. Regs., Part II. and the Staff Manual respectively. Title pages will be prepared in manuscript.

WAR DIARY
or
INTELLIGENCE SUMMARY.
(Erase heading not required.)

Army Form C. 2118.

Place	Date	Hour	Summary of Events and Information	Remarks and references to Appendices
Trenches	21		Trenches at Wulverghem –	
—"—	22		Combined bombardment of enemy line opposite Mortar Farm 3 & 4 Pm. Our Stokes Batty fired 650 rounds with good effect –	[illegible]
—"—	23		Quiet day – Brigade Relief – 15th R.I.R. relieved 8th R.I.R. in Right Subsector + 10th R.I.R. relieved 9th R.I.R. in left subsector – 8th withdrew to Brigade reserve & 9th to Div'l reserve at KORTEPYP	[illegible]
—"—	24		Our Stokes T.M. Batty bombarded enemy line otherwise all quiet –	
—"—	25		Very quiet	
—"—	26		—"—	
—"—	27		—"—	
—"—	28		Our Stokes Trench Mortar Batty bombarded enemy line from 9am to 10.30am. firing 995 Rounds with great effect – Enemy retaliation weak –	[illegible]
—"—	29		Nothing of interest – Enemy very inactive – Brigade relief – 8th R.I.R. relieved 15th R.I.R. in right subsector & 9th R.I.R. relieved 10th R.I.R. in left subsector – 10th R.I.R. withdrew into Brigade Reserve + 15th R.I.R. into Divisional Reserve at KORTEPYP –	X

1577 Wt. W10791/1773 500,000 1/15 D. D. & L. A.D.S.S./Forms/C. 2118.

REPORT ON RAID BY 10TH R. IRISH RIFLES.

Party consisted of Lieut. Hackett. (Leader).

Lieut. McKee.

2nd Lt. Haslett.

and 70 other rank and file.

Left our trenches in good order at 9.30 p.m. and advanced towards German trenches, which they were to reach at 10 p.m. The party was led correctly by 2nd Lieut. Haslett to the exact spot in the German wire which was found to be well cut. The Germans appear to have been alarmed by another raid to the South which started before its time; they were "standing to" in their trenches in fair numbers and as our party reached the wire opened rapid Rifle fire and threw Bombs. We retaliated with Bombs which lit in the German trenches; C.S.M. Whelan and Sergt. McCune did particular good work in this respect. The 3 Officers with C.S.M. Whelan, Sergt. McCune and Sergt. Shaw appear to have got too far ahead of their men and were not in sufficient force to rush the trench.

All preparations went without a hitch but I consider the failure of the raid was due to:-

(1) The raid on the right starting before its time.

(2) The party was too big for the purpose intended and could not be handled properly in the dark.

I am convinced that the 3 Officers and N.C.Os mentioned above did everything in their power to gain their object as they are a most determined set of men.

Casualties Rank and File, 8 mostly slight.

Sgd. N.G. Burnand, Lt. Col.
Commg. 10th Bn. R. Irish Rifles.

Instructions regarding War Diaries and Intelligence Summaries are contained in F. S. Regs., Part II. and the Staff Manual respectively. Title pages will be prepared in manuscript.

WAR DIARY
or
INTELLIGENCE SUMMARY.
(Erase heading not required.)

Army Form C. 2118.

Place	Date	Hour	Summary of Events and Information	Remarks and references to Appendices
Trenches E of WULVERGHEM	Sept 30th		Quiet Day. a series of Raids took place all along the IXth Corps front at 10 pm. The 10th R.I.R. carrying out the Raid for 107th Bde. Report of O.C. attached.	[illegible]
			[signature] Brig. General 107 Infy Bde	
			1/10/16	

1577 Wt. W10791/1773 500,000 1/15 D. D. & L. A.D.S.S./Forms/C. 2118.

Vol 12

Army Form C. 2118.

107 Infy Bde

WAR DIARY
or
INTELLIGENCE SUMMARY.
(*Erase heading not required.*)

Instructions regarding War Diaries and Intelligence Summaries are contained in F. S. Regs., Part II. and the Staff Manual respectively. Title pages will be prepared in manuscript.

Place	Date October	Hour	Summary of Events and Information	Remarks and references to Appendices
Trenches	1		Trenches Wulverghem Sector –	
	2		—"— Our Trench mortars bombarded Enemy front line with good effect at 4 pm.	[illegible]
	3		—"—	
	4		—"—	
	5		—"— Combined bombardment of Enemys line from 8.30 am to 10 am. Brigade relief – 15th R.I.R. relieved 8th R.I.R. in right Subsector and 10th R.I.R. ~~the~~ relieved 9th R.I.R. in left Subsector. 8th R.I.R. withdrew to Kortepyp and 9th R.I.R. to Bde Reserve.	[illegible]
	6th		—"—	
	7th		—"—	
	8th		—"— We discharged Gas from our trenches at 1.30 a.m. accompanied	
	9th		—"— by bombardment of enemy line with Trench Mortars – At 3 am. Party of 2 Officers & 14 O.R. of 10th R.I.R. raided the enemy's trenches bringing back 3 Prisoners –	[illegible]
	10th		—"— Usual Trench Mortar activity –	
	11th		—"— Brigade relief – 8th R.I.R. relieved 15th R.I.R. and 9th R.I.R. relieved 10th R.I.R.	[illegible]
	12th		—"— At 2 am. our Artillery & Trench Mortars opened an intense bombardment of Enemy trenches the Stokes guns firing 1123 Rounds rapid – at 2.15 am. a raiding Party of 9th R.I.R. entered Enemy trenches doing damage & bringing back one Prisoner –	[illegible]

1577 Wt. W10791/1773 500,000 1/15 D. D. & L. A.D.S.S./Forms/C. 2118.

Instructions regarding War Diaries and Intelligence Summaries are contained in F. S. Regs., Part II. and the Staff Manual respectively. Title pages will be prepared in manuscript.

WAR DIARY
or
INTELLIGENCE SUMMARY.
(Erase heading not required.)

Army Form C. 2118.

107 Infy Bde

Place	Date	Hour	Summary of Events and Information	Remarks and references to Appendices
Trenches	13th		Wulverghem Sector – Trench mortar + artillery activity chiefly on our side –	
"	14th		" – At 3 P.m the enemy commenced a heavy bombardment of our trenches continuing till 4.30 P.m. – Our trenches suffered considerably – Casualties slight –	
"	15th		" } Trench mortars + artillery active –	
"	16th		"	
"	17th		" At 4 P.m. we bombarded the enemy with trench mortars for 2 hours – Brigade relief – 15th R.I.R. relieved 8th R.I.R. who withdrew into Bde Reserve + 10th R.I.R. relieved 9th R.I.R. who withdrew into Divl Reserve at KORTEPYP –	
"	18th		" } Nothing of importance to record – our Trench Mortars were offensive practically every day always having the upper hand	
"	19th		"	
"	20th		"	
"	21		"	
"	22		"	
"	23		" Bde Relief 8th R.I.R. relieved 15th R.I.R. in Right Subsector and 9th R.I.R. relieved 10th R.I.R. in Left subsector – 10th R.I.R. withdrew to Brigade reserve and 15th R.I.R. to Divl Reserve –	

1577 Wt. W10791/1773 500,000 1/15 D. D. & L. A.D.S.S./Forms/C. 2118.

Instructions regarding War Diaries and Intelligence Summaries are contained in F. S. Regs., Part II. and the Staff Manual respectively. Title pages will be prepared in manuscript.

WAR DIARY
or
INTELLIGENCE SUMMARY.
(Erase heading not required.)

Army Form C. 2118.

107 Infty Bde

Place	Date	Hour	Summary of Events and Information	Remarks and references to Appendices
Trenches	24		Wulverghem Section – Quiet Period –	
"	25		—"— Quiet Period –	
"	26		—"— Quiet Period –	
"	27		—"— Quiet Period –	
"	28		—"— Quiet Period –	
"	29th		—"— Brigade relief – 15th R.I.R. relieved 8th R.I.R. and 10th R.I.R. Relieved 9th R.I.R. – 9th R.I.R. withdrew to Brigade reserve and 8th R.I.R. to Divl Reserve –	
	30th		—"—	
	31st		—"— at 2.10 am. the 15th R.I.R. sent over a raiding Party of 60 men to enter the German trenches at U.1.a 27.68 – they succeeded in getting in but were bombed out again – Casualties 1 officer + 2 men wounded + 2 men killed –	

1/11/16

[illegible] Captain Bde Major 107 Infty Bde

Instructions regarding War Diaries and Intelligence Summaries are contained in F. S. Regs., Part II. and the Staff Manual respectively. Title pages will be prepared in manuscript.

WAR DIARY
or
~~INTELLIGENCE~~ SUMMARY.
(Erase heading not required.)

Army Form C. 2118.

H.Q. 107th Inf Bde

Vol 13

Place	Date	Hour	Summary of Events and Information	Remarks and references to Appendices
	November			
Trenches	1st		Wulverghem Sector - Quiet Day	
	2nd		" "	
	3rd		" Our Trench Mortars bombarded the German Trenches at T 6 b 99 at 3 P.M. Enemy retaliated with Minenwerfers and 5.9 shells	
	4th		" Enemy bombarded our front line at 2.30 P.M. but were soon silenced - Brigade relief. 8th R.I.R. relieved 15th R.I.R. in right Subsector and 9th R.I.R. relieved 10th R.I.R. in left Subsector. 15th R.I.R. withdrew to Brigade reserve and 10th R.I.R. to Divisional reserve at KORTEPYP.	
	5th		" Enemy opened fire at 8.55 with 77 MM. shells doing little damage - at 4 P.M. enemy shelled round Bde H.Q. killing one of the Brigadier's Horses and wounding the other.	
	6th		" Enemy artillery again active on front line and also round Brigade H.Q. Our Tr. Batty bombarded German line from 3 to 3.30 P.M.	
	7th		" Very wet & windy day - No activity on either side until 4.30 P.M. when Enemy artillery was again unusually active - Their ammn supply seems to have increased lately -	

Army Form C. 2118.

Instructions regarding War Diaries and Intelligence Summaries are contained in F. S. Regs., Part II. and the Staff Manual respectively. Title pages will be prepared in manuscript.

WAR DIARY
or
~~INTELLIGENCE SUMMARY.~~
(Erase heading not required.)

H.Qrs 107th Inf Bde

Place	Date	Hour	Summary of Events and Information	Remarks and references to Appendices
Trenches	November		Wulverghem Sector	
"	8th		" " Nothing to report	J.L.D.
"	9th		" " " "	J.L.D.
"	10th		" " Brigade relief 15th R.I.R. relieved 8th R.Ir.R. in right subsector and 10th R.Ir. Rifles relieved 9th in left sub sector – 8th R.Ir. Rifs withdrew into Brigade reserve and 9th to Divl reserve at KORTEPYP	J.L.D.
"	11th		" " Quiet two days. Nothing to report	J.L.D.
"	12th		" "	
"	13th		" " Situation in line normal. Major Dery (Bde Major) departed to take over duties G.S.O. 2 33rd Division. Result general mourning in Bde.	J.L.D.

1577 Wt. W10791/1773 500,000 1/15 D. D. & L. A.D.S.S./Forms/C. 2118.

Army Form C. 2118.

Instructions regarding War Diaries and Intelligence Summaries are contained in F. S. Regs., Part II. and the Staff Manual respectively. Title pages will be prepared in manuscript.

WAR DIARY
or
~~INTELLIGENCE~~ SUMMARY.
(Erase heading not required.)

H.Q's. 107th Inf Brigade.

Place	Date	Hour	Summary of Events and Information	Remarks and references to Appendices
WULVERGHEM SECTOR	Nov 14th		Enemys artillery fairly active shelling communication trenches and ground in rear of front line. No trench mortar activity.	
"	15th		Combined artillery and trench mortar shoot on the enemy's lines. The result appeared to be very satisfactory. Enemy retaliated with a few shells on SURREY LANE. No damage done.	
"	16th		Very quiet day. Bn reliefs took place. see	App
"	17th		Our artillery and Trench mortars active; they bombarded the enemy's line in conjunction with a raid by the Brigade on our left. Enemy shelled WULVERGHEM Cross roads and front line of Right subsector	
"	18th		Increased activity by the enemy artillery. The ~~...~~ LOOP and the reverse slope in rear of the front line were shelled. No damage done.	
"	19th		Our artillery and Trench mortars bombarded the enemy's front line at T.6.B.9.8 – results very good. Enemy retaliated with 18 rounds. The following drafts arrived for the 9th, 10th, and 15th Bns Royal Irish Rifles. 9th Bn 107. O.R's. 10th Bn 70 O.R's, 15th Bn 76. O.R's.	

1577 Wt. W10791/1773 500,000 1/15 D. D. & L. A.D.S.S./Forms/C. 2118.

Army Form C. 2118.

Instructions regarding War Diaries and Intelligence Summaries are contained in F. S. Regs., Part II. and the Staff Manual respectively. Title pages will be prepared in manuscript.

WAR DIARY
or
~~INTELLIGENCE SUMMARY.~~
(*Erase heading not required.*)

H.Q's 107th Inf Brigade.

Place	Date	Hour	Summary of Events and Information	Remarks and references to Appendices
WULVERGHEM SECTOR	Nov 20th		Very quiet day.	
"	21st		Very quiet day; 107th Brigade Order No 92 issued reference Bn reliefs on 22nd Instant	App. I.
"	22nd		Quiet day; our howitzers shelled MESSINES and the trenches in the vicinity. 107th Inf Bde Order No 93 issued re clearing trenches during a combined trench mortar and artillery bombardment taking place on the 23rd Inst. Inter Bn reliefs took place	App. II
"	23rd		~~At~~ From 11.30 a.m to 12.55 pm our Trench Mortars and artillery carried out a combined bombardment of the enemy's trenches in front of the 109th Inf Brigade. One heavy trench mortar fired from 107th Brigade area, necessitating the clearing of some trenches. The enemy replied with 150 shells, the majority falling in the vicinity of NORTHUMBERLAND AVENUE. no damage was done.	~~App.~~ TmB.

1577 Wt. W10791/1773 500,000 1/15 D. D. & L. A.D.S.S./Forms/C. 2118.

Instructions regarding War Diaries and Intelligence Summaries are contained in F. S. Regs., Part II. and the Staff Manual respectively. Title pages will be prepared in manuscript.

WAR DIARY
or
~~INTELLIGENCE SUMMARY.~~
(Erase heading not required.)

Army Form C. 2118.

H. Q's. 107th Inf. Brigade.

Place	Date	Hour	Summary of Events and Information	Remarks and references to Appendices
	NOV.			
WULVERGHEN SECTOR	24th		Fairly quiet day. At 10 p.m. in the evening Enemy opened fairly heavy bombardment on trenches of our Left subsector. We retaliated heavily.	
"	25th		Quiet day. 107th Brigade Order No 94 issued re discharge of gas to take place on 107th and 108th Brigade fronts at 5 p.m. on 21st Inst. Addendum No 1 to above order issued later making slight alterations in the details	App III
"	26th		Addendum No 2 to Order No 94 issued ordering the 10th and 15th R. Irish Rifles to send out patrols two hours after Zero. At 5 p.m. a message was received from 10th R.I.R. stating that the wind for the discharge was unfavourable. All operations were cancelled.	
"	27th		Enemy's artillery was somewhat active in the morning, but quiet for the rest of the day. Order No 95 issued re reliefs on the 28th Instant Order No 96 issued re combined bombardment to take place on 29th Inst	App IV App V.
"	28th		Quiet day. 8th R.I.R relieved 15th, who withdrew to NEUVE ÉGLISE; 9th R.I.R. relieved the 10th, who withdrew to KORTEPYP.	

Tom B.

1577 Wt. W10791/1773 500,000 1/15 D. D. & L. A.D.S.S./Forms/C. 2118.

Instructions regarding War Diaries and Intelligence Summaries are contained in F. S. Regs., Part II. and the Staff Manual respectively. Title pages will be prepared in manuscript.

WAR DIARY
or
~~INTELLIGENCE SUMMARY.~~
(Erase heading not required.)

Army Form C. 2118.

HQ's 107th Inf Brigade.

Place	Date	Hour	Summary of Events and Information	Remarks and references to Appendices
WULVERGHEM SECTOR.	Nov			
	29th		Very quiet day; ~~as the~~ the combined bombardment was cancelled.	
			Order no 98 issued postponing the combined bombardment until 2pm 30th Inst	App VI.
			Order No 97 issued ordering gas discharge to take place at 5 p.m on 30th Inst	App VII
	30th		Combined trench mortar and artillery bombardment of the enemy's lines took place at 2 p.m. Hostile retaliation was not heavy and enemy's trenches were seen to be damaged. Gas discharge was postponed until the 1st Instant.	
				T.McB.

T. McB. Buchan Capt
Brigade Major.
107th Brigade.

1/12/16.

1577 Wt. W10791/1773 500,000 1/15 D. D. & L. A.D.S.S./Forms/C. 2118.

Headquarters.

36th Division "G"

Herewith War Diaries for December 1916 from Units of this Brigade.

6493

N.S. Burnard.

Lieut-Colonel.

Commanding, 107th Infantry Brigade.

2nd January 1917.

Instructions regarding War Diaries and Intelligence Summaries are contained in F. S. Regs., Part II. and the Staff Manual respectively. Title pages will be prepared in manuscript.

December 1916.

WAR DIARY
or
~~INTELLIGENCE SUMMARY.~~
(Erase heading not required.)

H.Q's 107th Inf Brigade.

Vol 14

Army Form C. 2118.

Place	Date	Hour	Summary of Events and Information	Remarks and references to Appendices
WULVERGHEM SECTOR	Dec 1st		Artillery and trench mortars very quiet. The orders for the gas discharge were cancelled	App I
"	2nd		Enemy's artillery active intermittently throughout the day. 107th Brigade Order No 99 issued re Bn reliefs on the 4th Instant.	App II
"	3rd		Enemy fairly active. 107th Brigade Order No 100 issued re moves of transport lines to DRANOUTRE Area	App III
"	4th		Enemy's artillery active from 10.a.m to 12.Noon. The 10th R.I.R relieved the 9th R.I.R in the left subsector, the 9th R.I.R withdrawing to WAKEFIELD. The 15th R.I.R relieved the 8th R.I.R in the right subsector, the 8th R.I.R withdrawing to NEUVE-EGLISE. Bns took over their new frontages: i.e. Right subsector from U.1/10 to T.6/5, both inclusive and the left subsector from T.6/6 to N.36/4.	

T.Om.B.

1577 Wt. W10791/1773 500,000 1/15 D. D. & L. A.D.S.S./Forms/C. 2118.

Instructions regarding War Diaries and Intelligence Summaries are contained in F. S. Regs., Part II. and the Staff Manual respectively. Title pages will be prepared in manuscript.

WAR DIARY

or

~~INTELLIGENCE SUMMARY.~~

(*Erase heading not required.*)

Army Form C. 2118.

December 1916. H.Q.'s 107th Inf Brigade.

Place	Date	Hour	Summary of Events and Information	Remarks and references to Appendices
WOLVERGHEM	Dec 5th		Very considerable artillery activity on both sides. M.G. Coy moved from KORTEPYP to TYRONE FARM and the 107th T.M. Battery from KORTEPYP to DONNEGAL FARM. Transport of 8th R.I.R moved from KORTEPYP to DRANOUTRE LINES.	
"	6th		Our medium and light T.M's bombarded the enemy's lines from 7 a.m to 7.30 a.m. Enemy retaliated fairly heavily. Transport of 15th R.I.R. moved from KORTEPYP to DRANOUTRE LINES.	
"	7th		From 7.30 a.m to 8 a.m our medium and light T.M's bombarded the enemy's lines. Enemy's retaliation very feeble. Rest of the day quiet.	
"	8th		Our 2" Trench mortars started firing at 2.50 p.m. The enemy retaliated very heavily causing no casualties. Our artillery retaliation feeble.	
"	9th		107th Brigade Order No 101 issued re Bn reliefs on the 10th Instant. At 10.30 a.m our medium mortars commenced to bombard the enemy's line in the vicinity of MORTAR FARM. The enemy retaliated heavily with artillery and trench mortars, doing considerable damage to our trenches. Our artillery retaliation was feeble.	App IV
				T and B

1577 Wt. W10791/1773 500,000 1/15 D. D. & L. A.D.S.S./Forms/C. 2118.

Instructions regarding War Diaries and Intelligence Summaries are contained in F. S. Regs., Part II. and the Staff Manual respectively. Title pages will be prepared in manuscript.

WAR DIARY
or
~~INTELLIGENCE SUMMARY.~~

(*Erase heading not required.*)

Army Form C. 2118.

December 1916. H.Q's 107th Inf Brigade.

Place	Date	Hour	Summary of Events and Information	Remarks and references to Appendices
WULVERGHEM SECTOR	Dec 10th		The enemy shelled BOYLES FARM and the trenches in the right subsector. Our artillery replied and eventually silenced the enemy. In the afternoon WULVERGHEM was also shelled. The 8th R.I.R relieved the 15th R.I.R in the right subsector, the 15th R.I.R. withdrawing to Dive Reserve. The 9th R.I.R relieved the 10th R.I.R who withdrew into Brigade Reserve.	
"	11th		There was very considerable Artillery and Trench mortar activity on both sides. AGNES STREET was damaged and one direct hit by a heavy minenwerfer on our front line caused considerable damage and two casualties	
"	12th		A quiet day.	
"	13th		A very quiet day.	
"	14th		Enemy's artillery active during the afternoon against trenches U.1/10, U1/11 DURHAM ROAD and AGNES STREET; damage was done to the latter.	
				Form B.

Instructions regarding War Diaries and Intelligence Summaries are contained in F. S. Regs., Part II. and the Staff Manual respectively. Title pages will be prepared in manuscript.

WAR DIARY
or
~~INTELLIGENCE SUMMARY.~~
(*Erase heading not required.*)

Army Form C. 2118.

December 1916 — AQ's 107th Inf Brigade

Place	Date	Hour	Summary of Events and Information	Remarks and references to Appendices
WULVERGHEM SECTOR	Dec 15th		Our stokes mortars took part in an Combined Trench mortar and artillery bombardment in the sector of the 109th Brigade. The enemys retaliation was heavy and one of our guns were put out of action and ~~three~~ men killed and two wounded. The enemy also retaliated on this Brigade Sector, damaging trench N. 36/3. 107th Brigade order No 102 issued	App V.
"	16th		Quiet day. Inter Battalion reliefs carried out in accordance with or No 102 [see appendix V]. 107th Inf Brigade Order No 103 issued re discharge of Gas to take place on the night of the 17th instant	App VI
"	17th		Enemy artillery active during the afternoon, causing some casualties and damage to our Trenches. Addendum No I to 107th Brigade Order No 103 issued re patrols to go out after the Gas discharge. At 4.55 p.m telegram received from 10th R. Irish Rifles to say that Gas would not be discharged. Wind was under 4 miles per hour.	App VII

T.om 15.

1577 Wt. W10791/1773 500,000 1/15 D. D. & L. A.D.S.S./Forms/C. 2118.

Army Form C. 2118.

WAR DIARY
or
~~INTELLIGENCE SUMMARY.~~
(Erase heading not required.)

Instructions regarding War Diaries and Intelligence Summaries are contained in F. S. Regs., Part II. and the Staff Manual respectively. Title pages will be prepared in manuscript.

December 1916 H.Q's 107th Inf Brigade.

Place	Date	Hour	Summary of Events and Information	Remarks and references to Appendices
WULVERGHEM SECTOR.	Dec 18th		Slight increase of enemy artillery activity. No trench mortar activity	
	19th		Fairly quiet day.	
	20th		Enemy artillery active shelling THE BARRIER, STONE STREET, MESSINES-WULVERGHEM Road and WULVERGHEM with 5.9's. Very little damage done	
	21st		Occasional shelling of WULVERGHEM. At 3.30pm Enemy shelled whole of Brigade Front with 5.9's and 77.m.m's. Order No 104 issued re reliefs to take place on the 22nd Inst.	App VIII
	22nd		Neighbourhood of WULVERGHEM and St QUENTIN'S CABT shelled with 5.9's.	
	23rd		Order No 105 issued re discharge of gas to take place tonight and Addendum No I issued to above order re patrols to go out 2 hours after zero and investigate the effects of the Gas. The above operations were carried out with only 3 casualties. For full report see — — —	App IX. App IX
	24th		At 8.a.m the Enemy commenced to shell the whole of our front line. Several direct hits on AGNES STREET and SURREY LANE. Our artillery replied effectively.	

Toh. B.

1577 Wt. W10791/1773 500,000 1/15 D. D. & L. A.D.S.S./Forms/C. 2118.

Army Form C. 2118.

Instructions regarding War Diaries and Intelligence Summaries are contained in F. S. Regs., Part II. and the Staff Manual respectively. Title pages will be prepared in manuscript.

WAR DIARY
or
~~INTELLIGENCE SUMMARY.~~
(Erase heading not required.)

Dec 1916 H.Q's 107th Inf Brigade.

Place	Date	Hour	Summary of Events and Information	Remarks and references to Appendices
WULVERGHEM SECTOR.	Dec 25th		The Enemy's artillery was very active. During the morning he intermittently shelled and trench mortared our front line. At 5 p.m. he commenced to shell 60 pdr Battery position in the vicinity of Brigade Headquarters with 5.9's and 4.2's, about 300 shells falling in all.	
"	26th		Enemy's artillery again very active.	
"	27th		Artillery again active. 107th Inf Brigade Order No 106 issued re reliefs on the 28th Instant.	App XI
"	28th		107th Inf Brigade Order No 107 issued re taking over a portion of 108th Brigade Area.	App XII
"	29th		Artillery less active until 2.15 p.m when he shelled trenches T.6.1 to T.6.6, obtaining several direct hits. The new Brigade frontage, extending up to Trench to U.1/3 inclusive, was taken over at 6 p.m.	
"	30th		Slight enemy artillery activity	
"	31st		Very considerable enemy artillery activity, especially against the left subsector. One elephant dugout was hit killing one man and wounding 6 who were inside. Operation Order No 108 issued re combined artillery and T.M Bombardment taking place on the 2/1/17	App XIII
			T.O.M. Buchan Capt Brigade Major 107th Inf Brigade	TOM B.

1577 Wt. W10791/1773 500,000 1/15 D. D. & L. A.D.S.S./Forms/C. 2118.

Instructions regarding War Diaries and Intelligence Summaries are contained in F. S. Regs., Part II. and the Staff Manual respectively. Title pages will be prepared in manuscript.

WAR DIARY
or
~~INTELLIGENCE SUMMARY.~~
(Erase heading not required.)

Army Form C. 2118.

Vol 15

January 1917. H. Q's. 107th Infantry Brigade.

Place	Date	Hour	Summary of Events and Information	Remarks and references to Appendices
WULVERGHEM SECTOR.	January 1st		Artillery on both sides active. In the afternoon enemy's trench mortars became very active in the left subsector breaking in two elephant dugouts and causing six casualties.	
	2nd		At 12 noon we carried out a combined Artillery and Trench mortar shoot. The enemy's retaliation was not heavy and our shoot appeared to have excellent results. Operation Order No 109 issued re reliefs taking place on 3rd January.	SEE APPX
	~~3rd~~ 3rd		Artillery of both sides active throughout the day. Reliefs took place in accordance with Order No 109.	
	4th		Artillery very active both in the back area and in the front line.	
	5th		Artillery and Trench mortars again very active, damaging our trenches considerably	
	6th		A much quieter day with slight activity in the afternoon.	
	7th		At 4 a.m the enemy opened a very severe bombardment on our sector and on the sector to the North. At 4.45 the bombardment ceased. Our trenches were ~~were~~ very badly damaged but we had only 3 casualties.	TMB

Instructions regarding War Diaries and Intelligence Summaries are contained in F. S. Regs., Part II. and the Staff Manual respectively. Title pages will be prepared in manuscript.

Army Form C. 2118.

WAR DIARY
or
~~INTELLIGENCE SUMMARY.~~
(*Erase heading not required.*)

Jan 1917. H.Q's. 107th Inf Brigade.

Place	Date	Hour	Summary of Events and Information	Remarks and references to Appendices
WOLVERGHEM	Jan 8th		Artillery on both sides fairly active. ~~Inter Battalion reliefs took place in accordance with~~ Order No 110. issued re inter Bn reliefs.	App II
"	9th		Considerable artillery activity. Some damage done to SURREY LANE and U.1/8. Inter Bn Reliefs took place in accordance with Order No 110	
"	10th		Enemy's trench mortars active	
"	11th		Artillery on both sides quiet.	
"	12th		Enemy's artillery again active. During the night Trenches T.6./1.2.3 were heavily shelled and considerably damaged.	
"	13th		Artillery fairly active.	
"	14th		Very quiet day, owing to heavy fog. Brigade Order No 111 issued re reliefs on the 15th Instant.	App III
"	15th		Fairly quiet day. Reliefs took place in accordance with order No 111	
"	16th		Increase in artillery activity. Trenches U.1/8. U.1/9. U.1/10. T.6/1.2.3 fairly heavily shelled	

T.O. [illegible]

1577 Wt. W10791/1773 500,000 1/15 D. D. & L. A.D.S.S./Forms/C. 2118.

Instructions regarding War Diaries and Intelligence Summaries are contained in F. S. Regs., Part II. and the Staff Manual respectively. Title pages will be prepared in manuscript.

WAR DIARY

or

~~INTELLIGENCE SUMMARY.~~

(Erase heading not required.)

Army Form C. 2118.

January 1917 H.Q's 107th Inf Brigade.

Place	Date	Hour	Summary of Events and Information	Remarks and references to Appendices
	January			
WULVERGHEM SECTOR.	17th		Very quiet day.	
"	18th		Quiet day.	
"	19th		At 3.45 p.m the enemy shelled T.6/4.5.6 and SPRING WALK doing some damage.	
"	20th		At 4 p.m the enemy bombarded trench N.36/4 and the trenches on our left fairly heavily. Brigade Order No 112 issued re reliefs to take place on 21st inst	App IV
"	21st		Brigade Order No 113 issued re cooperation with 47th Brigade in the event of their carrying out a raid Reliefs carried out in accordance with order No 112! Quiet day.	App V
"	22nd		Enemy's artillery fairly active in our sector shelling T.6/1.2.3. At 4 p.m a heavy bombardment commenced of the trenches on our right. At 5.45 p.m the Division ordered the Bn in Brigade Reserve to stand to. This was wired out to them at 5.55 p.m. At 6.35 p.m both Bns reported that they were ready to move. At 6.45 p.m the Division said on the telephone that they could dismiss again. 47th Brigade wired that their raid would not be carried out next day.	
"	23rd		Artillery quiet. Div orders received for the relief of this Brigade by the 108th Brigade. 6.30 p.m 47th Brigade wired that their raid would not take place on the next day	

[signature]

2353 Wt. W2544/1454 700,000 5/15 D. D. & L. A.D.S.S./Forms/C. 2118.

Army Form C. 2118.

Instructions regarding War Diaries and Intelligence Summaries are contained in F. S. Regs., Part II. and the Staff Manual respectively. Title pages will be prepared in manuscript.

WAR DIARY
or
~~INTELLIGENCE SUMMARY.~~
(Erase heading not required.)

January 1917. H. Q.'s 107th Inf Brigade

Place	Date	Hour	Summary of Events and Information	Remarks and references to Appendices
	January			
WULVERGHEM SECTOR.	24th		Enemy's artillery active intermittently all day, shelling the majority of our trenches.	
			Brigade Order No 114 issued re the relief of this Brigade by the 108th Brigade.	App VI
"	25th		Enemy's activity continues. Moves in accordance with Order No 114 took place	
"	26th		Fairly quiet day " " " " " " " "	
"	27th		Brigade reliefs completed. About 4pm the Enemy became active against the right subsector causing some delay in the reliefs. at 7pm the G.O.C. 108th Brigade assumed command of the WULVERGHEM Sector.	
BAILLEUL	28th		Brigade Headquarters moved to BAILLEUL	
"	29th		Nothing to report	
"	30th		" "	
"	31st		" "	

T. O. M. Buchan Capt
Brigade Major
107th Inf Brigade

T O M B

Army Form C. 2118.

Vol 16

Instructions regarding War Diaries and Intelligence Summaries are contained in F. S. Regs., Part II. and the Staff Manual respectively. Title pages will be prepared in manuscript.

WAR DIARY
or
INTELLIGENCE SUMMARY.
(Erase heading not required.)

February 1917. H.Q.'s 107th Inf Brigade.

Place	Date	Hour	Summary of Events and Information	Remarks and references to Appendices
	Feby			
BAILLEUL	1st		The Brigade in rest and training in progress.	
	2nd		Nothing to report	
	3rd		" "	
	4th		" "	
	5th		" "	
	6th		" "	
	7th		107th Brigade order No 115 issued re moves of Bns on the 10th Inst	App I.
	8th		Nothing to report.	
	9th		" " "	
	10th		Moves of Bns took place in accordance with Brigade order No 115	App I.
	11th		Nothing to report	
	12th		" " "	
	13th		Brigade in rest and training in progress	
	14th		" " " "	
	15th		" " " "	
	16th		" " " "	

2353 Wt. W2544/1454 700,000 5/15 D. D. & L. A.D.S.S./Forms/C. 2118.

Instructions regarding War Diaries and Intelligence Summaries are contained in F. S. Regs., Part II. and the Staff Manual respectively. Title pages will be prepared in manuscript.

WAR DIARY
or
INTELLIGENCE SUMMARY.
(Erase heading not required.)

Army Form C. 2118.

Place	Date	Hour	Summary of Events and Information	Remarks and references to Appendices
BAILLEUL	17th		Brigade in rest and training in progress	
	18th		" " "	
	19th		" " "	
	20th		Detachment of 6 STOKES guns moved up to DOUVE sector to assist 109 Infy. Bde.	
	20th		in bombardment and raid on enemy trenches.	
	21st		Brigade in rest and training in progress	
	22nd		107 Bde. Order No116 issued re moves of Battns to the line in relief of 109 Bde	App. II
	23rd		Brigade in rest and training in progress. Part of M. G. Coy & T M B. to KORTEPYP	
	24th		107 M. G. Coy and 107 T. M. Battery moved to trenches relieving 109th Bde.	App. II
	25th		moves of Battns took place in accordance with Brigade Order No116	
ENGLISH FM.	26th		Do Do Do. Brigade Hd. Qrs moved to ENGLISH FARM.	
DOUVE	27th		Quiet day in line — nothing to report	
SECTOR	28th		Do. do Do. do	

J. G. Duffin Capt.
Staff Capt.
for Brigade Major
107 Infy. Bde.

2353 Wt. W2544/1454 700,000 5/15 D. D. & L. A.D.S.S./Forms/C. 2118.

ROLL OF OFFICER CASUALTIES OF 107th INFANTRY BRIGADE

DURING MONTH OF JUNE 1917

++

UNIT	RANK & NAME	NATURE OF CASUALTY	DATE	REMARKS
8th R.I.Rifles	Lt (A/Capt) A.T. BLACKWOOD.	Wounded	7.6.17.	
-do-	2nd Lt. J.M.CLARK	"	"	
-do-	" H.M.LANCASHIRE	"	"	
-do-	" G.N.C.A.H. MACARTNEY.	"	"	
-do-	" (A/Capt) T.CRESSWELL	"	"	
-do-	" W.F.HUNTER	"	"	
-do-	" F.J.T.BARKER	"	"	
-do-	" F.W.H.CAUGHEY	"	"	
-do-	" L. HUGHES	"	"	
-do-	" D.A. MOYLES	"	"	
9th R.I.Rifles	Capt C.H.HARDING, M.C.	"	"	
-do-	Lt. R.P.MACGREGOR, M.C.	"	"	
-do-	2nd Lt.P.St J.H.KELLEHER	"	"	
-do-	" T.A. ROCHE	"	"	
-do-	" L.J.ROSS.	"	"	
-do-	Major H.R.HASLETT.	"	26.6.17.	
10th-do-	Lt. R. McLAURIN	Killed	7.6.17.	
-do-	2nd Lt. J. MARTIN.	Wounded	"	
-do-	" H. ROSS	"	"	
15th R.I.Rifles	Capt N.B.HIND.	"	"	
-do-	2nd Lt W.H. ADDEY	"	"	
-do-	" T.S.BEATTIE	"	"	
-do-	" W.R. PATEY	"	"	Slightly at duty
-do-	" E.E.H.TAYLOR	"	"	-do-
-do-	" A.W.F.GILMORE	"	"	-do-
-do-	" W.F. MORRISON	"	"	-do-
107th M.G.Coy.	Lieut H.W. WALKER	Killed	6.6.17	-do-

Army Form C. 2118.

Instructions regarding War Diaries and Intelligence Summaries are contained in F. S. Regs., Part II. and the Staff Manual respectively. Title pages will be prepared in manuscript.

WAR DIARY
or
~~INTELLIGENCE SUMMARY.~~

(*Erase heading not required.*)

March 1917 H.Q.'s 107th Inf Brigade

Vol 17

Place	Date	Hour	Summary of Events and Information	Remarks and references to Appendices
	March			
DOUVE	1st		Reliefs took place in the left subsector in accordance with Brigade Order No 117	App I
SECTOR	2nd		Quiet day	
	3rd		Reliefs carried out in right subsector according to Brigade Order No 118	App II.
	4th		Artillery fairly active	
	5th		Nothing to report	
	6th		" " "	
	7th		Reliefs took place in left subsector in accordance with order No 119	App III
	8th		Quiet day.	
	9th		Reliefs carried out in right subsector in accordance with order No 120	App IV.
			Warning order received from 36th Division that 3rd New Zealand (Rifle) Brigade would relieve 107th Brigade between the 11th and 13th Instants. Bns instructed to reconnoitre the new line.	
	10th		Quiet day	
	11th		107th M.G. Coy relieved and 107th T.M. Bty relieved in the line by M.G. Coy & T.M.Bty of 3rd New Zealand (Rifle) Brigade and by M.G. Coy 2nd New Zealand Brigade	App V
			107th Brigade Order No 122 issued re relief of 107th Inf Brigade by 3rd New Zealand	
				T.M.R.

2353 Wt. W2544/1454 700,000 5/15 D. D. & L. A.D.S.S./Forms/C. 2118.

Army Form C. 2118.

WAR DIARY
or
~~INTELLIGENCE~~ SUMMARY.
(Erase heading not required.)

Instructions regarding War Diaries and Intelligence Summaries are contained in F. S. Regs., Part II. and the Staff Manual respectively. Title pages will be prepared in manuscript.

March 1917 — H. Qs 107th Inf Brigade

Place	Date	Hour	Summary of Events and Information	Remarks and references to Appendices
DOUVE SECTOR	11th (continued)		(Rifle) Brigade and by the 2nd New Zealand Brigade in the DOUVE SECTOR and the subsequent relief of the 47th Inf Brigade by the 107th Inf Brigade in the SPANBROEK SECTOR.	App VI
"	12th		Administrative orders relating to the above were issued by the Staff Captain	App VII
			Addendum No I to order No 122 issued ordering the 109th M.G Coy & 109th T.M Battery to relieve the 49th M.G Coy and 49th T.M Battery in the left subsector of the SPANBROEK Sector.	App VIII
"			Reliefs took place in accordance with march table to order No 122.	
"	13th		Reliefs took place in accordance with march table to order No 122	
"	14th		G.O.C 107th Inf Brigade handed over command of DOUVE SECTOR South of river DOUVE to GOC 3rd New Zealand Rifle Brigade and assumed command of SPANBROEK Sector at 12 noon. Reliefs completed in accordance with order No 122 by 7pm.	
SPANBROEK SECTOR.	15th		A quiet day. A redistribution of units took place as instructed in 107th Brigade Order No 123	App IX

2353 Wt. W2544/1454 700,000 5/15 D. D. & L. A.D.S.S./Forms/C. 2118.

Army Form C. 2118.

WAR DIARY
or
INTELLIGENCE SUMMARY.
(*Erase heading not required.*)

Instructions regarding War Diaries and Intelligence Summaries are contained in F. S. Regs., Part II. and the Staff Manual respectively. Title pages will be prepared in manuscript.

March 1917. H.Q's 107th Inf Brigade.

Place	Date	Hour	Summary of Events and Information	Remarks and references to Appendices
SPANBROEK	16		A very quiet day.	
SECTOR	17.		A quiet day. Brigade Order No 124 issued re reliefs taking place on the 19th March	App X
"	18		Slight artillery activity on both sides.	
"	19.		Slight T.M. activity. Reliefs carried out in accordance with order 124	
"	20		Trench mortars on both sides active	
"	21		Enemy trench mortars active	
"	22		Quiet day.	
"	23		Artillery very active. Our artillery fired a group concentration.	
"	24.		At 4 a.m. the enemy commenced a heavy bombardment of the front and support lines and communication trenches in the area of our right subsector. Shortly after the commencement of the bombardment a sentry post observed the enemy leaving his trenches close to the WULVERGHEM-WYTSCHAETE Road. The S.O.S. was sent up and Lewis Gun fire opened on the enemy who retired again to their trenches. Our artillery opened fire quickly and with effect. The Brigade Support and Reserve Bns were ordered to stand to. At 5-20 a.m. the situation became quiet again. Very considerable damage was done	T.W.B.

2353 Wt. W2544/1454 700,000 5/15 D. D. & L. A.D.S.S./Forms/C. 2118.

(SPECIAL) 1:10,000 MAP 8150/2.

SECRET.

GOSTTAVERNE LINE

DOTTED BLACK LINE

BLACK LINE

IX CORPS GREEN LINE

BLUE LINE

RED LINE

19th DIV.

16th DIV.

36th DIV.

Wytschaete

Oosttaverne

Vierstraat

Wambeke

CONVERSION TABLE

MINUTES — HOURS.

Minutes	Hours	Mins	Minutes	Hours	Mins
61 mins.	1 hour	1 min.			
62		2			
64		4			
65		5			
67		7			
69		9	220 mins.	3 hours	40 mins.
70		10	224		44
71		11	228		48
72		12	229		49
73		13	230		50
77		17	232		52
82		22	224		54
85		25	226		56
90		30	240	4 hours	0 mins.
91		31	244		4
100		40	245		5
104		44	246		6
105		45	248		8
108		48	249		9
110		50	250		10
113		53	255		15
115		55	264		24
116		56	272		32
118		58	275		35
119		59	280		40
120	2 hours	0 mins.	284		44
122		2	286		46
125		5	288		48
127		7	300	5 hours	0 mins.
129		9	304		4
130		10	318		18
131		11	322		22
132		12	326		26

SECOND ARMY BARRAGE MAP.

June, 1917.

CORPS BOUNDARY

DIVISIONAL BOUNDARY

Appendix 16.

ENEMY ATTITUDE DURING THE TOUR.

For the first three days of the tour the enemy was apparently only spasmodically active, and contented himself with holding a line of posts in shell holes, O.23.Central with possibly a reserve of posts some 250 yards behind. It was not until the night of the 22nd/23rd that work to any extent was reported in the groups of trees in O.29.d. and in the Wood in O.29.b.

Since then he has apparently been endeavouring to make something like two strong points at these places and the fact that there is not much signs of completed work on recent aeroplane photographs at these points is due to the harassing fire of our artillery.

On the 24th, 25th/26th the enemy apparently discontinued their activity at work, perhaps owing to our artillery activity, but on the night of the 27th stronger working parties than ever were discovered.

A confirmation of this is found in the decrease in enemy artillery activity (thus encouraging our artillery to be quieter) in proportion to the increase in his work.

Another strong point outside our sector has been made and is garrisoned at O.29.b.90.63. From this part of the ridge all the front part of our sector is under observation and the trenches will be correspondingly unhealthy until the enemy is driven from this part of the ridge.

The enemy's delay in starting to work at these places may be explained by his waiting to see what our policy would be. Of this he must have been fully and accurately informed by the constant and close patrol work of his air service.

28th June, 1917.

Appendix V

PLAN OF ATTACK AND ACCOUNT OF OPERATIONS
WHICH TOOK PLACE ON 7th JUNE 1917

++

107th INFANTRY BRIGADE

In the middle of May instructions were received from the 36th Division to the effect that the 107th Inf. Brigade would take part in a general attack by the Second Army with a view to capturing the MESSINES - WYTSCHAETE Ridge and that the attack would take place early in June. The 107th Inf. Brigade was to attack on the Right of the Divisional front, and the 109th Inf. Brigade on the Left. One Battalion from the 108th Inf. Brigade, in Divisional Reserve, would be put at the disposal of the 107th Inf. Brigade for carrying out the attack. The 107th Inf. Brigade was thus composed as follows :-

BRIGADE COMMANDER	...	Brigadier General W.M.WITHYCOMBE, C.M.G.
8th R.I.Rifles	...	Lt.Col. C.G. COLE-HAMILTON, D.S.O.
9th R.I.Rifles	...	Lt.Col. P.J. WOODS, D.S.O.
10th R.I.Rifles	...	Lt.Col. N.G. BURNAND, D.S.O.
15th R.I.Rifles	...	Lt.Col. F.L. GORDON, D.S.O.
12th R.I.Rifles	...	Lt.Col. W.R.GOODWIN. (This Battalion was attached to this Brigade from 108th Inf. Brigade.)
107th M.G. Coy.	...	Capt. R.H. FORBES.
107th T.M. Bty	...	Capt. I. GROVE-WHITE.

It was decided to carry out the attack on a two Battalion frontage and two main objectives were decided upon, the first marked in BLUE on the attached map and the second in BLACK.

The BLUE Line was given ~~for~~ as the objective for the two leading Battalions, and the BLACK Line as the objective for the third and fourth Battalions, and in order to allow the necessary time for these Battalions to get up there was to be a pause for two hours on the BLUE Line.

The tasks allotted to Battalions were as follows :- the 8th and 9th R.I. Rifles were to attack the BLUE Line, the 8th on the Right and the 9th on the Left. Each Battalion was to carry out the attack on a two Company frontage, one Company consisting of two waves. The first two waves were to halt at the RED Line, while the third and fourth waves passed through and straight on to the BLUE Line, the first two waves re-joining and then following in support.

The 12th R.I. Rifles were allotted the task of mopping up the area between the old German front line and the BLUE Line. On completion of this task they were to consolidate the RED Line.

The 15th and 10th R.I. Rifles were given the ~~atsk~~ task of capturing the BLACK Line, the 15th on the Right and the 10th on the Left. A minor objective marked in GREEN on the attached map was given to each Battalion, the first two waves halted and re-formed on this line, while the third and fourth waves passed through to the BLACK Line. The 15th R.I. Rifles were given a two Company frontage on the GREEN Line and a one company frontage on the BLACK Line. The 10th R.I. Rifles were given a two Company frontage throughout. One Company of the 15th R.I. Rifles was allotted the task of mopping up the area between the BLUE and the GREEN line in 10th sub-sectors, and on completion of its task to rejoin its Unit and act as a reserve.

After capturing the BLACK Line the 10th and 15th R.I. Rifles were instructed to push out outposts to a line marked in MAUVE on the attached map.

The RED, BLUE and BLACK Lines were all to be consolidated, and in addition certain strong points, as marked on the map, were to be constructed.

The guns of the 107th Machine Gun Coy. were to be kept under the orders of the Division until Zero plus 55, and were to be employed in putting up a creeping barrage in conjunction with the artillery. The remaining 6 guns were under the orders of the Brigade Commander, and it was decided to send them over immediately in rear of the last wave of the 9th R.I. Rifles to SPANBROEKMOLEN, where they were to take up positions to cover the advance of the Infantry. At Zero plus 55 the 10 guns providing the barrage were to come under the orders of the Brigade Commander and instructions were issued to the O.C. 107th Machine Gun Coy. to move four of these guns up to strong points, one to SKIP END, one to OCCULT END and two to OCHRE END, and the remaining 6 up to the BLACK Line, two in the Right sub-sector and 4 in the Left sub-sector.

Two guns only of the 107th Trench Mortar Battery were to accompany the attack, these two guns with their carriers were instructed to move in rear of the last wave of the 8th and 9th R.I. Rifles and to establish themselves in the BLUE Line, one in each sub-sector. After the BLACK Line had been captured both guns were to move forward and take up positions in the vicinity.

At Zero hour Units of the Brigade were disposed as shewn on the attached tracing, with

Brigade Headquarters at	REGENT STREET Dugouts.	N.29.c.50.25.
H.Q. 8th R.I.Rifles.	S.P.6.	N.35.b.70.30.
H.Q. 9th R.I.Rifles.	S.P.7.	N.35.b.55.80.
H.Q. 10th R.I.Rifles	S.P.7.	-do-
H.Q. 15th R.I.Rifles.	BEEHIVE Dugouts	N.34.b.47.40.
H.Q. 12th R.I.Rifles.	S.P.6.	N.35.b.70.30.
H.Q. 107th M.G. Coy.	REGENT STREET Dugouts.	N.29.c.50.25.
H.Q. 107th T.M. Bty.	S.P.7.	N.35.b.55.80.

3.10 a.m. At 3.10 a.m. mines were exploded along our front at SPANBROEKMOLEN, IN DE KRUISTRAAT and BONE POINT and the creeping Barrage opened on the enemy Front Line with a standing barrage on the various Strong points and Emplacements. 10 Machine Guns of 107th M. Gun Coy. also swept and searched the ridge. The effect of the mines was the destruction of the whole enemy front line system; though the size of the craters combined with the bad visibility owing to the mist and the twilight caused a certain amount of loss of direction during the early part of the operations.

The leading waves of the attack, 8th R.I.Rifles bei "B" & "C" Companies and 9th R.I.Rifles "A" & "B" Companies followed by their respective Moppers up. "A" and "C" Coys. 12th R.I.Rifles got quickly out of their jumping off trenches and followed closely on the barrage, despite the speed with which the latter moved and the very difficult ground which was pock marked with shell holes.

At the same time the remaining 6 guns of the 107th M.Gun Company, the Brigade forward party, and the Brigade Intelligence Section Established themselves on the Eastern Lip of the SPANBROEKMOLEN Crater. Owing to the darkness the Machine Guns could not fire; but prepared their positions and dug themselves in, while the Signallers quickly brought forward the cable from the ruined cellar at N.30.c.2.9 up to where it had previously been buried and established communication with Brigade Headquarters. Forward communication was establidhed later by runner relay, telephone and Visual.

The enemy barrage was put down along our front line, but was at no time heavy and the 8th R.I.R. reached the RED Line practically without opposition, while the 9th R.I.R. found their first obstacle at HOP POINT, which was speadily taken by "B" Company under Captain C.H. Harding M.C.

The Mopping up of the ground as far as the RED Line was completed by two Companies of the 12th Rifles by 4.40 a.m. and several batches of prisoners sent back. The Moppers up carried on with the consolidation of two Strong Points OCCULT END and HOP END.

4.0 a.m. At 4 a.m. the Attack moved on to the BLUE Line, being made by "A" and "D" Companies of the 8th R.I.Rifles and "C" and "D" Companies of the 9th R.I.Rifles with the other Companies in Support and with "B" and "D" Companies of the 12th R.I.R. as their respective Moppers up.

4.5 a.m. At 4.5 a.m. the Machine Guns ceased their Barrage fire. On the right the 8th R.I.R. met with some opposition from undestroyed enemy Machine Guns in ENFER WOOD and EARL FARM; and the wire in places on the STEENBEEK was uncut- but thanks to the prompt action and initiative of the Platoon Commanders the resistance of these was quickly overcome without serious casualties and the advance at no time held up.

On the Left the 9th R.I.R.also took a number of Machine Guns and prisoners in PICK WOOD and SKIP POINT.

4.50 a.m. The BLUE Line was reached in good time and the work of consolidation begun as soon as possible; three Strong Points being made at OCHRE END, ENFER POINT and SKIP POINT.

The Moppers up had still some fighting to do in L'ENFER WOOD; and as touch had not been maintained by the troops of the 25th Division on our right, a Platoon of "D" Company 12th R.I.Rifles wasordered up to make a defensive flank;

5 a.m. By 5 a.m. however clear light had come and the gaps which existed between Units were shortly afterwards filled up.

7.0 a.m. On completion of their task the Moppers up returned to the other Companies of the 12th R.I.Rifles in the RED LINE which they consolidated and garrisoned. In the meantime at 4.25 a.m. 4 Guns of the 107th Machine Gun Company moved forward and took up positions at SKIP END, OCCULT END and O.25.d.50.80 (OCHRE END being already occupied by the 25th Division).

The 15th and 10th R.I.Rifles left their assembly trenches at 4.50 and 5.10 a.m. respectively and went forward to go through the Battalions in the BLUE LINE and attack the further objectives. The enemy barrage which was kept up intermittently all day ~~day~~ on the STEENBEEK Valley and western slopes of the ridge, was not heavy or accurate enough to cause any great difficulty, though "D" Company of the 15th R.I.Rifles had some casualties.

Our Barrage lifted at 6.50 a.m. and the attack on the GREEN Line went forward encountering practically no opposition; the BLACK Line however, especially on the Left when the Attack was being carried out by "C" and "D" Companies of the 10th R.I.Rifles, gave some trouble PICK HOUSE being very strongly held. It was here that the Brigade lost the first and only Officer killed during the day, Lieut. R. McLAURIN of the 10th R.I. Rifles. With the help of rifle grenade fire and fire from a captured Machine Gun the flanks of the position were turned and the garrison which included a Regimental Commander and 30 other Officers taken prisoners.

The ground between the BLUE and the BLACK Lines ~~aw~~ was mopped up by parties from the attacking Battalions told off for the purpose.

To cover the consolidation of the selected strong points LUMM POINT, MOAT and PICK POINTS, an outpost line was put out some 100 yards in front, and 6 machine guns moved forward and took up positions - one at O.25.b.20.40, 3 60 yards North of LUMM FARM and two at O.26.c.60.80.

At 6:15 and 7:55 a.m. carrying parties were sent up to the BLUE and BLACK Lines with S.A.A., Grenades, Shovels, Picks, Wire, etc.

At 8:30 a.m. the machine guns moved from SPANBROEKMOLEN, 3 guns to the neighbourhood of GODERIS FARM and one each to O.26.a.80.99; 65.72 and 60.80.

From 8 a.m. on the Commanding Officers made tours of their lines, re-organized the men and directed the consolidating of the ~~first~~ positions.

Forward Battalion Headquarters were established as follows

8th R.I.Rifles	O.31.b.30.75. (3:40 p.m.)
9th R.I.Rifles	Near SKIP POINT
10th R.I. Rifles	OCEAN LANE N. of GODERIS FARM.
15th R.I. Rifles	Dugout in ENFER WOOD.

11:55 a.m. One platoon of the 9th R.I.Rifles was sent to reinforce the 10th R.I.Rifles; and

12:40 p.m. the 15th R.I.Rifles were ordered to reinforce "D" (their advanced Company) with either their support or reserve Company.

1:0 p.m. Pack Mules were sent up with water, S.A.A. and bombs to the advanced troops.

At 2 p.m. the 12th R.I.Rifles were ordered to go forward, hold and consolidate the MAUVE Line from O.27.d.2.9 to O.27.a.70.55; this was carried out without many casualties and Battalion Headquarters established at LUMM FARM.

When information came from Division of enemy massing for a counter-attack another Company of the 9th R.I.Rifles was ordered forward to support the 10th R.I.Rifles in the BLACK Line. This counter-attack did not however develop on our front, but was directed against the ANZAC Corps on our Right.

By 4 p.m. a Brigade of the 11th Division was on its way through to proceed to the attack on the final objective OOSTAVERNE Line; and the O.C. 121 Field Coy. R.E. reported that our consolidation of the BLUE and BLACK Lines was quite satisfactory

4 p.m. Lt. HAIGH, M.C. took up a party of 80 men with stakes and wire on pack mules to the BLACK Line, and had a good obstacle laid out in front of it by nightfall.

Orders were received from Division at 7:50 p.m. that the Brigade was to be relieved by the 108th Brigade and the relief was eventually completed as follows :-

	To	Time
8th R.I.R.	N.28.a and b (Ft VICTORIA)	9 a.m. 8/6/17.
9th R.I.R.	N.28.c and d	" "
10th R.I.R.	FRENCHMAN'S FARM	2 a.m. "
15th R.I.R.	BEEHIVE DUG-OUTS.	1.30 a.m. "

Brigade Headquarters were moved to S.KEMMEL DUGOUTS about 5 a.m. 8/6/17.

<u>Action of Trench Mortar Battery.</u>

For three minutes from 3.10 a.m. 4 Stokes Mortars ea carried out an intense bombardment of selected pointsin enemy line. Two Mortars went forward with the 8th and 9th R.I.Rifles to the BLUE Line and took up positions at O.26.c 00.65 and O.25.b.50.30. Subsequently they went forward to the BLACK LINE and at 8.45 a.m. established themselves at O.26.b.20.30 and O.26.a.40.50; ammunition was brought up to these points, but these guns were not called upon to fire during the action.

Appendix XVI

STATEMENT OF CASUALTIES WHICH OCCURRED IN IO7th INFANTRY BRIGADE

DURING MONTH OF JUNE 1917.

UNIT	KILLED		WOUNDED		MISSING	
	Officers	O.R.	Officers	O.R.	Officers	O.R.
8th R.I. Rifles.	-	32	IO	140	-	13
9th R.I. Rifles.	-	29	6	119	-	IO
IOth R.I. Rifles.	1	20	2	83	-	2
15th R.I. Rifles.	-	15	6	IO2	-	-
IO7th M.G. Coy.	1	3	-	6	-	-
IO7th T.M. Battery.	-	3	-	2	-	-

Instructions regarding War Diaries and Intelligence Summaries are contained in F. S. Regs., Part II. and the Staff Manual respectively. Title pages will be prepared in manuscript.

WAR DIARY
or
~~INTELLIGENCE~~ SUMMARY.
(Erase heading not required.)

Army Form C. 2118.

March 1917 — H.Q's 107th Infantry Brigade.

Place	Date	Hour	Summary of Events and Information	Remarks and references to Appendices
	March			
SPANBROEK			to our trenches. Bde order No 125 issued re reliefs on the 25th inst	App XI
SECTOR	25th		Very quiet day, reliefs took place in accordance with order No 125. Complete by 12 p.m.	
"	26		Our field guns carried out wire cutting at N 30.c.43.33. The enemy retaliated on ULSTER ROAD.	
"	27		Very quiet day — nothing unusual to report	
"	28		" " " " " "	
"	29		Bde Order No 126 issued re moves of T.M. Battery 107th & 108th Bde Transport ~~nothing unusual to report~~. Bde Order No 127 issued re reliefs	App. XII App. XIII
"	~~30~~		on the 31st inst. nothing unusual to report	
"	30		Nothing unusual to report — Capt. Buchan to Hospital with measles	
"	31st		Moves in accordance with O.O. No 126 took place — Relief in accordance with O.O. No 127 took place. Nothing unusual to report.	

[signature] Capt
Staff Capt
for Brigade Major
31/3/17

2353 Wt. W2544/1454 700,000 5/15 D. D. & L. A.D.S.S./Forms/C. 2118.

Army Form C. 2118.

WAR DIARY
or
~~INTELLIGENCE SUMMARY.~~
(Erase heading not required.)

Instructions regarding War Diaries and Intelligence Summaries are contained in F. S. Regs., Part II. and the Staff Manual respectively. Title pages will be prepared in manuscript.

April 1917. H.Q's 107th Inf Brigade.

Vol 18

Place	Date	Hour	Summary of Events and Information	Remarks and references to Appendices
SPANBROEK SECTOR	April 1st		Nothing to report.	
			Nothing to report.	
	2nd		Nothing to report.	
	3rd		Nothing to report.	
	4th		Nothing to report.	
	5th		On the evening of April 5th 47th Bde. 16 Division carried out a raid on the enemy lines in N.24 C. and N.24 D. in which our Machine guns in the left sub-sector co-operated. On our bombardment opening at 8.45 PM enemy put a shrapnell barrage along our front line and also shelled possible assembly points such as S.P. 6 (N35B) LONG LANE (N36 A) – PICCADILLY TRENCH (N29 A) – REGENT ST. DUGOUTS (N29 C) – Junction of PALLMALL and RESERVE LINE (N29D) – Junction of KETCHEN AV. and front line (N 24 C.) The above points were consequently considerably damaged – Our casualties as the result of the Bombardment 5 Killed – 14 wounded	
	6th		Inter Brigade relief vide Bde. O.O. No 128 carried out	Appendix I

[signature]

2353 Wt. W2544/1454 700,000 5/15 D. D. & L. A.D.S.S./Forms/C. 2118.

Army Form C. 2118.

WAR DIARY
or
~~INTELLIGENCE~~ SUMMARY.
(Erase heading not required.)

Instructions regarding War Diaries and Intelligence Summaries are contained in F. S. Regs., Part II. and the Staff Manual respectively. Title pages will be prepared in manuscript.

April 1917. H.Q's 107th Inf Brigade.

Place	Date	Hour	Summary of Events and Information	Remarks and references to Appendices
SPANBROEK SECTOR	April 7th		Inter-Bde relief vide Bde. O.O. No 128 carried out.	Appendix I.
DRANOUTRE	8th		Do " " " Do. Bde Hd Qrs established at DRANOUTRE	Appendix I.
"	9th		Nothing to report. Battns at work.	
"	10th		Do. Do. Do Do. Capt BUCHANAN (Brigade Major) rejoined from Hospital. Acting Brigade Major consequently much relieved!	
"	11th		Nothing to report	
"	12th		" " "	
"	13th		" " " Brigade Order No 129 issued	App II.
"	14th		Detachments of Bns in the KEMMEL Area moved back to rejoin their HQ's in the METEREN Area. Brigade Order No 130 issued	App III
HAZEBROUCK	15th		The Brigade accompanied by No 2 Coy Train and 1 Sect 110th Field Ambce moved to HAZEBROUCK. Brigade order No 131 issued	App IV.
ARQUES	16th		Brigade Group moved to ARQUES-ST MARTIN AU LAERT-HALLINES area. Order No 132 issued	App V

TMcB

2353 Wt. W2544/1454 700,000 5/15 D. D. & L. A.D.S.S./Forms/C. 2118.

Army Form C. 2118.

Instructions regarding War Diaries and Intelligence Summaries are contained in F. S. Regs., Part II. and the Staff Manual respectively. Title pages will be prepared in manuscript.

WAR DIARY
or
~~INTELLIGENCE~~ SUMMARY.
(Erase heading not required.)

April 1917. HQ's 107th Inf Brigade.

Place	Date	Hour	Summary of Events and Information	Remarks and references to Appendices
WESTRECOURT	17th		Brigade Group moved to Training area. For dispositions see appendix V	
"	18th		Training Commences. Wet day	
"	19th		" Continued Wet day.	
BOISDINGHEM	20th		" " Brigade H.Q's moved from WESTBECOURT to BOISDINGHEM.	
"	21st		" "	
"	22nd		" "	
"	23rd		" "	
"	24th		" "	
"	25th		" "	
"	26th		" "	
"	27th		" "	
"	28th		The training during the above period has been progressive i.e. the period was divided into four parts – 3 days platoon training, 3 days company, 3 days Bn, 3 days Brigade. In these 12 days an entirely new system of warfare had to be learnt and adopted viz the platoon as the unit armed with its own particular weapons. The period available was not really long enough to allow of sufficient being taught, but	TMB.

2353 Wt. W2544/1454 700,000 5/15 D. D. & L. A.D.S.S./Forms/C. 2118.

Instructions regarding War Diaries and Intelligence Summaries are contained in F. S. Regs., Part II. and the Staff Manual respectively. Title pages will be prepared in manuscript.

WAR DIARY
or
~~INTELLIGENCE SUMMARY.~~

(*Erase heading not required.*)

Army Form C. 2118.

April 1917. H.Qs. 107th Inf Brigade.

Place	Date	Hour	Summary of Events and Information	Remarks and references to Appendices
BOIS DINGHEM	April 28th		Nevertheless very considerable progress was made. The men were very keen and took considerable interest throughout. The greatest difficulty was the junior officer. It was difficult to make the platoon commander understand that he was in command of his platoon and his difficulty was considerably increased by his lack of imagination or initiative. At the end of the 12 days junior officers were just beginning to understand the importance of their position. On the whole very considerable progress was made. In addition all men fired on the range, threw live bombs and were practised in Bayonet fighting.	
"	29th		Brigade Order No 133 issued vide	App VI
"	30th		" " No 144 " Brigade Group marched to HAQUES area vide App VII	App VII

T. M. Buchanan Capt
Brigade Major 107th Inf Bde

2353 Wt. W2544/1454 700,000 5/15 D. D. & L. A.D.S.S./Forms/C. 2118.

Instructions regarding War Diaries and Intelligence Summaries are contained in F. S. Regs., Part II. and the Staff Manual respectively. Title pages will be prepared in manuscript.

WAR DIARY
or
INTELLIGENCE SUMMARY.
(Erase heading not required.)

Army Form C. 2118.

HQ 107 Infy Bde

May 1917. H.Q.s 107th Inf Brigade

Vol 19

Place	Date	Hour	Summary of Events and Information	Remarks and references to Appendices
HAZEBROUCK	May 1st		The Brigade Group marched from ARQUES area to Billets in the neighbourhood of HAZEBROUCK	
METEREN	2nd		The Brigade marched from HAZEBROUCK to the METEREN area.	
"	3rd to 12th incl		During this period the Brigade found working parties for the Corps amounting to approximately 1800 men. The 8th R.I.R. moved down to MOULLE on the 6th inst returning on the 12th inst and fired a musketry course during the six days. Owing to so many men being away training of signallers and intelligence sections only could be carried out. A school was formed at Brigade H.Q.s for 12 young officers and twenty two Sgts. The course lasted one week. The programme covered a large variety of subjects but most time was devoted to schemes, with the object of improving the imagination and initiative of the officers and senior N.C.O's. The results of the course were very satisfactory.	
			During this period the Brigade was in Divisional Reserve and orders were issued for moving forward in case of heavy fighting.	App I.
				T.M.B.

2353 Wt. W2544/1454 700,000 5/15 D. D. & L. A.D.S.S./Forms/C. 2118.

Instructions regarding War Diaries and Intelligence Summaries are contained in F. S. Regs., Part II. and the Staff Manual respectively. Title pages will be prepared in manuscript.

WAR DIARY
or
~~INTELLIGENCE~~ SUMMARY.

(*Erase heading not required.*)

Army Form C. 2118.

May 1917. H.Q's 107th Inf Brigade

Place	Date	Hour	Summary of Events and Information	Remarks and references to Appendices
	May			
METEREN	11th		Brigade Order No 136 issued and addendum thereto re move forward of the 107th M.G. Coy and T.M. Bty	App II.
"	12th		Brigade Order No 137 issued re move Eastwards of the 107th Brigade on the 14th Inst. 8th R. Irish Rifles returned from TILQUES to the METEREN Area. Addendum to order No 136 issued	App III / App IV
"	13th		The M.G. Coy and T.M. Battery moved into the Line relieving the 108th M.G. Coy and T.M. Bty	
DRANOUTRE	14th		The Brigade, less M.G. Coy and T.M. Bty & working parties, moved into Bivouacks in the area just south of DRANOUTRE	
"	15th to 23rd		The majority of Brigade away on working parties. Signallers, Scouts and Lewis Gun classes kept for training and a second junior officers school was formed / Signalling scheme was carried out in conjunction with contact aeroplanes	
"	24th		A raid was carried out by a party of the 15th R.I.R. on the enemys trenches at N.36.a.70.90 in accordance with Brigade Order No 138 vide	App V
			The report on the raid is attached vide	App VI
			Brigade Order No 139 issued vide	App VII
"	25th–28th		Nothing to report. 10th R. Irish Rifles raid was postponed until 29th Inst.	

2353 Wt. W2544/1454 700,000 5/15 D. D. & L. A.D.S.S./Forms/C. 2118.

Army Form C. 2118.

Instructions regarding War Diaries and Intelligence Summaries are contained in F. S. Regs., Part II. and the Staff Manual respectively. Title pages will be prepared in manuscript.

WAR DIARY
or
~~INTELLIGENCE SUMMARY.~~
(*Erase heading not required.*)

May 1917 — H.Q.s 107th Inf Brigade

Place	Date	Hour	Summary of Events and Information	Remarks and references to Appendices
	May			
DRANOUTRE	29th	10.pm	A raid was carried out by the 10th R. Ir. Rif. (vide Appendix VII). They entered enemy's trench which they found unoccupied, and remained nearly an hour without seeing any enemy, when they withdrew without casualty.	
	30th	10 a.m	All Battalions, less Working parties, Transport, and Q.M.'s Stores moved to BERTHEN Training Area in accordance with Bde. O.O. 140 (vide Appendix VIII)	
	31st		Nothing to report.	

2353 Wt. W2544/1454 700,000 5/15 D. D. & L. A.D.S.S./Forms/C. 2118.

Army Form C. 2118.

Instructions regarding War Diaries and Intelligence Summaries are contained in F. S. Regs., Part II. and the Staff Manual respectively. Title pages will be prepared in manuscript.

WAR DIARY
or
~~INTELLIGENCE~~ SUMMARY.
(Erase heading not required.)

June 1917 — A.Q's 107th Inf Brigade — Vol 20

Place	Date	Hour	Summary of Events and Information	Remarks and references to Appendices
55.d.6070 DRANOUTRE	June 1st		All Bns in the BERTHEN area training, practising the attack for the M.O. The Ground was marked representing as nearly as possible the MESSINES WYTSCHAETE Ridge and practise attacks were carried out over this ground. During this period divisional instructions for the attack were coming in and instructions were being issued to Bns.	
BERTHEN Area	2nd		Brigade H.Q's moved down to the BERTHEN area. Several working parties rejoined their units. Brigade carried out another practice attack scheme. Brigadier General W.M. Withycombe CMG rejoined the Brigade from England and resumed command.	
"	3rd		The B.G.C visited Divl HQs and discussed the forthcoming offensive. Also visited M.G. Coy and T.M. Bty to see that their instructions were clear. The T.M. Bty was moved back from KEMMEL HILL to S.S.C.	
"	4th		12th R. Irish Rifles came down from the forward area to practice the attack with the remainder of the Brigade. Order No 141 issued for the move back to the concentration area in S.S.C and D. See	App I

T.O.M.B.

2353 Wt. W2544/1454 700,000 5/15 D. D. & L. A.D.S.S./Forms/C. 2118.

Instructions regarding War Diaries and Intelligence Summaries are contained in F. S. Regs., Part II. and the Staff Manual respectively. Title pages will be prepared in manuscript.

Army Form C. 2118.

WAR DIARY
or
~~INTELLIGENCE SUMMARY.~~
(*Erase heading not required.*)

June 1917. H.Q's 107th Inf Brigade.

Place	Date	Hour	Summary of Events and Information	Remarks and references to Appendices
BERTHEN	5th		Brigade Order No 142 issued giving the orders for the assembly of troops on the night of Y/Z day and also the orders for collecting ~~surplus ammn~~ extra ammunition, bombs etc. ~~Zero day notified~~ SEE	App II
			Zero day notified by the Division as being 7th June.	
			Brigade Order No 143 issued giving the orders for the attack on the MESSINES – WHYTSCHAETE Ridge SEE	App III
DRANOUTRE S.5.d.60.70	6th		All Bns marched to the concentration area in S.5.c and d and Brigade HQs to S.5.d.60.70. The men were bivouacked for the day in hybells and fitted out with S.A.A. bombs etc. Zero hour notified by the division for 3.10 a.m on the 7th. Brigade HQs moved to battle position at REGENT STREET dugouts at 10 pm. At 9.15 pm Battalions commenced to march	
In the line	7th		to their assembly trenches and at 2.42 am all units reported that they were ready in their assembly trenches. A time table of occurrences during the 7th June is attached SEE	App IV
			The plan of attack and an account of the operations is attached SEE	App V
			The instructions issued to units prior to the final orders are ~~is~~ attached SEE	App VI

T.O. M.B.

2353 Wt. W2544/1454 700,000 5/15 D. D. & L. A.D.S.S./Forms/C. 2118.

Instructions regarding War Diaries and Intelligence Summaries are contained in F. S. Regs., Part II. and the Staff Manual respectively. Title pages will be prepared in manuscript.

WAR DIARY

or

~~INTELLIGENCE SUMMARY.~~

(Erase heading not required.)

June. H. Q's 107th Inf Brigade

Army Form C. 2118.

Place	Date	Hour	Summary of Events and Information	Remarks and references to Appendices
In the Line	7th		Suggestions for the future learnt from these operations are shewn in Appendix	VII
			During the night of the 7th/8th the Brigade was relieved in its positions by the 108th Brigade and withdrew to the area East of the LINDENHOEK – DAYLIGHT CORNER Road and South of the LINDEN HOEK – STORE FARM	
M.26.B.4.1	8th		road with Brigade H.Q. at M.26.B.4.1. All Bns were in their bivouacks by 11.30 a.m. The Brigade was in Divl Reserve.	
			Brigade Order No 144 issued at 11.30 pm for the relief of the Brigade by 32nd Brigade next day.	App VIII
S.5.d.6.7.	9th		On relief by 32nd Brigade the Brigade withdrew to bivouacks in S.4 and 5	
S.4.d.10.10	10th		Brigade H.Q's moved to S.4.d.10.10. Working party of 500 men sent away.	
"	11th		Nothing to report.	
"	12th		B.G.C. addressed the Brigade. Order No 145 issued	App IX
"	13th		Battalions, M G Coy. and T.M.B. marched to Area 13. Further working parties, 500 men for 250th Tunnelling Coy, and 100 men for 121 Coy. R.E. sent away.	
~~S.4.d.2.2~~ "	14/15/16		Men of Battns not on working parties were trained in S 1, 2 and 4.	T.O.H.B.
"	15		The Army Commander visited Bde. HQ at S4d1.1.	

2353 Wt. W2544/1454 700,000 5/15 D. D. & L. A.D.S.S./Forms/C. 2118.

Instructions regarding War Diaries and Intelligence Summaries are contained in F. S. Regs., Part II. and the Staff Manual respectively. Title pages will be prepared in manuscript.

Army Form C. 2118.

WAR DIARY
or
~~INTELLIGENCE SUMMARY.~~
(Erase heading not required.)

June

H^d Qrs 107th Inf. Bde

Place	Date	Hour	Summary of Events and Information	Remarks and references to Appendices
54 d 1.1.	17		Order no. 146 with Administrative Instructions and After Order issued see Order subsequently cancelled at 8.30 p.m.	App. X / App. XI.
"	18		Order no. 147 issued see App. XI. 107th Bde. relieved 33rd Bde in area E. of LINDENHOEK. Working parties ceased work on completion of day's task and rejoined their units, being relieved by the 56th Bde.	
"	19		Order no. 148 issued, see App. XII. The 107th Bde. relieved the 32nd and 34th Bdes. in the line E of WYTSCHAETE-MESSINES Road. Bde HQ moved to REGENT ST DUGOUTS, opening there at 9 p.m.. Battns commenced to move about 9 p.m. and relief was complete at 2 a.m. on 20th	App. XII.
In the line REGENT dugouts "	20		Considerable artillery activity. Enemy shelling was scattered. Casualties to noon 20th Two ORs killed and 13 O.R's wounded and Three officers wounded	
"	21.		Artillery activity continued. Front line in left subsector heavily shelled in the afternoon. Casualties to noon 21st Two OR's killed Two officers and 14 OR's wounded.	
"	22		Bombardment of front line in left subsector continued. Patrols out nightly but cannot definitely locate Enemy. He does not appear	

T. O. M. B.

2353 Wt. W2544/1454 700,000 5/15 D. D. & L. A.D.S.S./Forms/C. 2118.

Instructions regarding War Diaries and Intelligence Summaries are contained in F. S. Regs., Part II. and the Staff Manual respectively. Title pages will be prepared in manuscript.

Army Form C. 2118.

WAR DIARY
or
~~INTELLIGENCE~~ SUMMARY.
(*Erase heading not required.*)

June 1917. Hqs 107th Inf Brigade.

Place	Date	Hour	Summary of Events and Information	Remarks and references to Appendices
[illegible]			to be holding any definite line in proximity to our outpost line.	
Regent Dugouts	22		~~Artillery activity continued~~. Casualties to noon 22nd 8 ORs killed 6 ORs wounded 4 ORs missing.	
"	23		Artillery activity continued. Casualties to noon 23rd Two ORs killed 5 ORs wounded. Brigade Order No 149 issued re reliefs on 24th inst.	App XIII
"	24.		Enemy's artillery activity was confined to right subsector. Casualties to noon 24th. Two ORs killed, 16 ORs wounded.	
"	25		Enemy's artillery less active. Casualties to noon 25th 7 ORs wounded	
"	26		Enemy's artillery still less active. Casualties to noon 26th 2 ORs killed and 11 wounded. Brigade Order No 150 issued re relief of the Brigade by 111th Inf Brigade	App XIV
"	27		Enemy artillery activity normal. Right Bn HQs shelled with 8 inch. L'ENFER Wood shelled from 11.30 a.m to 1 p.m. The 10th R. Irish Rifles sent out two patrols to endeavour to capture a prisoner. Patrols found the enemy at work with strong covering parties and returned to our lines. The 8th and	T. O[illegible]

2353 Wt. W2544/1454 700,000 5/15 D. D. & L. A.D.S.S./Forms/C. 2118.

Army Form C. 2118.

Instructions regarding War Diaries and Intelligence Summaries are contained in F. S. Regs., Part II. and the Staff Manual respectively. Title pages will be prepared in manuscript.

WAR DIARY
or
~~INTELLIGENCE SUMMARY.~~

(*Erase heading not required.*)

June 1917 — H. Qs 107th Brigade

Place	Date	Hour	Summary of Events and Information	Remarks and references to Appendices
In the line 2 REGENT Dugouts	June 28th		9th R. Irish Rifles were relieved in the support trenches by the Bns of 111th Brigade all reliefs being completed by 1.30 am on the 29th Enemy's artillery quiet. All reliefs were completed by 1.50 am on the 29th	
OUTTERSTEENE	29th		G.O.C 111th Brigade took over command of the Brigade Sector and Brigade HQs and 8th and 9th R. Irish Rifles and M.G. Coy and T.M. Bty moved to OUTTERSTEENE AREA	
"	30th		10th and 15th R. Irish Rifles moved to OUTTERSTEENE Area	
			An appendix is attached showing the attitude of the enemy during the period the Brigade was in the line	App XV
			An appendix is attached showing casualties for the month of June	App XVI
			T. O. M. Buchan Capt Brigade Major 107th Inf Brigade 30/6/17.	

2353 Wt. W2544/1454 700,000 5/15 D. D. & L. A.D.S.S./Forms/C. 2118.

Army Form C. 2118.

Instructions regarding War Diaries and Intelligence Summaries are contained in F. S. Regs., Part II. and the Staff Manual respectively. Title pages will be prepared in manuscript.

WAR DIARY
or
~~INTELLIGENCE SUMMARY.~~

(Erase heading not required.)

July 1917 — H. Q's 107th Inf Brigade

Vol 21

Place	Date	Hour	Summary of Events and Information	Remarks and references to Appendices
	July			
OUTTERSTEENE	1st		Nothing to report	
	2nd, 3rd, 4th		Brigade order No 151 issued re move to TILQUES training area and transfer of Division to 5th Army. Two days spent in training in Musketry and of specialists. One day Brigade route march.	App I
CAESTRE	5th		Brigade moved to CAESTRE Area. See Order No 151	
RENNESCURE	6th		Brigade moved to RENNESCURE area. See order No 151/1	
WESTBECOURT	7th		Brigade marched to TILQUES Training area. See order No 151/2 — Disposition of units. Brigade H.Qs WESTBECOURT; 8th R.I.R. LA WATTINE; 9th R.I.R QUERCAMP; 10th R.I.R LE POVRE; 15th R.I.R. ACQUIN; 107th M.G.Coy VAL D'ACQUIN; 107th T.M.B NORDAL	
"	8th		Training commenced. An appendix is attached shewing the syllabus of training to be carried out.	App II
"	9th–19th		Training carried out continuously commencing with platoon training and gradually working up through Company and Battalion training to Brigade schemes. The Bns were situated too far away from the	

TMB.

Instructions regarding War Diaries and Intelligence Summaries are contained in F. S. Regs., Part II. and the Staff Manual respectively. Title pages will be prepared in manuscript.

Army Form C. 2118.

WAR DIARY
or
~~INTELLIGENCE~~ SUMMARY.
(*Erase heading not required.*)

July 1917. H. Q's. 107th Brigade.

Place	Date	Hour	Summary of Events and Information	Remarks and references to Appendices
	July		training area to allow as much benefit to be obtained from the training as would otherwise have been possible	
ESQUERDES	20		Moves of the Brigade units took place in accordance with Order No 152	App III
"	21st		Training continued. Brigade order No 153 issued re the move the Brigade to the WINNEZEELE No 3 area	App IV
"	22nd–24th		Further training including a Brigade day on the 22nd and 24th Instants.	
"	25th		The transport of the Brigade Group moved to NOORDPEENE commencing at 4 a.m in the morning. The Personnel of the Brigade Group Embussed at 3 p.m. and reached their destination at 8 p.m. all the embussing programme worked very satisfactorily	
LOOFE-HOOK	26th		Brigade did not move	
"	29		Brigade Order No 154 issued ordering the move of the Brigade to the WATOU area on the night of 30/31	App V
			Brigade order No 155 issued giving general instructions for the forthcoming offensive	App VI
"	30		Brigade moved off to WATOU No 3 area in accordance with order No 154.	
			[signature]	

2353 Wt. W2544/1454 700,000 5/15 D. D. & L. A.D.S.S./Forms/C. 2118.

Instructions regarding War Diaries and Intelligence Summaries are contained in F. S. Regs., Part II. and the Staff Manual respectively. Title pages will be prepared in manuscript.

WAR DIARY

or

~~INTELLIGENCE SUMMARY.~~

(Erase heading not required.)

Army Form C. 2118.

Aug 1917. HQ's 107th Brigade

Place	Date	Hour	Summary of Events and Information	Remarks and references to Appendices
WATOU No 3 Area	31st		Brigade arrived in Billets, all moves being completed about 3 a.m. An appendix is attached showing reinforcements for the month	App VII
			" " " " " Battle casualties for the month	App VIII
			T. O. M. Buchan Capt Brigade Major 107th Brigade	

2353 Wt. W2544/1454 700,000 5/15 D. D. & L. A.D.S.S./Forms/C. 2118.

Instructions regarding War Diaries and Intelligence Summaries are contained in F. S. Regs., Part II. and the Staff Manual respectively. Title Pages will be prepared in manuscript.

WAR DIARY
or
INTELLIGENCE SUMMARY

(Erase heading not required.)

Army Form C. 2118.

August 1917. H.Q.'s 107th Inf Brigade.

Place	Date	Hour	Summary of Events and Information	Remarks and references to Appendices
WATOU Area	August 1st	10 a.m	Message received from the Division warning the Brigade to be ready to move at two hours notice. — All units warned.	
		1.30 pm	Above notification cancelled	
		4 pm	B.G.C. attended conference at Div. HQs.	
		9 pm	Conference of all C.O's at Brigade H.Q's. B.G.C. informed all C.Os that situation was that 55th and 15th DIVS were on Black Line. If they were unable to capture Green Line themselves 16th and 36th DIVS would be allotted the task. The Brigade would anyhow probably remain in present position.	
		10.30 pm	Telephone message from Division ordering Brigade to be ready to entrain at HOPOUTRE at 4 a.m next morning and to move to neighbourhood of YPRES into Divl Reserve to 55th Division. All units warned and eventually after many changes in details Brigade order No 156 was issued at 12 midnight. see App.	

T. [signature] B

2449 Wt. W14957/M90 750,000 1/16 J.B.C. & A. Forms/C.2118/12.

Army Form C. 2118.

WAR DIARY
or
INTELLIGENCE SUMMARY
(Erase heading not required.)

Instructions regarding War Diaries and Intelligence Summaries are contained in F. S. Regs., Part II. and the Staff Manual respectively. Title Pages will be prepared in manuscript.

August 1917 H Qs 107th Brigade.

Place	Date	Hour	Summary of Events and Information	Remarks and references to Appendices
Should read Aug. 2nd C. Falls	August 8th		The personnel of the Brigade entrained at G.4.d.c.o. at 8 am and 10 am, detraining again at GOLDFISH CHATEAU. The transport proceeded by road to GOLDFISH CHATEAU.	
	"	8am	The B.G.C. called at 55th Dn HQs when order No 157 was issued giving units their orders for the move up from detraining point to old British trenches East of YPRES and ~~relieve~~ for relief then of 164 Inf Brigade.	See App I.
		12.45pm	B.G.C reached H.Qs of 164 Brigade in WIELTJE dugouts.	
		1.30pm	Telegram received from 55th Dn ordering the 107th Brigade to relieve the 165th and 166th Brigades see	App III & IV
		3pm	B.G.C held Conference of C.Os and explained details to them.	
		6pm	Brigade order 158 ordering relief of 165 and 166 Brigades issued	App V
		3.40pm	Reliefs of 164 Brigade reported complete	
		6pm	Brigade Intelligence officer visited 117th Bde on left and established liaison with them	T.O'm B.

2449 Wt. W14957/M90 750,000 1/16 J.B.C. & A. Forms/C.2118/12.

Army Form C. 2118.

Instructions regarding War Diaries and Intelligence Summaries are contained in F. S. Regs., Part II. and the Staff Manual respectively. Title Pages will be prepared in manuscript.

WAR DIARY
or
INTELLIGENCE SUMMARY

(Erase heading not required.)

August 1917. H.Q.'s 107th Brigade

Place	Date	Hour	Summary of Events and Information	Remarks and references to Appendices
WIELTJE	August		During above period enemy were attacking 165 Brigade and Division on right but were driven off.	
	3rd	5.am	Relief of 156 Brigade reported complete.	
		6.am	Relief of 155 Brigade reported complete	
		12.10pm	Wire sent to Division reporting unsatisfactory condition of our right flank and the lack of touch with Division on right. See App	App VI
		3.45pm	Situation reported quiet. See	App VII
		5.50pm	Telegram received from Div stating left of 15th Div approximately at D.14.c.9.4 and left flank being extended. 10th R.I.R. informed.	
		8.20pm	Wire received from Division that 15th Div were sending up one platoon to fill up gap between their left and our right. 10th R.I.R. informed. Two Bns of the 108th Bde and two Bns of the 109th Brigade relieved 166th and 165th Inf Brigades in the old British Trenches, coming under the orders of G.O.C. 107th Brigade. These Bns were as follows	

T. Ohw B.

2449 Wt. W14957/M90 750,000 1/16 J.B.C. & A. Forms/C.2118/12.

Army Form C. 2118.

WAR DIARY
or
~~INTELLIGENCE SUMMARY~~
(Erase heading not required.)

Instructions regarding War Diaries and Intelligence Summaries are contained in F. S. Regs., Part II. and the Staff Manual respectively. Title Pages will be prepared in manuscript.

August 1917 — HQs 107th Brigade

Place	Date	Hour	Summary of Events and Information	Remarks and references to Appendices
WIELTJE	August		108th Bde 9th R.I. Fusiliers, 13th R.I. Rifles — 109th Bde 14th Rifles and 11th R. Inniskilling Fusiliers	
	4th		The remaining guns of 165 and 166 M.G. Coys left in the line were relieved during the night by guns of the 108th and 109th M.G. Coys.	
	4th	5.10 am	Situation reported to Division as unchanged.	
		2.30 pm	B.G.C assembled C.O's of Bns of 108th and 109th Bdes under his command and discussed the situation and probable action with them	
		4.15 pm	Situation reported to Division SEE	App VIII
		9 pm	15th R.I.R instructed to occupy CAPRICORN support; this was successfully carried out during the night.	
			Carrying parties of 50 men per Bn from the Bns of 108 and 109 Bdes attached to this Brigade were sent up with wire and stakes to the BLACK LINE.	
		8 PM	Bde Order No. 159 issued see	App IX

T. Ohn[?] B.

2449 Wt. W14957/M90 750,000 1/16 J.B.C. & A. Forms/C.2118/12.

Army Form C. 2118.

Instructions regarding War Diaries and Intelligence Summaries are contained in F. S. Regs., Part II. and the Staff Manual respectively. Title Pages will be prepared in manuscript.

WAR DIARY
or
INTELLIGENCE SUMMARY
(Erase heading not required.)

August 1917, H.Q's 107th Brigade

Place	Date	Hour	Summary of Events and Information	Remarks and references to Appendices
WIELTJE	4th	10.30 P.M.	Div! Order No. 126 received ordering one battalion each of the 108th and 109th Inf. Bdes. to withdraw from the forward area.	
	5th	3.50 AM	Situation reported to Division see	app. X
		6.30 AM	9th R. Ir. Fus. report that they have moved out. 11th R. Ir. Rif. also moved out during the day.	
		10.30 AM	Bde Order no 160 issued see	app. XI
		12.20 PM	Div. wire that 14th R. Ir. Rif. will also probably move back following day.	
		3 PM	14th R. Ir. Rif. ordered to move out in accordance with Div! instructions.	
		5.25 P.M.	Div. wire that 13th R. Ir. Rif. will also move out following day.	
		4.15 P.M.	Situation reported to Division see	app. XII
		4.15 P.M.	Bde. Order No. 169 wired see	app. XIII
	6th	12.2 AM	Div! Order no. 127 received confirming moves of 13th and 14th R. Ir. Rif.	
		4.10 AM	Situation reported to Division see	app. XIV
		10 A.M.	8th and 9th R. Ir. Rif. instructed with reference to putting out wire on BLACK LINE; this work was carried out during the night.	
		3.20 PM	Situation reported to Division see	app. XV
		6 P.M.	Div! order no. 128 received giving orders for relief of the Bde. by the 108 and 109 Bde., each 2 Bns on the night of the 7/8th.	
		9 P.M.	Two prisoners of 49 R.I.R. came in on the right of 8th R. Ir. Rif. and gave themselves up.	
		10 P.M.	10 R. Ir. Rif. discovered an unwounded prisoner in CAMEL TRENCH, having hidden there since 31st July.	
		9.25 PM	Removal of Coy. of 15th R. Ir. Rif. from BLUE LINE N. of WIELTJE-GRAVENSTAFEL road to DURHAM TRENCH completed.	

YRB

2449 Wt. W14957/M90 750,000 1/16 J.B.C. & A. Forms/C.2118/12.

Army Form C. 2118.

WAR DIARY
or
INTELLIGENCE SUMMARY
(Erase heading not required.)

Instructions regarding War Diaries and Intelligence Summaries are contained in F. S. Regs., Part II. and the Staff Manual respectively. Title Pages will be prepared in manuscript.

August 1917 HQrs 107th Brigade

Place	Date	Hour	Summary of Events and Information	Remarks and references to Appendices
WIELTJE	6th	11PM	Bde Order no 162 issued see	App. XVI
	7th	4AM	Situation reported to Divn see	App. XVII
		2PM	Wounded German prisoner found by 8 R. Ir. Rif. in hiding since 31st July.	
		11.30PM	Special situation report sent to Divn see	App. XVIII
			An appendix is attached showing the situation of our line and the enemy's as far as known in the shape of a disposition map see	App. XIX
WIELTJE	8th	4.30am	B.G.C. 107th Brigade handed over command of sector to G.O.C 108th Bde.	
BRANDHOEK		6am	Brigade H.Qrs opened in BRANDHOEK area	
		7am	All units reported arrival in BRANDHOEK area.	
"	9th		All units resting and cleaning up.	
"	10th		Nothing to report. 107th Brigade Instructions for the offensive issued see	App XX
"	11th	2pm	Orders received from Division for Brigade to take over line on the night of 12/13th August.	
		4pm	Brigade Order No 163 issued for the relief of two Bns of the 108th Bde and two Bns of the 109th Bde in the line on the night of the 12/13th August see	App XXI

T.O.M.B.

Army Form C. 2118.

Instructions regarding War Diaries and Intelligence Summaries are contained in F. S. Regs., Part II. and the Staff Manual respectively. Title Pages will be prepared in manuscript.

WAR DIARY
or
~~INTELLIGENCE SUMMARY~~
(Erase heading not required.)

August 1917 — H.Q's 107th Brigade.

Place	Date	Hour	Summary of Events and Information	Remarks and references to Appendices
BRANDHOEK	Aug 12th		Bns moved up to relief – 10th and 15th in front line 8th and 9th in support in our old British Trenches.	
WIELTJE	13th		Brigade H.Q's relieved 109th Bde H.Q's in WIELTJE at 5.30. a.m and G.O.C 107th Bde assumed command of the sector. Enemy's artillery was not active during the day. Our artillery very active. Carrying parties of 100 men each from the 8th and 9th R.I.R were detailed to carry up S.A.A to the Black Line for the M.G. Coy. Owing to heavy gas shelling during the night the parties failed in their tasks	
"	14th		Brigade orders for the relief of the Brigade by the 108th and 109th Bde issued, the 108th on the right and the 109th on the left. Hostile artillery generally quieter than usual during the day. Our artillery carried out practice barrages, the first could be plainly observed and appeared good but the remainder did not seem sufficiently heavy	App. XXII

T.B.W.B.

2449 Wt. W14957/M90 750,000 1/16 J.B.C. & A. Forms/C.2118/12.

Army Form C. 2118.

WAR DIARY
or
~~INTELLIGENCE~~ SUMMARY
(Erase heading not required.)

Instructions regarding War Diaries and Intelligence Summaries are contained in F. S. Regs., Part II. and the Staff Manual respectively. Title Pages will be prepared in manuscript.

August 1917 — H.Q's 107th Brigade.

Place	Date	Hour	Summary of Events and Information	Remarks and references to Appendices
WIELTJE	14.		Carrying parties of 8th and 9th again detailed to carry up ammunition for M.G. Coy and completed their task with success. Units leaving the Black Line left 100 rounds per man for the M.G's. 108 and 109th Bde H.Q's relieved 107th Bde H.Q's at 8 p.m. and 107th Bde returned to BRANDHOEK. All units informed that August 16th was Z day.	
BRANDHOEK	15.		Bns reported all in camps by 8 a.m. Bde Order No 165 issued for assembly of the Brigade on ~~the~~ morning of the 16th Instant see	App XXIII
			Brigade H.Q's opened at MILL COTTS at 8 p.m.	
MILL COTTS	16.		Zero hour at 4.45 a.m. Bns reported all in assembly positions by 5.45 a.m. No heavy shelling of assembly trenches or casualties on way up. By 11.20 am reports received to the effect that both 108 and 109 Bdes appear to be more or less on Black Line. At 3.30 pm B.M. attended conference at WIELTJE of G.O.C's 108 and 109th Bdes and G.S.O.1. Situation very unclear but in meantime 107th Bde were to relieve 108 and 109 in the line that night. It might be necessary to make	

BRB

2449 Wt. W14957/M90 750,000 1/16 J.B.C. & A. Forms/C.2118/12.

Army Form C. 2118.

WAR DIARY
or
INTELLIGENCE SUMMARY
(Erase heading not required.)

Instructions regarding War Diaries and Intelligence Summaries are contained in F. S. Regs., Part II. and the Staff Manual respectively. Title Pages will be prepared in manuscript.

August 1917. H.Qs 107th Brigade.

Place	Date	Hour	Summary of Events and Information	Remarks and references to Appendices
MILL COTTS		5.5am	Reliefs reported complete	
		9.45am	From reports of observers it appears uncertain whether Enemy holds HILL 35 or not.	
		10am	B.G.C rings up G.S.O.1, tells him this and says he will send out patrols if G.S.O.1 will stop heavies, from 12.30 pm – 2 pm.	
		10.10am	O.C. 9th R.I.R instructed accordingly	
		10.25am	Bde order for reliefs same night by 183rd Bde issued see	App XXV
			Reports from Patrols establish the fact that HILL 35, IBERIAN and POND FARM are held by the Enemy. see	App XXVI
		3.45pm	Situation Reported to Division see	App XXVII App XXVIII
		9pm 3.30pm	Reliefs commenced	

T. O...

2449 Wt. W14957/M90 750,000 1/16 J.B.C. & A. Forms/C.2118/12.

Army Form C. 2118.

WAR DIARY
or
~~INTELLIGENCE SUMMARY~~

(Erase heading not required.)

Instructions regarding War Diaries and Intelligence Summaries are contained in F. S. Regs., Part II. and the Staff Manual respectively. Title Pages will be prepared in manuscript.

August 1917. H.Q's 107th Bde.

Place	Date	Hour	Summary of Events and Information	Remarks and references to Appendices
MILL COTTS	16th		attack next day but G.S.O. 1. would ring up on return to Division.	
		6.15pm	B.G.C. held conference of C.O's and issued orders for relief verbally.	
		7pm	G.S.O. 1. rang up B.G.C and informed him that Bde would attack and capture the line IBERIAN – HILL 35 – SOMME – POND FARM next morning. Barrage would be 100 yards in 7 mins. B.G.C explained that he would have to use 4 Bns for attack, as frontage even then would be 850 yards per Bn. In consequence he would require troops to hold BLACK LINE. G.S.O. 1. said he would ring up again.	
			B.G.C continued conference with C.O's giving orders for attack next day. Group Commanders were asked to come over.	
		8pm	Col Place rang up B.G.C and said attack was cancelled.	
		8.15pm	C.O's instructed to continue ordinary reliefs.	
		8.30pm	Bde Order No 161 issued see	App XXIV
		9pm	Reliefs commenced, 9th R.I.R moving to front line on right and 8th R.I.R on left. 10th and 15th in old British front line trenches.	

T. McD.

2449 Wt. W14957/M90 750,000 1/16 J.B.C. & A. Forms/C.2118/12.

Army Form C. 2118.

WAR DIARY
or
INTELLIGENCE SUMMARY
(Erase heading not required.)

Instructions regarding War Diaries and Intelligence Summaries are contained in F. S. Regs., Part II. and the Staff Manual respectively. Title Pages will be prepared in manuscript.

August 1917 — H.Qs 107th Brigade.

Place	Date	Hour	Summary of Events and Information	Remarks and references to Appendices
VLAMERTINGHE	18th	4.50 am	Relief reported complete and G.O.C. 183rd Brigade assumed Command of the Sector. Brigade H.Qs opened at VLAMERTINGHE at 7 am. Brigade Order No 168 issued for the move of the Brigade to the WINNEZEELE No 3 area. A map is attached showing the disposition of units our front line on handing over to the 183 Bde. A copy was sent to G and a copy to 183 Bde.	App XXX
LODGE HOEK	19		The Brigade moved by bus to the WINNEZEELE No 3 area. Transport moved by road. Units were all in camp by 8.30 a.m and transport by 1 p.m. An account of the operations from Aug 2nd to Aug 18th is attached vide	App XXXI
"	20		Nothing to report.	
"	21/22		Brigade Order No 169 issued re move to IVth Corps vide	App XXXII
			Administrative order for the above move by train issued vide	App XXXIII
BARASTRE	23/24th		Brigade moved by rail to BARASTRE. HQs in village, all units in camp in O.16 Central.	

TB

2449 Wt. W14957/M90 750,000 1/16 J.B.C. & A. Forms/C.2118/12.

Army Form C. 2118.

WAR DIARY
or
INTELLIGENCE SUMMARY
(Erase heading not required.)

Instructions regarding War Diaries and Intelligence Summaries are contained in F. S. Regs., Part II. and the Staff Manual respectively. Title Pages will be prepared in manuscript.

August 1917 H.Q.s 107th Inf Bde.

Place	Date	Hour	Summary of Events and Information	Remarks and references to Appendices
BARASTRE	25th		Nothing to report	
"	26th		Brigade Order No 170 issued giving orders for move to YTRES Area next day. Brigade order No 171 issued for relief of South African Bde on 28th Inst.	App. XXXIV
NEUVILLE	27th		Brigade moved to YTRES area and Bde H.Q.s to NEUVILLE.	
METZ	28th		Bde H.Q.s moved to METZ. Reliefs carried out in accordance with order No 171. At 10 p.m G.O.C. 107th Bde assumed command of the Sector.	App XXXV
"	29th/31st		All three days passed very quietly.	
			A statement showing reinforcements received during the month is attached see	App XXXVI
			A statement showing casualties for the month is attached see	App XXXVII
			On the 25th instant the 1st Royal Irish Fusiliers joined the Brigade. On the 31st Inst the 8th and 9th Royal Irish Rifles were amalgamated into one Bn to be known as the 8/9 Royal Irish Rifles. The surplus personnel left over after the amalgamation was sent to the 10th and 15th R Irish Rifles, completing their establishment, and the remainder to other Bns in the Division. All surplus Off warrant officers and NCO's of the rank of corporal and above were sent to the Base.	

T.O.M. Buchan Capt
Brigade Major 107th Bde

2449 Wt. W14957/M90 750,000 1/16 J.B.C. & A. Forms/C.2118/12.

Appendix XXXI

REPORT ON OPERATIONS FROM 2nd to 18th AUGUST, 1917.

2nd August. Early in the morning of August 2nd the Brigade moved out from the WATOU area and entrained at POPERINGHE for YPRES. After detraining at GOLDFISH CHATEAU the Brigade relieved the 164th Brigade, together with two Battalions of the 16th Divn, and came into Divisional Reserve to the 55th Division. Brigade Headquarters moved into WIELTJE dugouts. While the relief was still in progress and before it had been completed, orders were received from the 55th Division for the Brigade to take over the whole Divisional Front that night, relieving the 165th and 166th Brigades.

At 9-P.M. the relief commenced and was reported complete by 5-A.M. on the 3rd instant. A Map is attached marked appendix I shewing dispositions of the Brigade on taking over the line. The 10th Royal Irish Rifles were in the front line on the right and 15th Royal Irish Rifles on the left; the 9th R. Irish Rifles were in support in the right and the 8th R. Irish Rifles on the left.

About mid-day on the 3rd instant, a report was received from O.C. Right Sub-sector stating that the situation on our right was unsatisfactory, as the Brigade on our right was not holding the line up to its left boundary - the STEENBEEK - and consequently there was no touch between the Brigades. The Division was informed and on that night the Brigade on our right sent up a platoon to fill up the gap. From that date the position was more satisfactory, though the presence of the enemy in BECK HOUSE caused some slight annoyance.

On our left flank touch was kept with the Division on our left by means of patrols, their nearest post being in CANVAS Trench.

On the evening of the 3rd instant two Battalions of the 108th Brigade and two Battalions of the 109th Brigade moved up into the Old British Trenches and came under the orders of the G.O.C., 107th Brigade.

August 4th to August 8th.

During this period the enemy's infantry shewed no signs of activity on the Brigade front until the night of the 7/8th when the enemy apparently attempted to raid our left Battalion . At about 10-30 P.M. a party of 30 to 40 men were seen to be approaching our trenches on the extreme left. The S.O.S. was sent up and the party driven off. The artillery barrage came down quickly and was very effective.

Our Infantry was continuously active patrolling throughout the period and by the 7th instant had definitely located the enemy's line as shewn on the attached map marked Appendix II.

In addition CAPRICORN support was occupied and posts pushed out around the Eastern edge of POMMERN REDOUBT.

The enemy's artillery was continuously active throughout the period, especially on the trenches in the neighbourhood of the BLUE LINE. The BLACK LINE was subjected to comparatively light shelling. Owing to this fact, one Company from each of the Support Battalions was withdrawn on the 6th instant from the BLUE LINE and placed in our original trenches in the neighbourhood of WIELTJE Dug-outs. Previously to this the two Battalions of the 108th and the 109th Brigades had been withdrawn from the old British Trenches and had rejoined their Brigades.

5/6th. On the night of the 5th/6th August the 10th R.I.R. were relieved in the right subsector by the 9th R.I.Rifles and the 15th R.I.R. were relieved in the Left subsector by the 8th R.I.R.

7/8th On the night of the 7/8th August the Brigade was relieved by two Battalionsof the 108th Brigade and two Battalions of the 109th Brigade, the 108th Bde H.Qrs taking over command of the sector. The Brigade withdrew into BRANDHOEK area.

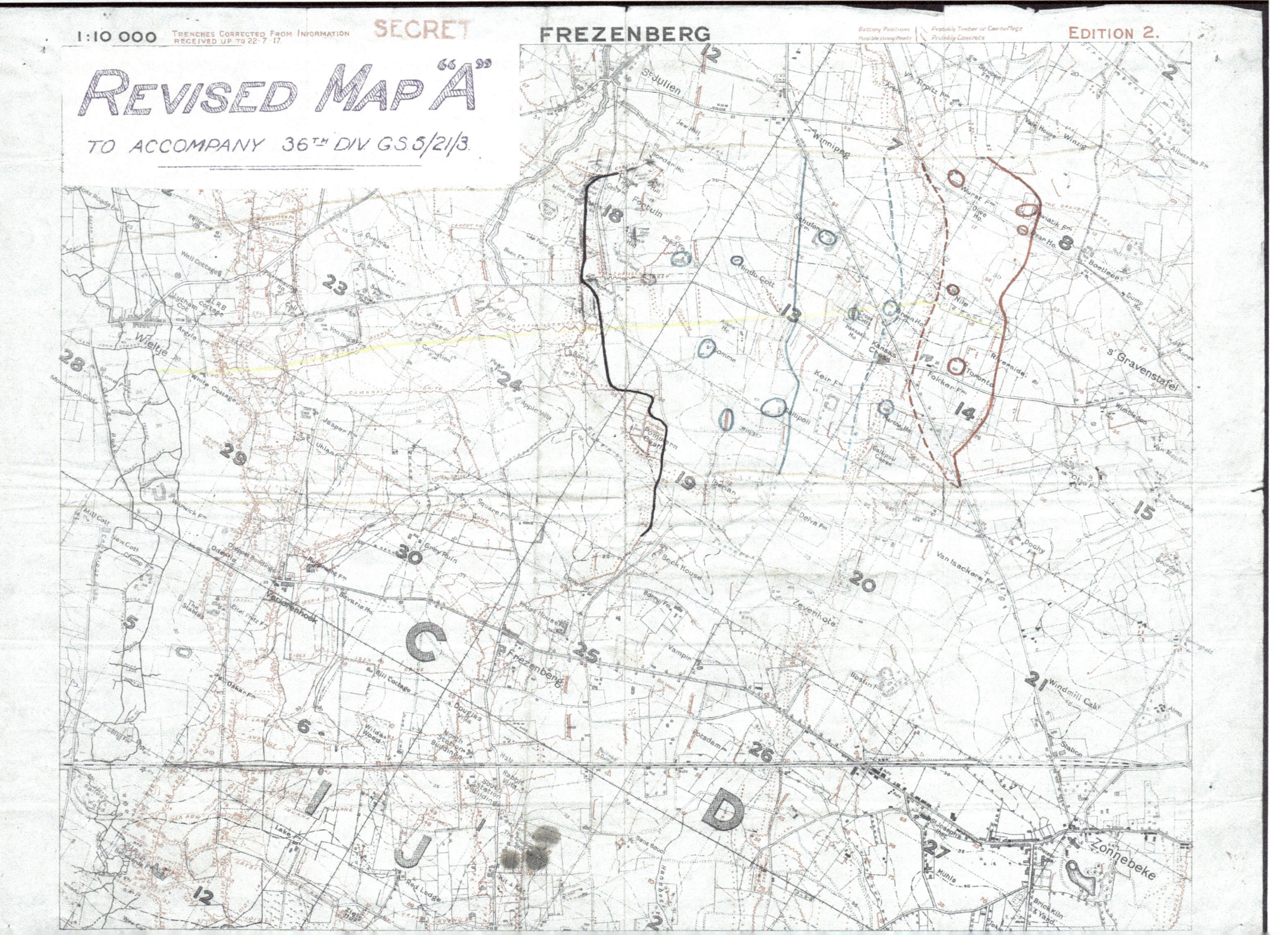
1:10 000
TRENCHES CORRECTED FROM INFORMATION RECEIVED UP TO 22·7·17.
SECRET
FREZENBERG
EDITION 2.
REVISED MAP "A"
TO ACCOMPANY 36TH DIV GS.5/21/3.
St Julien
Winnipeg
Wieltje
s'Gravenstafel
Frezenberg
Zonnebeke
Vampir
Zevenkote
Van Isackere Fm
Windmill Cabt
Station
Potsdam
Beck House
Delva Fm
Gallipoli
Keir Fm
Schuler
Hindu Cott
Somme
Toronto
Tokker Fm
Nile
Square Fm
Grey Ruin
Uhlan
Jasper Fm
White Cottage
Well Cottage
Bellevue
Warwick Fm
Mill Cott
Oskar Fm
Bill Cottage
Douglas Villa
Wilde Wood
Red Lodge
Lake Fm
Sans Souci
Muhle
Brick Kiln & Yard
Bavaria Ho.
Borry Fm
Bostin Fm
Apple Villa
Bank Fm
Von Hugel
Fortuin
Jew Hill
Alma
Dochy Fm
Wimbledon
Van Meulen
Korek
Boetleer
Winzig
Albatross Fm
2
7
8
12
13
14
15
18
19
20
21
23
24
25
26
27
28
29
30
5
6
C
D
I
J

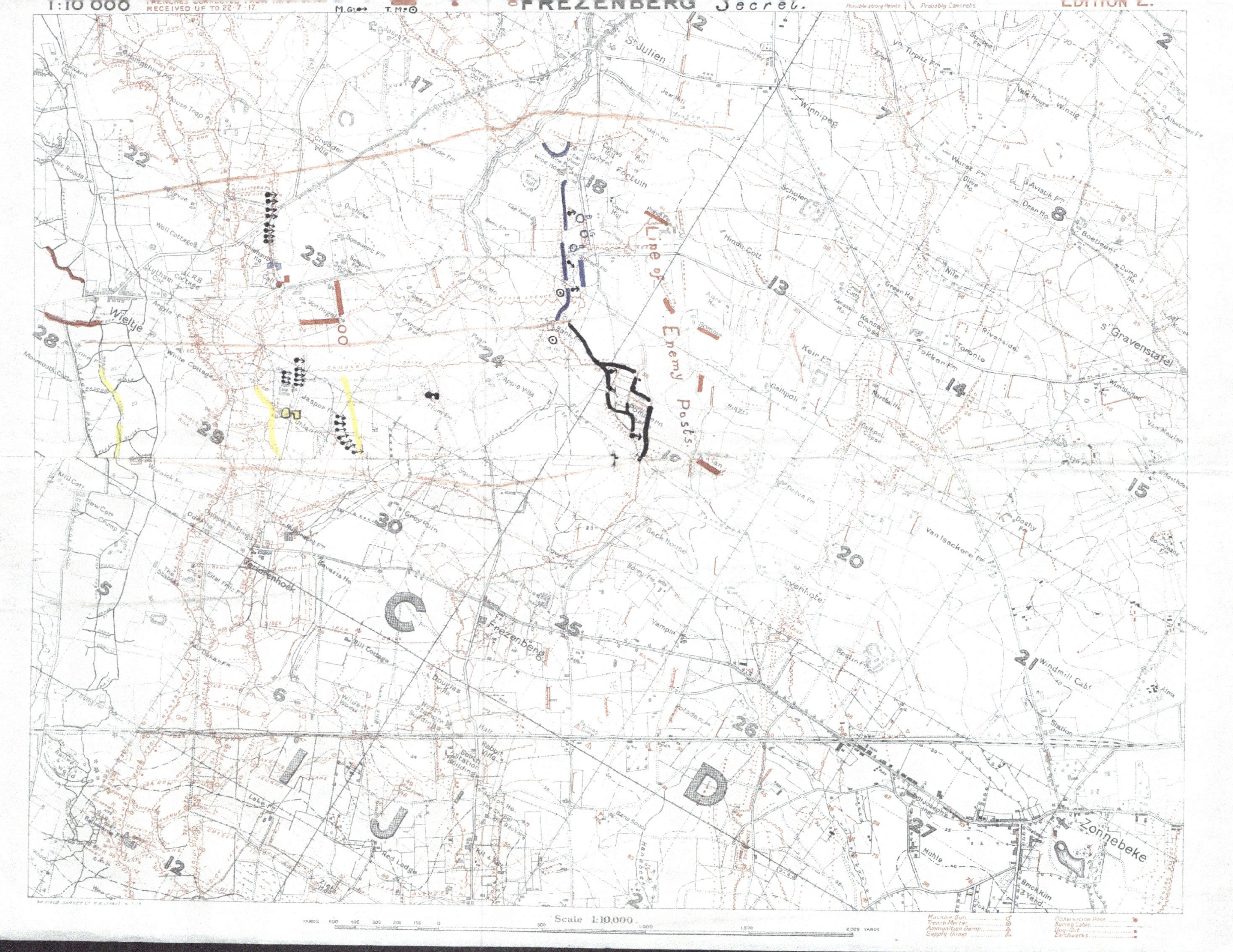
1:10 000
RECEIVED UP TO 22-7-17.
FREZENBERG Secret.
EDITION 2.
Line of Enemy Posts.
St Julien
Winnipeg
Fortuin
s' Gravenstafel
Wieltje
Apple Villa
Frezenberg
Zonnebeke
Windmill Cabt
Van Isackere Fm
Zevenkote
Vampir
Beck House
Gallipoli
Kansas Cross
Fokker Fm
Toronto
Riverside
Hindu Cott
Schuler Fm
Wurst Fm
Aviatik Fm
Dean Ho
Boetleer
Grey Ruin
Bill Cottage
Wilde Wood
Red Lodge
Lake Fm
Muhle
Station
Brick Kiln & Yard
Well Cottage
White Cottage
Jasper Fm
Mill Cott
Scale 1:10,000

appendix XIX

11

Instructions regarding War Diaries and Intelligence Summaries are contained in F. S. Regs., Part II. and the Staff Manual respectively. Title Pages will be prepared in manuscript.

WAR DIARY
or
INTELLIGENCE SUMMARY
(Erase heading not required.)

Army Form C. 2118.

October 1917. HQ 107th Inf. Bde.

Vol 24

Place	Date	Hour	Summary of Events and Information	Remarks and references to Appendices
METZ	1st		Order 177 issued for Bn. Reliefs see	App. I.
	1st/3rd		In the line; our patrols continually active, and a programme of night firing by artillery, M.G's, Stokes Mortars and Lewis guns carried out every night.	
	3rd		Inter battalion relief took place quietly.	
	5th		at 10.30 p.m. gas was successfully projected into HAVRINCOURT from front of Bde on our left (108th) Order 178 issued see	App. II.
	8th		Minor operation referred to in O/178 postponed owing to enemy having been found earlier in their post than usual.	
		8.45 p.m.	An enemy raiding party of 1 officer and 8 O.R. entered B Sap in the right subsector and tried to cut off a post of the 15 R. Ir. Rif.; they were attacked by a party of 3 men with the bayonet and driven out leaving a slightly wounded prisoner in our hands, and the officer dead just outside the trench. Our only casualty was one man slightly wounded.	
	9th		The minor operation of the 10th R. Ir. Rif. referred to in O/178 was carried out most successfully at 4 p.m.; the party went out by day and cut the enemy wire by hand. Shortly after 6 p.m. an enemy party of 11 approached the post; the NCO was taken prisoner, slightly wounded, and all the others accounted for by rifle fire at close range. We had no casualties.	
			Reliefs in accordance with O/179 were duly carried out see	App. III.
	3rd/10th		We continued our night firing programmes of harassing fire as before; the enemy artillery shewed normal activity, occasionally shelling battery positions heavily. The weather became broken, cold and wet, greatly interfering with the work on the line, which had hitherto been proceeding quickly and well.	

2449 Wt. W14957/M90 750,000 1/16 J.B.C. & A. Forms/C.2118/12.

Army Form C. 2118.

Instructions regarding War Diaries and Intelligence Summaries are contained in F. S. Regs., Part II. and the Staff Manual respectively. Title Pages will be prepared in manuscript.

WAR DIARY
or
INTELLIGENCE SUMMARY
(Erase heading not required.)

Place	Date	Hour	Summary of Events and Information	Remarks and references to Appendices
METZ	10th	25th	A normal period in the line; we carried out harassing fire by night with M.G's Lewis and Stokes Guns in conjunction with the Field Artillery. Patrols were active nightly; on the early morning of the 14th an attempt on an enemy post by the	
	14		1st R. Ir. Fus. was unsuccessful, as the enemy opened fire before our party	
	25		could explode their ammonal tube. On the evening of the 25th inst. a patrol of the same Regt. occupied an enemy outpost at dusk and brought back a wounded prisoner of the 84th. I.R.. On the night 25/26th the 8/9 R. Ir. Rif. blew two gaps in the enemy wire with ammonal tubes.	
			Inter Battalion Reliefs were carried out on the 15th. 21st. and 27th in accordance with Orders 180 181 and 182	see App. IV, V, VI.
			The work of revetment in the line was carried on rapidly despite most unfavourable weather; by the 25th inst. baby elephant shelters had been provided for all the front line garrison. Work on new cookhouses in METZ and EQUANCOURT was carried out.	
	25/6	11 p.m.	An officer's patrol of 9 O.R. when examining enemy wire opposite E Sap met an enemy party about 30 strong. Numerous casualties were inflicted on enemy by rifle fire and bombs at close range; but three of our men were wounded and did not return with the rest of the patrol.	
			During the last few days of the month enemy artillery of light calibres was rather more active against our front system.	
	31		O/183 issued see	App VII
			Statement shewing casualties during October attached.	App. VIII
			" " reinforcements " " "	App. IX

2449 Wt. W14957/M90 750,000 1/16 J.B.C. & A. Forms/C.2118/12.

19

Army Form C. 2118.

WAR DIARY
or
~~INTELLIGENCE SUMMARY~~

(Erase heading not required.)

107th Infy Brigade

Vol 25

Instructions regarding War Diaries and Intelligence Summaries are contained in F. S. Regs., Part II. and the Staff Manual respectively. Title Pages will be prepared in manuscript.

1917 Headquarters 107th Inf. Bde.

Place	Date	Hour	Summary of Events and Information	Remarks and references to Appendices
	November			
METZ.	1st.		Normal activity on both sides.	
	2nd		Reliefs took place in accordance with 7/183 issued 31/10/17	
		10.15 p.m.	An enemy patrol of 7 attempted to get into B Sap but was driven off by the Garrison (1st R. Ir. Fus.) leaving a wounded prisoner in our hands, who died in the C.C.S. Hostile artillery rather active.	
	3rd.		Our trenches heavily shelled about 8.45 p.m. in retaliation for a raid by 109th Bde on our left. Our patrols active	
	4th/7th		Our patrols continued their activity and with view to future operations blew numerous gaps in enemy outpost wire with ammonal tubes, and cut gaps by hand on left subsector. Usual night firing programmes, M G's and Stokes Coöperating with artillery, carried out.	
	5th		7/184 issued – the night of relief being changed on account of hostile activity on previous relief nights – see	App I.
	7th		Reliefs carried out in accordance with 7/184. Enemy prisoner taken just before relief by 8/9 R. Ir. Rif. having lost his way and wandered into our wire. Enemy artillery very active on left Coy. of right Subsector between 10 p.m. and midnight; over 700 shells were fired and considerable damage inflicted to trenches – Our casualties 1 officer and 2 O.R. wounded.	
	8th/12th		Enemy artillery quieter. Our night firing continued as usual; and further gaps were cut in enemy wire by our patrols.	
	11th		7/185 issued for Bn reliefs, see	App II

2449 Wt. W14957/M90 750,000 1/16 J.B.C. & A. Forms/C.2118/12.

Army Form C. 2118.

WAR DIARY
or
~~INTELLIGENCE SUMMARY~~
(Erase heading not required.)

Instructions regarding War Diaries and Intelligence Summaries are contained in F. S. Regs., Part II. and the Staff Manual respectively. Title Pages will be prepared in manuscript.

1917 Headquarters 107th Inf Bde.

Place	Date (November)	Hour	Summary of Events and Information	Remarks and references to Appendices
METZ.	11th		G.S 3/1 – First Divisional Instructions for the Offensive – received.	
	12th		B.G.C. attended conference at Divl. HQ at 10 a.m.. A conference of Comdg Officers of units was held at Bde HQ at 2 30 p.m.	
		7 30	MO 30 – 107th Bde. Instructions for the Offensive – issued; this and subsequent instructions are attached complete. See	App III
			After Order to O/185 issued. See	App IV
	13th		Reliefs in accordance with O/185, and readjustment of front took place. During the following days heavy fog favoured the preparations for the offensive operations. All work of revetment was abandoned, and concentrated solely on preparation of the trenches back to the reserve lines for assembly purposes. Enemy artillery was much quieter owing to impossibility of observation. We continued night harassing fire as usual.	
	15th		Orders for relief of left subsector, less outposts, issued, O/186 See	App V
	17th		Orders for moves on 18/19th inst issued, O/187 See	App VI
			Reliefs in accordance with O/186 took place, and command of the left subsector passed to B. G. C. 185 Inf Bde at 10.10 p.m. During the night the enemy raided E Sap under cover of a box barrage and took 6 prisoners of the 1st R. Ir. Fus.	
	18th		Movements took place in accordance with O/187	
	19th		Relief of the Bde. in the line completed and command of the right subsector passed to B G C 154 Inf Bde. at 2 p.m. Concentration of the Bde in the YTRES-LECHELLE area completed	
		12 noon	O/188 and march table issued See	App. VII

Army Form C. 2118.

WAR DIARY
or
INTELLIGENCE SUMMARY
(Erase heading not required.)

Instructions regarding War Diaries and Intelligence Summaries are contained in F. S. Regs., Part II. and the Staff Manual respectively. Title Pages will be prepared in manuscript.

Headquarters 107th Inf. Bde.

Place	Date	Hour	Summary of Events and Information	Remarks and references to Appendices
	November			
LECHELLE	19th	3.15 pm	The Divisional Commander addressed the officers of the Bde. at YTRES and explained the course of future operations.	
	20th		The Bde. moved forward to the concentration area near the SLAG HEAP S of HERMIES in accordance with O/188. Moves were completed at 8.30 a.m., but in spite of the success of the attack no further order was received for the Bde. to go forward until 1.30 p.m. when it was ordered to go to SQUARE COPSE SW of HAVRINCOURT where assembly was complete at 3.15 p.m. The men lay there in the open under very heavy rain till 8 p.m. when orders were received to move to HAVRINCOURT. Owing to the difficulty of crossing the canal, and the congested state of the roads, which were very heavy going on a dark night, the concentration of the Bns. in the old enemy trenches and dugouts near HAVRINCOURT was not complete till 3 a.m.	
HAVRINCOURT	21st.			
		8 am	Order no 189 issued see	App. IX
			The moves to assembly positions in accordance with O/189 began at 3.30 p.m. and	
W of GRAINCOURT		4.30 pm	Bde. HQ was established in an old German dugout. The attack as detailed in O/189 did not take place owing to BOURLON village not having been captured.	
		8 pm	The Bde. was assembled in the HINDENBURG SUPPORT line ready to move forward. A warning order was issued to the 10 and 15 R. Ir. Rif. to be prepared to attack following morning. 8/9 R. Ir. Rif. ordered up to man KANGAROO ALLEY, S of BAPAUME-CAMBRAI road owing to reports of enemy counterattack E of canal.	
		10 pm	Orders for attack received by telephone from Divn. and communicated to Comdg. Officers personally. Written orders did not come till 4.30 a.m.	
	22	8.45 am	O/190 issued see	App. X

2449 Wt. W14957/M90 750,000 1/16 J.B.C. & A. Forms/C.2118/12.

Army Form C. 2118.

Instructions regarding War Diaries and Intelligence Summaries are contained in F. S. Regs., Part II. and the Staff Manual respectively. Title Pages will be prepared in manuscript.

WAR DIARY
or
INTELLIGENCE SUMMARY

(Erase heading not required.)

Headquarters 107th Inf. Bde.

Place	Date	Hour	Summary of Events and Information	Remarks and references to Appendices
	November			
W of GRAINCOURT	22nd		Attack in accordance with O/190 was carried out by the 15th and 10th R. Ir. Rif.; 500 yards of the HINDENBURG support line was bombed and cleared of the enemy, but progress could not be made beyond this point, as the enemy was found in force in the trench and the attacking forces came under heavy M G fire, suffering numerous casualties, especially in officers. The trench gained was held and consolidated in spite of counter attacks.	
		11 p.m.	Telephone orders received from Divn for further attack on HINDENBURG SUPPORT line	
	23rd	4 a.m.	Conference of Comdg. Officers at Bde. HQ with Tank Bn officers.	
		8.30 a.m.	O/191 issued for attack at 10.30 a.m. see	App. XI
		10.30 a.m.	Attack supported by tanks began. On the right one tank was ditched, and the other took a wrong direction; in consequence the 15th R. Ir. Rif. were held up by M. G. fire in exactly the same way as on the previous day. On the left the 8th. R. Ir. Rif. took ROUND TRENCH and LOCK No. 5, but in face of determined enemy opposition and heavy M. G. fire little impression could be made on the HINDENBURG SUPPORT line, and the Bns coming up for the second phase of the attack suffered heavy casualties.	
		4 p.m.	We established outpost positions in ROUND TRENCH and LOCK No. 5; otherwise the Bns withdrew to the positions held previous to the attack. The evening and night passed quietly. The 10th R. Ir. Rif extended to the right to support the 186th Bde.	
	24th	1 a.m.	Orders received by 'phone from Divn. for further attack. Conference of Comdg. Officers at Bde. HQ	
		10 a.m.	Enemy about 50 strong attempted to raid 15th R. Ir. Rif. in trench captured on 22nd inst, but were repulsed leaving 2 dead and an M. G. in our hands	
		11.10 a.m.	Order 192 issued, see	App. XII

2449 Wt. W14957/M90 750,000 1/16 J.B.C. & A. Forms/C.2118/12.

Instructions regarding War Diaries and Intelligence Summaries are contained in F. S. Regs., Part II. and the Staff Manual respectively. Title Pages will be prepared in manuscript.

WAR DIARY
or
INTELLIGENCE SUMMARY

Army Form C. 2118.

(Erase heading not required.)

1917 Headquarters 107th Infantry Brigade.

Place	Date November	Hour	Summary of Events and Information	Remarks and references to Appendices
W of GRAINCOURT	24th.	3.10 pm.	Artillery bombardment opened but as guns had not been registered shooting especially on nearest portion of objective was inaccurate, several shells falling among our assembled troops and causing casualties. The enemy manned his trench in force, and our attack could not develop. The 1st R. Ir. Fus. remained in the HINDENBURG SUPPORT line, relieving the 15th R. Ir. Rif who withdrew to KANGAROO ALLEY, S of BAPAUME CAMBRAI road. The Coy. of the 10th R. Ir. Rif who had extended to the right were withdrawn to support the 1st R. Ir. Fus.	
	25th.		The night passed quietly. Orders were received from Division to consolidate the line held; and the Bde. Works Party, under Lieut. J.H. HAIGH M.C. and the Bn Works Officers, which had done consistently good work in carrying grenades, S.A.A etc. to the Bns. in the line, during the evening wired 350x E of the CANAL.	
	26th.		Orders received to hand over to the 109th Bde the portion of the line between the CANAL and the SAINS LEZ MARQUION-HAVRINCOURT road. This adjustment was completed by 3.30 p.m. Arrangements made for relief of the Bde. by the 108th. Bde were cancelled owing to the relief of the Divn. by the 2nd Divn. Order no 193 issued see	App. XIII
HERMIES	27th.	3 a.m.	Relief by the 99th Bde. complete; the move back to HERMIES was accomplished in the teeth of a severe blizzard, and it was after 6 a.m. before Bns were complete in the accomodation provided, consisting of bivouacs and old trenches.	
		4 am	Orders for further move received from Division.	
		8.30 am	Order 194 issued see	App XIV
BARASTRE		2.30 pm	Moves took place in accordance with O/194 and the Bde. was concentrated in camps in the BARASTRE area.	
	28th.		Warning orders for move by train to FOSSEUX area received.	
		10 pm	O/195 issued see	App. XV.
			Advance transport sent on to new area.	

2449 Wt. W14957/M90 750,000 1/16 J.B.C. & A. Forms/C.2118/12.

Army Form C. 2118.

WAR DIARY
or
INTELLIGENCE SUMMARY

(*Erase heading not required.*)

Instructions regarding War Diaries and Intelligence Summaries are contained in F. S. Regs., Part II. and the Staff Manual respectively. Title Pages will be prepared in manuscript.

1917 Headquarters 107th Infantry Brigade

Place	Date	Hour	Summary of Events and Information	Remarks and references to Appendices
	November			
BERNEVILLE	29th		Bde. entrained at YTRES Station, and detrained at BEAUMETZ-RIVIÈRE, from where they marched to BERNEVILLE. The whole Bde. Group was billetted in this village	
	30th		Divl warning order no. 155 received for move to MONT ST ELOI area for training.	
		12.30 a.m.	Telephone message received from Divn. ordering Brigade to be ready to move on the shortest notice. Bns. found some difficulty in getting ready owing to the fact that the transport which had been moving by road had not yet arrived.	
		2.20 p.m.	Instructions received by wire from Division to move to COURCELLES-LE-COMTE via WAILLY and MOYENNEVILLE.	
		2.30 p.m.	Head of column pass the starting point just outside BERNEVILLE. An order was sent to the transport to turn on the road and follow column.	
COURCELLES-LE-COMTE		12 midnight	Concentration of Brigade in Camps in COURCELLES complete	

Instructions regarding War Diaries and Intelligence Summaries are contained in F. S. Regs., Part II. and the Staff Manual respectively. Title Pages will be prepared in manuscript.

WAR DIARY
or
~~INTELLIGENCE SUMMARY~~
(Erase heading not required.)

107th Infantry Bde. HQ.

Army Form

Vol 26

Place	1917 December Date	Hour	Summary of Events and Information	Remarks and references to Appendices
COURCELLES-LE-COMTE	1		36th Div. transferred to V Corps. Order no. 196 issued for move to BEAULENCOURT see. Owing to considerable congestion on roads the Bde was much delayed en route and was not completely installed in new billets till 6.30 p.m.	App. I.
BEAULENCOURT	2.		Order no. 197 issued for move to LECHELLE area see. Very scanty accomodation was provided for the Bde in the new area. 50 to 60 men had to be billetted in one Nissen hut. Bde. HQ established just N of LITTLE WOOD at YTRES.	App. II.
YTRES.	3.	10am	Telephone order received from Divn to stand to and be ready to move on half an hours notice. Stood to all day but unpacked limbers 5 p.m. as no further orders being received.	
	4.	9 30am	Order received from Division to move forward. Order 198 issued for move see. Units were clear of LECHELLE area 1 p.m. and marched by track just N of METZ to the valley at NE corner of HAVRINCOURT WOOD, where a halt was made for dinners. At dusk the Bns. moved up to positions in neighbourhood of BEAUCAMP occupying an old trench system and dugouts; the 8/9 R. Ir. Rif. occupied LINCOLN AVENUE on HIGHLAND RIDGE while the 15 R. Ir. Rif. were accomodated in tents on NE edge of HAVRINCOURT WOOD.	App III
METZ-EN-COUTURE.		2 pm	Bde HQ opened at cross roads METZ. The Bde was detailed as Corps Reserve.	
	5	1 am	2 Bns. worked at digging reserve line on HIGHLAND RIDGE under CRE 61 Divn. Very cold frosty weather set in. This work was continued on following night.	
	6	11 am	O/198/1 issued for withdrawal of 8/9 R. Ir. Rif. to METZ see	App IV
		5 pm	8 guns of the 107 M.G. Coy. being already in the line under orders of DMGO the remaining 8 guns were ordered forward to positions in support on N slope of HIGHLAND RIDGE.	

2449 Wt. W14957/M90 750,000 1/16 J.B.C. & A. Forms/C.2118/12.

Army Form C. 2118.

Instructions regarding War Diaries and Intelligence Summaries are contained in F. S. Regs., Part II. and the Staff Manual respectively. Title Pages will be prepared in manuscript.

WAR DIARY
or
~~INTELLIGENCE SUMMARY~~
(Erase heading not required.)

HQ 107 Inf. Bde.

Place	Date 1917 December	Hour	Summary of Events and Information	Remarks and references to Appendices
METZ-EN-COUTURE	7		Thaw following on the previous frost made ground very heavy.	
		10.30pm	O/199 issued for relief of 109 Bde in right subsector of Divl front by 107 Bde. see	app V
	8		After order no. 199 issued see	app VI
	9		Relief took place in accordance with O/199, but owing to the extreme darkness of the night and the very heavy going in the forward area was not complete until 6 a.m.	
S. of MARCOING (in old HINDENBURG front line)		10 am	Command of the right subsector of Divl front passed to B G C 107 Inf. Bde. 107 T.M. Batty. relieved 109 T.M. Batty. in accordance with after order no. 199. The passing of command of the M.G. Coys. was cancelled and Capt P. J. MULHOLLAND (109 M.G. Coy.) remained in command of the right sector M.G's, while Capt J. S. CRESSALL (107 M.G. Coy.) took over command of the left group under B.G.C. 108 Bde.	
		1.45pm	O/200 issued see	app VII
		11.45pm	The bombing attack by the 10 R. Ir. Rif. was successful in the HINDENBURG front line, (EMDEN TRENCH) but in the other two trenches strong opposition was met with and the bombing parties had to retire, the officer in each case having become a casualty.	
	10/11		The period passed quietly. A great deal of work was done in clearing the trenches, which were in a very bad state owing to the severity of the weather. The three blocks were entirely rebuilt and the trenches in front filled with wire. There was considerable artillery activity on both sides.	
	12		15 R. Ir. Rif. the 10 R. Ir. Rif. in the right subsector in accordance with O/201 see	app VIII
	13		Relief of 11/13 R. Ir. Rif. and 2 R. Ir. Rif. by the 1 R. Ir. Fus. and 10 R. Ir. Rif. carried out, and the two first named Bns. came under command of B G C 107 Inf. Bde. in accordance with O/202 see	app IX
	14		Moves were not completed owing to tired condition of men until 1.45 a.m.	

2449 Wt. W14957/M90 750,000 1/16 J.B.C. & A. Forms/C.2118/12.

Army Form C. 2118.

WAR DIARY
or
INTELLIGENCE SUMMARY

(Erase heading not required.)

Instructions regarding War Diaries and Intelligence Summaries are contained in F. S. Regs., Part II. and the Staff Manual respectively. Title Pages will be prepared in manuscript.

HQ 107 Inf. Bde.

Place	Date (1917 December)	Hour	Summary of Events and Information	Remarks and references to Appendices
S of MARCOING	14	7 am	Prisoner captured by 15 R. Ir. Rif. in front of their trench.	
			Relief of the 107 Bde. by the 189 Bde. (less 1 Bn.) carried out in accordance with O/203 and was complete at 12.10 p.m. On relief the Bde. concentrated in METZ	see App. X
METZ EN COUTURE	15		from where it marched to the ETRICOURT area in accordance with the march table issued with O/203.	
MANANCOURT		3 p.m.	Bde. HQ established in Nissen Huts just on N outskirts of MANANCOURT. The Bns. were accommodated under canvas. The weather was very severe and the men in an exhausted condition owing to exposure and lack of sleep.	
	16	3.30 pm	Orders for further move issued see O/204	App. XI
			Heavy snow fell all night, followed by severe frost	
	17		Moves took place in accordance with O/204. Locations of units were altered by Divn, and instructions accordingly issued to Bns. see	App. XII
			Owing to the roads being blocked by snowdrifts great difficulty was experienced by the transport; and the motor lorries supplied for the move nearly all broke down.	
IVERGNY		6 p.m.	Bde. HQ opened at IVERGNY. Bns. did not arrive in billets till between 9 p.m. and midnight owing to condition of roads.	
	18		11/13th R. Ir. Rif. rejoined 108 Bde.. 10 R. Ir. Rif. and 1 R. Ir. Fus. came into 107 Bde area at GRAND RULLECOURT and IVERGNY respectively. 2 R. Ir. Rif. had gone straight into 108 Bde. area at WARLINCOURT on arrival.	
		5 pm	Orders received from Divn to put all available men on to work of clearing roads; a stretch of road was allotted to each unit.	
		11 p.m.	Bde. Transport which had come by road began to arrive at IVERGNY having been on the march since 8 a.m.	

Army Form C. 2118.

Instructions regarding War Diaries and Intelligence Summaries are contained in F. S. Regs., Part II. and the Staff Manual respectively. Title Pages will be prepared in manuscript.

WAR DIARY
or
~~INTELLIGENCE SUMMARY~~

(Erase heading not required.)

HQ. 107 Inf. Bde.

Place	Date 1917 December	Hour	Summary of Events and Information	Remarks and references to Appendices
IVERGNY.	19		Work continued on roads.	
	20		1 R. Ir. Fus. transferred to billets in SUS ST LEGER. Work on roads continued	
			For an account of the operations from Nov 20th – Nov 27th 1917 see	App. XIII
"	21–24		Frost continued. All units employed on keeping the roads clear, training Lewis Gunners, shooting on the Rifle Range.	
"	25	2 pm	Message received by phone saying Brigade would move to CORBIE area on 27th and part of transport on 26th.	
		3.30 pm	Warning order sent out to units see	App. XIV
			Orders for move of Bde Transport to PUCHEVILLERS ~~issued~~ and thence to CORBIE issued Order No 205	App. XV
"	26		Orders for move of the Brigade by Train to CORBIE area issued. Order No 206	App. XVI
"	27.		Brigade moved to CORBIE by Train and transport by road. Snow and frost considerably delayed the transport and the Brigade Group was not complete in Billets until 4 a.m. for dispositions see	App. XVII
CORBIE	28–31st		Snow and frost continued. Bns all training.	
			A table showing casualties for the month is attached as ~~[illegible]~~	App. XVIII
			A Table showing ~~casualties~~ reinforcements for the month is attached a	App. XIX

T. O. M. Buchan Capt
Brigade Major
107 Inf Bde

2449 Wt. W14957/M90 750,000 1/16 J.B.C. & A. Forms/C.2118/12.

Army Form C. 21[illegible]

Instructions regarding War Diaries and Intelligence Summaries are contained in F. S. Regs., Part II. and the Staff Manual respectively. Title Pages will be prepared in manuscript.

WAR DIARY
or
~~INTELLIGENCE SUMMARY~~

(Erase heading not required.)

H.Q's 107th Inf Brigade — January 1918

Place	Date	Hour	Summary of Events and Information	Remarks and references to Appendices
CORBIE	1am 1/5th		Brigade remained in the CORBIE area. All Bns training. Time mainly devoted to smartening up the men in carriage and dress. Large Lewis Gun classes formed in each Bn to make up the Reserve of Lewis Gunners.	
			Brigade Order No 207, re move of Brigade to PROYART area on 7th inst.	App. I
"	7th		Brigade moved by march route to PROYART area. New dispositions as shewn in March Table to Appendix I.	
ROSIERES	8th		Brigade commander went up to the line to visit 24th Inf Regiment and to reconnoitre the area to be taken over. Order No 208 issued.	App. II
"	9th		Brigade moved to NESLE area dispositions as shewn in order No 208.	
VOYENNES	10th		Brigade commander and reconnoitring parties visited the line. Order No 209 issued for move to French Southern area. Div orders for the Relief of the French issued, and also preliminary Instructions for the Relief issued by the Brigade	App III
ESTOUILLY	11th		Brigade moved to ESTOUILLY area. Order No 210 issued for the Relief of the 24th French Regiment. Preliminary Bde Defence Scheme issued	see App IV & App V
"	12th		Bns and M.G. Coy moved in to relieve the French. All reliefs complete by 12 midnight. Brigade Major and Bde Sig Officer ~~were~~ came to live with the French for the night.	

T.O[illegible] B.

2449 Wt. W14957/M90 750,000 1/16 J.B.C. & A. Forms/C.2118/12.

Instructions regarding War Diaries and Intelligence Summaries are contained in F. S. Regs., Part II. and the Staff Manual respectively. Title Pages will be prepared in manuscript.

Army Form C. 2118.

WAR DIARY
or
~~INTELLIGENCE SUMMARY~~
(Erase heading not required.)

H.Q's 107th Inf Bde — January 1917.

Place	Date	Hour	Summary of Events and Information	Remarks and references to Appendices
L'EPINE de DALLON. A.3.d. 70.20	Jan 13th		at 10 a.m Bde Commander 107th Inf Bde assumed command of the sector. The following points on the relief are worth noting. (1) M.G's. The French had 36 M.G's to our 16. The extra positions were taken over by Lewis Guns, the L.G's taking the most advanced positions (2) advanced parties. advanced parties of Intelligence officer, Signal officer and 2 signallers per Bn, 1 officer per Coy, 1 N.C.O per Bn, and 1 man per M.G. position were sent up the day before. (3) Guides The French provided guides who were accompanied by the English advanced parties. This worked very well. (4) Rear parties. The French left behind the Chef de Batallion, 1 officer per Coy and 1 man per M.G. position for 24 hours. (5) Bombs & Rockets French Bombs, Rockets and Verey Lights were taken over and used. The mobile Reserves were drawn on that night for S.A.A and Mills Bombs.	

T.O.M. B.

2449 Wt. W14957/M90 750,000 1/16 J.B.C. & A. Forms/C.2118/12.

Army Form C. 2118.

WAR DIARY
or
~~INTELLIGENCE SUMMARY~~
(Erase heading not required.)

Instructions regarding War Diaries and Intelligence Summaries are contained in F. S. Regs., Part II. and the Staff Manual respectively. Title Pages will be prepared in manuscript.

H.Q's 107th Bde — January 1917.

Place	Date	Hour	Summary of Events and Information	Remarks and references to Appendices
L'EPINE de DALLON.	Jan 14th to 21st		Period passed quietly. Division took over command of the line on Jan 14th and established their H.Q's in OLLEZY. The French artillery covered the Brigade front until the night of the 16/17th. On the 18/19th January the 15th R.I.R relieved the 8/9th R.I.R in the Right Subsector and the 10th R.I.R relieved the 1st R.I.F in the Left vide	App VI.
"	22nd		An enemy patrol rushed the Liaison post on our extreme right which was shared with 109th Bde, capturing one man of the 15th R.I.R, who was apparently severely wounded.	
"	23rd		The enemy rushed a post of 109th Bde on our right. A call for assistance was received and the artillery opened fire. All was quiet by 9.30 pm. A patrol of 1 officer, 1 Sgt and 5 O.R's of 10th R.I.R was rushed in "No Mans Land" and the officer and Sgt apparently captured. Bde Order No 211 issued for reliefs to take place on the night of the 24/25th	App VII
"	27th	11.30 pm	Two enemy prisoners of war who had escaped from French Camps at ROYE recaptured in outpost line by	1st R. Ir. Fus.
"	24th		Situation very quiet. Bde Defence Scheme issued on the 27th vide	App VIII
"	28th		Weather frosty with mist practically all day, preventing observation & restricting all activity	
"	29th		Bde Order No. 212 issued for Inter Bn. relief on night of 30th vide	App IX
"	30/31		Situation very quiet; weather still misty.	

R.O.W.

2449 Wt. W14957/M90 750,000 1/16 J.B.C. & A. Forms/C.2118/12.

Army Form C. 2118.

WAR DIARY
or
~~INTELLIGENCE SUMMARY~~
(Erase heading not required.)

Instructions regarding War Diaries and Intelligence Summaries are contained in F. S. Regs., Part II. and the Staff Manual respectively. Title Pages will be prepared in manuscript.

Headquarters 107th Inf. Bde.

Place	Date 1918 February	Hour	Summary of Events and Information	Remarks and references to Appendices
ÉPINE de DALLON	1st	10 a.m.	Corps Commander (Lt. Gen. Sir Ivor Maxse K.C.B., C.V.O., D.S.O.) visited the Bde. Sector, accompanied by the Div! Commander, and conferred with B. G. C. and Comdg. Officers.	
	1st to 3rd		A very quiet period in line; our patrols active.	
	3rd	10.45 pm	Order 213 issued for Bn. reliefs see	app. I.
	4th		Relief of 15 R. Ir. Rif. by 8/9 R. Ir. Rif. cancelled.	
			Order 214 issued for Relief of 8/9 R. Ir. Rif. by 1 R. Ir. Rif. see	App. II
	5th		1st R. Ir. Fus. relieved 10 R. Ir. Rif. in left subsector according to O/213.	
	6th		1st R. Ir. Rif. relieved 8/9 R. Ir. Rif. in Bde. Support and were incorporated in 107 Inf. Bde. On relief the 8/9 R. Ir. Rif. were disbanded according to the administrative instructions attached to O/214.	
		7 p.m.	Order 215 issued for successive reliefs see	app. III
	7th		10th R. Ir. Rif. relieved 1st R. Ir. Fus. in left subsector (see O/215)	
	8th		1st R. Ir. Rif. relieved 15th R. Ir. Rif. in right subsector. (see O/215)	
			2nd R. Ir. Rif. relieved 1st R. Ir. Fus. in Bde. Reserve and were incorporated in the 107th Bde, while the 1st R. Ir. Fus. were transferred to the 108th Inf. Bde, (see O/215)	
		8 p.m.	Amendments to Bde. Defence Scheme issued see	app. IV.
			Order 216 issued see	app. V
	9th		2nd. R. Ir. Rif. relieved 10th R. Ir. Rif. in left subsector (see O/215).	
			Amendment to O/216 issued see	app. VI
	10th		Redistribution of HQ etc. took place as detailed in O/216.	
HAMEL LOCK		6 p.m.	Bde. HQ opened at HAMEL LOCK.	
			The 15 R. Ir. Rif. relieved the 10 R. Ir. Rif. in Bde. reserve. On relief the 10 R. Ir. Rif. ceased to belong to the 107 Inf. Bde. and came under orders of the Div.n direct.	R.D.W.

2449 Wt. W14957/M90 750,000 1/16 J.B.C. & A. Forms/C.2118/12.

Army Form C. 2118.

WAR DIARY
or
~~INTELLIGENCE SUMMARY~~

Instructions regarding War Diaries and Intelligence Summaries are contained in F. S. Regs., Part II. and the Staff Manual respectively. Title Pages will be prepared in manuscript.

Headquarters 107th Inf. Bde. (Erase heading not required.)

1918

Place	Date February	Hour	Summary of Events and Information	Remarks and references to Appendices
HAMEL LOCK	10	11.55 pm	On completion of the above moves the Bde. reorganisation into 3 Bns. (the 1st. Bn. R. Ir. Rif., 2nd. Bn. R. Ir. Rif., and 15th Bn. R. Ir. Rif.) was completed. This period in the line passed very quietly and all the above moves were completed without interruption from the enemy. The weather was exceptionally fine.	
	12	12 noon	O/217 issued for relief of the Bde. in the line see	App. VII
			The Bde's. last few days in the line passed very quietly.	
	14	7 p.m.	15 R. Ir. Rif. attempted to raid enemy post opposite right of Bde. Sector. The party remained out over 5 hours but were unable to get in touch with enemy post, which was found alert; see O/218	App. VIII
			Amendment to Bde. Defence Scheme issued see	App. IX
	15		Reliefs in accordance with O/217 were completed without incident by 11.55 p.m.	
	16	9 a.m.	Command of Sector passed to B.G.C. 109 Inf. Bde. and 107 Bde. HQ. opened at DURY.	
DURY.			While the Bde was out of the line all Bns. were employed on work in the Battle zone. A Bde. Specialists School was established at DURY on the 18th inst. under command of Capt. P. MURPHY, 2 R. Ir. Rif.	
	20		O/219 issued see	App. X
G^D SERAUCOURT	22	3 p.m.	107 Bde took over centre subsector of Div! front and Bde. HQ opened at G^D SERAUCOURT. The reserve Bn. of the Bde. was employed on different working parties, burying cable, hutting, making gun positions etc. The 1 R. Ir. Rif worked on subsector F of the battle zone.	

RCW.

2449 Wt. W14957/M90 750,000 1/16 J.B.C. & A. Forms/C.2118/12.

Army Form C. 2118.

WAR DIARY
or
INTELLIGENCE SUMMARY

Instructions regarding War Diaries and Intelligence Summaries are contained in F. S. Regs., Part II. and the Staff Manual respectively. Title Pages will be prepared in manuscript.

Headquarters, 107th Inf. Bde. *(Erase heading not required.)*

February 1918

Place	Date	Hour	Summary of Events and Information	Remarks and references to Appendices
Gd SERAUCOURT	24	5.30 am	An enemy patrol attempted to raid an outpost of the right Coy. of 15 R. Ir. Rif. but was driven off before reaching our wire – our casualties were 2 O.R. wounded. Otherwise the period in the line passed very quietly. We had patrols out nightly.	
	26	9.30 pm	Enemy again attempted to raid one of our posts in the right Coy. Sector of 15 R. Ir. Rif. but was driven off leaving 1 dead in our hands (normal identification, 5th Grenadier Regt. 36 Div.) – our casualties 4 O.R. wounded by 1 bomb.	
	28	12.20 pm	Order received from Divn. to expect an enemy attack, and all units kept in a state of instant readiness. Nothing occurred.	
		11.50 pm	Inter Bn. reliefs in accordance with O 2 20 took place without interruption. Our patrols continued their activity.	See App. XI.

Rod.

2449 Wt. W14957/M90 750,000 1/16 J.B.C. & A. Forms/C.2118/12.

Instructions regarding War Diaries and Intelligence Summaries are contained in F. S. Regs., Part II. and the Staff Manual respectively. Title Pages will be prepared in manuscript.

WAR DIARY
or
~~INTELLIGENCE SUMMARY~~
(Erase heading not required.)

March 1918

Army Form C. 2118

March 1918 H.Qrs 107th Inf Brigade

Place	Date	Hour	Summary of Events and Information	Remarks and references to Appendices
GRAND SERAUCOURT	1st 20th		Bde held the line with one battalion in the Forward Zone one in the Battle Zone and one in Reserve. Inter battalion reliefs were carried out every six days. Brigade boundaries were as follows - Southern. Junction of BORELLIER TRENCH with St QUENTIN-VENDEUIL Road (B10c 6.4) B15a 7.0. - A29a 9.6 - 94 central. Northern - Junction of CABAL TRENCH and outpost line (B8c 90.65) Junction of PEIRIOLE ALLEY and MORBIHAN TRENCH (B14a 15.77) - A16c 1.0 A16c 05.70 For reliefs during this period see Appendices.	1 to 5
	1		On the night 1/2nd the enemy raided the 1st R. Ir. Rifles causing the following casualties one officer wounded 1 OR killed, 1 missing, 4 wounded. During first ten days of the month the enemy artillery was very quiet. After the 10th it became more active, organised shoots were carried out during the nights	
	21st 31st		See Narrative attached.	App VI
			Tom. Buchan Capt Brigade Major 107th Inf Bde	DWS.

1875 Wt. W593/826 1,000,000 4/15 J.B.C. & A. A.D.S.S./Forms/C. 2118.

36th Division.

B. H. Q.

107th INFANTRY BRIGADE

MARCH 1 9 1 8

Appendices attached :-

Narrative of Operations 21st-31st March.

Operation Orders.

Defence Scheme.

2502

NARRATIVE OF OPERATIONS COMMENCING
21ST MARCH, 1918.

107TH INFANTRY BRIGADE.

March 21st.

4.40 a.m. Enemy bombardment of Forward and Battle Zone commenced.

4.50 a.m. Order to MAN BATTLE STATIONS sent to all units.

5.0 a.m. Order to MAN BATTLE STATIONS received from Division. Brigade Intelligence Officer and Scouts proceeded to RACECOURSE REDOUBT.

5.15 a.m. Brigade Major 'phoned to G.S.O. 1 Divn. to say that no news had been received from the Forward Zone Battalion.

5.50 a.m. Battle Zone and Reserve Battalions report by 'phone that all their Companies have moved off to their battle stations, but that they have no reports in from them. All communication very hard to maintain as 'phone wires are constantly down and runners are slow and uncertain owing to fog and heavy shelling. H.E. and gas.

7.45 a.m. 2nd Bn Royal Irish Rifles report Battalion in position in Quarries - Reserve Battalion.

7.50 a.m. Division notified Reserve Battalion in battle station.

7.55 a.m. Above 'phoned to G.S.O.1 also that there is no 'phone communication forward of Brigade Headquarters.

8.15 a.m. Reported by 'phone to G.S.O.1 that M.G. in CONTESTCOURT had been knocked out. Instructed by him to have it replaced from Reserve M.G. Company. This was done through D.M.G.O.

8.45 a.m. Reserve Battalion ordered to send out patrol to RACECOURSE REDOUBT to get communication with Forward Zone Battalion.

8.50 a.m. Patrol ordered to be sent out from Battle Zone Battalion to ascertain situation in Forward Area.

9.15 a.m. Battle Zone Battalion report in position and this is

March 21st. 9.15 a.m. (Contd.)	reported to Division.
9.50 a.m.	Message received from 15th Bn. Royal Irish Rifles, Forward Zone Battalion, timed 8.0 a.m. which runs as follows:- "All communications forward and rearward gone. Latest information from the line 6.45 a.m., received 7.45 a.m. from Counter-attack Company says "Hostile Artillery fire intense in this Sector. Casualties nil." Very heavy shelling round redoubt. As far as known casualties 4 Killed and one wounded. Outposts watching lines of approach round redoubt. Fog still very thick."
10.0 a.m.	Above passed to Division.
10.5 a.m.	Report to Division that front line Battle Zone state that fire is diminishing.
11.25 a.m.	Asked G.S.O. II by 'phone for return of Officers from Corps School.
11.30 a.m.	Line through to 1st Bn. Royal Irish Rifles - Battle Zone Battalion.
11.55 a.m.	Message from O.C. 36th M.G.Battalion to O.C. "A" Coy., 36th M.G.Battn. to man the rear line of the Battle Zone was delivered to O.C. "A" Coy. 36th M.G.Battn.
12.0 noon.	Authority asked for to reinforce Battle Zone.with Reserve Battalion.
12.15 p.m.	Following messages received from Brigade Intelligence Officer:- "Racecourse Redoubt, 8.20 a.m. All lines including buried dised. Observation impossible owing to mist. Mustard gas thick in QUARRY VALLEY at G.3. a. and b., whole Battle Zone and Redoubts under gas and shell fire - 5.9 barrage on the GRUGIES - GRAND SERAUCOURT Road in G.3. at 5 a.m. - road much cut up." The following message to Signals from 15th Royal Irish

March 21st
12.15 p.m. (Contd). Rifles is forwarded as all communication is broken:-

"Battalion Headquarters has moved from GRUGIES to new Battalion Headquarters in cutting. Communication broken between I.T.D. and G.S. Visual impossible, it is feared S.O.S. signals will not be seen."

11.45 a.m. Racecourse Redoubt.

"At 10.30 enemy attack developed after heavy bombardment. They are still holding out. Enemy barraging Battle Zone. No gas.

12.30 p.m. Message from Brigade Intelligence Officer received states:- "Enemy attack on Battle Zone developing."

12.42 p.m. Authority given to reinforce Redoubt in Battle Zone with one Company and to withdraw remainder to open in rear of dug-outs.

12.43 p.m. Orders for above move given to Officer Commanding Battalion by 'phone.

12.50 p.m. Officer Commanding Battle Zone Battalion reports that his Counter-Attack Company has been seen moving forward to counter-attack.

12.55 p.m. This reported to Division.

12.55 p.m. Artillery report enemy in front line of Battle Zone.

1.0 p.m. Reserve Battalion, less one Company, is withdrawn to South of GRAND SERAUCOURT - ESSIGNY Road.

1.10 p.m. Artillery report enemy in CONTESCOURT.

1.25 p.m. Battle Zone Battalion informed of disposition of Reserve Battalion.

1.26 p.m. Confirmation of enemy being in Battle Zone.

1.30 p.m. Message from Brigade Intelligence Officer, timed 12.55 p.m. states:-

"Enemy attack was successful right of GRUGIES Road. Counter-attack launched and retook trench, but enemy appears

March 21st 1.30 p.m. (Contd.)	to have again ~~xxxxxxx~~ entered our line."
	Above passed to Division.
1.45 p.m.	Following received by pigeon from 15th Royal Irish Rifles:- "Still holding CENTRAL KEEP and centre railway cutting - Battalion Headquarters (Part) and two stations remain - 1.10 p.m. Casualties heavy. Bosche has passed us on both sides."
2.28 p.m.	Authority asked for to use some of Reserve Battalion to occupy left flank, alternative redoubt, of Battle Zone.
2.35 p.m.	Reserve Battalion reports by 'phone that his three Companies are as under:- 1 Coy. G.2.d.6.2. N.E. of road, facing N.E. 1 Coy. G.2.d.9.9. Facing N.E. 1 Coy. G.8.b.4.9. Facing N.E. Battn Hqrs. G.8.b.70.70.
2.43 p.m.	G.S.O.I Divn. gives authority to use these three Companies.
2.45 p.m.	Officer Commanding Reserve Battalion ordered by 'phone to occupy Redoubt at A.26.d. with his reserve Company.
3.0. p.m.	1 Company of Reserve Battalion ordered to position between Redoubts A.27.d. and G.11.a.
3.17 p.m.	Officer Commanding Battle Zone Battalion reports his C.A. Company hanging on at X Roads A.28.a.
3.24 p.m.	Right and Keep Platoons of Right Company of Battle Zone reported hanging on.
3.44 p.m.	Dispositions reported to G.S.O.II by 'phone.
4.10 p.m.	Large numbers of enemy reported entering FONTAINE and CONTESCOURT.
4.15 p.m.	Situation reported to G.S.O.I by 'phone.
4.20 p.m.	Reserve Battalion are now disposed as follows:- One Coy. in Redoubt to reinforce Coy. of 1st Bn.R.Ir.Rif. One Coy. in Alternative Redoubt at A.26.d. One Coy. in G.4. between the Redoubt in A.27.d. and G.11.a. One Coy. in reserve S. of the ESSIGNY - GRAND SERAUCOURT Road.

March 21st

4.22 p.m. Officer Commanding Reserve Battalion ordered to bring up his Reserve Company from S. of ESSIGNY-GRAND SERAUCOURT Road to the QUARRY, with a view to counterattacking the enemy in CONTESCURE.

4.30 p.m. Officer Commanding Reserve Battalion stated he would like two hours to make necessary arrangements for counter-attack. Attack arranged for 6.30 p.m. to be carried out by one Company. Artillery programme and orders for attack sent to Officer Commanding Reserve Battalion at 4.50 p.m. Watches were synchronised at 4.40 p.m.

4.47 p.m. Brigade on right report that their left troops in Front Line Battle Zone are in touch with 1st Bn. Royal Irish Rifles.

5.0 p.m. Officer Commanding "B" Coy. M.G.C. reports situation as 40 men in trench A.28.a.0.7. to A.22.c.1.1., also 2 M.Gs. and he is sending up another M.G.

5.51 p.m. Dispositions reported to G.S.O.II by 'phone.

6.23 p.m. Brigade on right report enemy in A.28.d.

6.30 p.m. Counter-attack on CONTESCURE launched. Artillery not sufficient to stop enemy machine guns and counter-attack failed. The Company carrying it out took a large number of casualties.

6.57 p.m. Situation reported to Division by 'phone.

7.0 p.m. Artillery report a party of the enemy in GUNNER COPSE. 1st Royal Irish Rifles report enemy trying to advance towards redoubt on West side of GRUGIES - GRAND SERAUCOURT Road.

7.45 p.m. Brigade Headquarters moved to Advanced Divisional Signal Station on ARTEMPS - SERAUCOURT Road.

8.15 p.m. At 8.3 p.m. O.C. 1st Bn. Royal Irish Rifles reports he

March 21st
8.15 p.m. (Contd.) examined A.28.d. and found no enemy there, he reports situation as follows:-

Right Company Keep held by 1 Officer and 34 O.R.

Redoubt held by $1\frac{1}{2}$ Coys. (Strength very weak).

In front of Battalion Headquarters - Runners etc., and remainder of Battalion, strength about 70 all told, prolong this line to a point a few yards across the GRAND SERAUCOURT - GRUGIES Road. The 2nd Battn. hold the left-hand redoubt.

At 8.15 p.m., O.C. 1st Bn. Royal Irish Rifles reports:-

My right/front Company Keep has gone. They were practically surrounded and have now moved to the redoubt. Their strength on moving was 23 - this includes men of Inniskilling Fusiliers and 15th Royal Irish Rifles who were kept by O.C. Right Front Company.

8.20 p.m. G.S.O.I on 'phone to Brigade Commander gives orders for Brigade to take up line from HAMEL to HAPPENCOURT CEMETERY. 108th Brigade to move first.

8.35 p.m. Orders for move sent to Battalions, 108th Brigade to move first, 2nd Battn. to move before 1st Battalion - 2nd Battn. to take up position from cemetery at HAPPENCOURT to L.6.c.1.9. and 1st Battn. to take up position from left of 2nd Battn. to X Roads immediately N.W. of HAMEL. Line to face S.E.

8.50 p.m. Situation now as follows:-

1 Coy. 2nd Bn. Royal Irish Rifles in G.4.

1 Coy. 1st Bn. and 1 Coy. 2nd R.Ir.Rifles. in redoubt and extending across GRUGIES - GRAND SERAUCOURT Road.

2 Coys. 2nd R.Ir.Rif. in alternative redoubt.

9.0 p.m. Brigade Headquarters left for BRAY ST. CHRISTOPHE.

10.40 p.m. Written orders for movement of Brigade to W. of CANAL received from Division by D.R.

March 21st 11.5 p.m. Revised orders sent to Battalions. 2nd Bn. to hold from HAMEL LOCK (inclusive) to G.1.d.e.7. 1st Bn. to hold from left of 2nd Bn. to ROUPY - GRAND SERAUCOURT Road (inclusive). Line to follow line of Canal and all crossings to be carefully guarded.

109th Brigade on left, 108th Brigade on right.

11.5 p.m. Brigade Headquarters at Town Major's Office, LAVESENE.

11.15 p.m. D.R. sent to HAPPENCOURT to receive reports from Battalions on their arrival in new positions.

March 22nd 1.15 a.m. Brigade Headquarters established 1 mile S. of BRAY ST. CHRISTOPHE. Forward Report Centre at Town Major's Office, LAVESENE.

109th Brigade also here.

2.30 a.m. Orders sent to 2nd Bn. Royal Irish Rifles to see that Engineers blow up all bridges after all are across.

3.0 a.m. Dispositions W. of Canal, and strengths of Battalions received.;

1st Bn. - Strength 5 Officers and 180 Other Ranks and three machine guns.

2nd Bn. - Strength, 6 Officers and 340 Other Ranks and one Stokes Mortar.

Rations, ammunition and shovels sent up to Battalions.

9.40 a.m. Brigade Intelligence Officer reports.-

Situation quiet on Brigade Front, but enemy reported coming round left flank of 1st Inniskillings. 2nd Bn. are ready to form defensive flank in this direction. (Division informed.)

10.0 a.m. Brigade Intelligence Officer reports.-

One Company, 1st Inniskillings, has given way. Two are hard pressed and likely to fall back.

Two Companies, 1st R.Ir.Rifles face the threatened flank.

March 22nd
10.0 a.m. (Contd.) The other two defend the marsh. (Division informed).

11.0 a.m. Reinforcements arrived for the 1st and 2nd R.Ir.Rif. under Captain Taylor, 1st R.Ir.Rifles. These were kept at Brigade Headquarters.

11.42 a.m. Brigade Intelligence Officer sends sketch of situation and reports:-
The attack against the 1st Inniskillings continues. No. signs of enemy advancing yet. The attack is being made chiefly on the left flank of the 109th Brigade. The enemy has not attempted to attack our front across the marsh. (Division informed.)

12.0 noon. Message from 2nd R.Ir.Rifles, timed 11.30 a.m., reports:- Large formed bodies of troops, apparently all arms, presumed to be enemy, seen through fog on E. side of Canal moving South between GRAND SERAUCOURT and ST.SIMON. (Division informed).

12.5 p.m. Report received, timed 11.40 a.m., that our heavies are firing short left of HAPPENCOURT - HAMEL Road. Large parties of enemy in GRAND SERAUCOURT and marching in fours past Quarries. (Division informed).

12.45 p.m. Message sent to Battalions to tell them that it is impossible to maintain the line at present held on account of troops on our left flank having given way. They will fall back on the line now held by 60th Brigade which runs from FLUQUIERES to CANAL (600 yards W. of HAPPENCOURT) 2nd Bn. to hold from CANAL to 400 yards North with 1st Bn. on their left.

1.0 p.m. Following message with sketch attached received from Brigade Intelligence Officer:-
11.25 a.m. - O.P. established at G.4.d.95.60.
11.30 a.m. - Support Company, 9th Inniskilling Fus. and and Company, 1st Bn. R.Ir.Rif. left of road extend more to the left.

March 22nd 1.0 p.m. (Contd.) 11.35. - Right of road the men on top of the ridge withdraw to some trenches on the reverse slope - Inniskillings on left of road also withdraw to trenches further back.

12.3. - These latter move forward again and close slightly t o to the right. The men on the other side also go up to the top of the ridge again.

12.7. - Enemy M.G. firing on ridge. Heavy M.G. fire on left.

Report from 1st R.Ir.Rif.,with sketch of his dispositions outlined, states:-

The right front keep of the 109th Brigade reported to have been lost, but the redoubt is holding out. As regards left of redoubt I have no information.

Rations and water have been issued.

One small bridge over the Canal has not been destroyed. The bridge is in front of the 2nd Bn. who have a M.G. trained on it.

1.20 p.m. G.S.O.I. on telephone stated we might have to retire on PITHON. The reinforcements of the 1st and 2nd.R.Ir.Rif. were marched back to the high ground N. of PITHON to form a bridgehead to cover any possible retirement.

A Staff Officer of the 107th Brigade and one of the 109th Brigade proceeded to line to ascertain situation and superintend any necessary retirement.

All three Brigade Headquarters went to PITHON.

2.0 p.m. Staff Officer of 107th Brigade returned from line and reported troops were holding the line W. of HAPPENCOURT, and no need for retirement. It was therefore decided to hold on where they were, Situation reported to G.O.C., 36th Division at PITHON.

4.10 p.m. Orders received from G.O.C., Division for retirement via PITHON to EAUCOURT. 108th Brigade to retire first, then 109th Brigade and 107th Brigade last.

4.20 p.m. Orders for above were sent to Battalions.

March 22nd.
[illegible].20 p.m. (Contd.) The reinforcements for the 1st and 2nd Battalions were ordered to remain on the high ground N. of PITHON to cover the retirement and crossing of the Canal.

6.30 p.m. Duplicate copies of above orders sent to Battalions.

7.10 p.m. Acknowledgement of first copies of orders received.

10.45 p.m. Last troops of 107th Brigade crossed Canal at PITHON railway bridge.

1st Battalion proceeded to EAUCOURT.

2nd Bn. and Brigade Headquarters in CUGNY.

MARCH 23rd
8.0 a.m. Rumour received that enemy cavalry are on S. side of CANAL.

Ordered 1st Battalion at EAUCOURT to put out outposts on N. and E. sides of village and ~~xxx~~ on road leading to HAM.

Ordered 2nd Battalion to put out outposts to N, E. and S. of CUGNY, and have remainder of Battalion ready to move if required.

9.0 a.m. G.S.O.2 telephones that both Battalions are at disposal of 108th Brigade if required.

10.40 a.m. Enemy reported to be in FLAVY, this report contradicted at 11.0 a.m. (Division informed.)

2nd Bn. Royal Irish Rifles ordered to take up a defensive position E. of CUGNY - 2nd Bn. R.Ir.Rif. in touch with 20th Division (K.R.R.) who are holding a line defending CUGNY about 400 yards up FLAVY Road.

11.30 a.m. Report brought in by M.M.P. that enemy are in ANNOIS.

2nd Bn. R.Ir.Rif. ordered to send a patrol/in this direction.

'B' Coy. M.G.C., report that they have two guns and belts for same. B.G.C. orders one gun to be put near cutting on CUGNY - FLAVY Road, R.21.Central. and one on CUGNY - DETROIT D'ANNOIS Road.

12.0 noon. Following report received from Brigade Intelligence Officer:-

"9th and 8th R.B. are falling back from FLAVY - MARTEL and intend to fall back on CUGNY. The Boche is advancing rapidly on left of FLAVY. Men are extending facing half left to the left of CUGNY - FLAVY Road.

March 23rd.
12.0 noon. Enemy reported on railway due N. of FLAVY. Division informed.

Party of stragglers of different regiments collected in CUGNY and sent to 2nd Bn. R.Ir.Rif.

12.5 p.m. Brigade Headquarters moved to cutting on CUGNY - VILLESELVE Road (Q.30.b.4.2.)

12.30 p.m. Following report from Brigade Intelligence Officer:-
"Enemy in ANNOIS and on the railway embankment left of it. Bosche advancing down the CUGNY Road from FLAVY. 2nd Bn. R.Ir.Rif. holding hedge left of FLAVY- CUGNY Road just outside village. There are three lines of troops extended in front of them."

12.45 p.m. Message from Division to say that 1st Bn.R.If.Rif. are returned to Brigade and ordering Brigade to form a flank from CUGNY Southwards, facing East along high ground in R.20., 26. and 32. to edge of BOIS de CORBIE.

1.0 p.m. Order issued to comply with above issued:-
2nd Bn.R.Ir.Rif. to hold from CUGNY to CROSS ROADS 500 yards South of CUGNY.
1st Bn. R.Ir.Rif. to hold from this point Southwards to N. edge of BOIS de CORBIE. Touch to be got with 14th Division on right and maintained with 20th Division on left.

1.5 p.m. K.R.R. in CUGNY sent message asking for shovels, these were obtained and sent up.

1.55 p.m. Brigade Intelligence Officer reports:-
"No enemy attack has developed from ANNOIS on FLAVY. Men seen coming from FLAVY were apparently our own stragglers. Enemy seen to be in the edge of wood this side of ANNOIS. It is difficult to locate his position. 2nd K.R.R. are in front of the 2nd R.Ir.Rif."

Reported to Division 2.0 p.m.

Brigade Major proceeds to CUGNY to superintend the taking up of positions by 1st and 2nd Bn. R.Ir.Rifles.

2.0 p.m. O.C. 14th Division Details reports personally his line as follows:-

March 23rd
2.0 p.m. (Contd.) "Enemy holds station and buildings West of Cemetery in FLAVY. 14th Division Details line runs - R.14.d.3.1. to LES DEUX ARBRES thence to R.22.d.90.90 to R.28.b.90.90.

Fairly Comfortable in his position.

2.20 p.m. Brigade Intelligence Officer reports:-

"The 14th Division are still holding the Western outskirts of FLAVY". Also sends sketch of position.

3.0 p.m. 2nd Bn. R.Ir.Rif. report, timed 2.40 p.m. -

No movement of enemy outside FLAVY and ANNOIS. He appears to bebheld."

3.15 p.m. Brigade Intelligence Officer reports:-

2.50 p.m. About 30 of our men have fallen back out of FLAVY and have extended across the road 300 yards from the nearest outskirts of the village.

2.55 p.m. Men are running out of FLAVY and forming up behind the sheds down the road."

3.45 p.m. Numbers of hostile aeroplanes fly low over BROUCHY, CUGNY and VILLESELVE, shooting at Battalions and other targets.

Situation report to Division as follows:-

"Brigade is holding line from R.32.b.90.15. round village of CUGNY to R.20.c.80.90. lines continuesmto the left held by mixed troops to Q.23.c.14. Beyond that the situation is uncertain and no touch can be gained with anybody there.

In front of us there is a line held by details of 14th Division from LES DEUX ARBRES to R.14.d.9.4., no one on their left, but French troops are on the right of the line held by us. Can we be informed who is on the left and where they are located."

Ttoops are still retiring on our left. The enemy in front of us holds ANNOIS beyond railway station FLAVY, and FLAVY beyond the cross roads. A body of troops that look like cavalry have put in an appearance North of Flavy.

4.20 p.m. Message from 2nd Bn.R.Ir.Rif., timed 3.45 p.m.-

"On our right we are not in touch with 1st Battalion, but

March 23rd
4.20 p.m.
(Contd.) we are in touch with an Entrenching Battalion holding the line immediately on our right."

4.25 p.m. Message from Brigade Intelligence Officer:-

"3.15. A Bosche observation balloon is up over FLAVY and seems very near our line.

3.57. Men who recently left FLAVY and formed up across the road have moved to the right.

4.0 p.m. Men from second line of troops in front of 2nd Bn. R.Ir.Rif. running to take up position on the right hand side of road. The men ran across road from left to right.

4.5. p.m. Men running from FLAVY reinforce their line on both sides of the road.

4.15. M.G. fire has caused the men immediately in front of FLAVY on both sides of the road to fall back slightly as if for cover.

4.18. Men in front of ANNOIS WOOD fell back 400 yards to the cover of the hedge running in front of the wood.

4.22. Enemy advancing from wood ¼ mile E. of FLAVY, our men on right of wood falling back slightly to the S.W. Advance continues."

5.15. p.m. 2nd Bn. R.Ir.Rif. report enemy are now South of FLAVY. Apparently regiment of Cavalry N. of FLAVY, also limbers.

5.22 p.m. Brigade Intelligence Officer reports:-

4.45 p.m. An attack is developing straight down the road on the right hand side.

4.50 p.m. The enemy troops attacking to the S.E. in massed formation, have opened out right and left.
The trench on right of road is occupied to where it joins the road now. The enemy is sending out small sections in front of this trench, the attack down the right of the road has otherwise stopped for the moment.

4.55 p.m. Reinforcements are moving up behind each of enemy attacking battalions."

5.25 p.m. 2nd Bn. R.Ir.Rif. report timed 5.10 p.m. states:-
"On right of FLAVY Road enemy are attacking in force. They are about 800 yards in front of right Company. The Entrenching Battalion that was holding between my right

March 23rd 5.25 p.m. (Contd.)	Company and the 1st Bn. has gone. I am joining up with the 1st Bn.
5.50 p.m.	Message received from Division saying that situation is improving, that 107th, 108th, 109th and 61st Brigades are to hold on to the ground they now have at all costs, and if they have withdrawn, they will endeavour to regain what has been given up unless the enemy has occupied it in force. (Copy of above message forwarded to Battalions.
5.55 p.m.	Message from 2nd Battalion, timed 5.30 p.m., to say that our troops are retiring on right of road and leaving him in the air.
5.55 p.m.	Message from 2nd Battalion, timed 5.35 p.m. to say enemy attacking on both sides of road and have started to use Trench Mortars.
6.0 p.m.	Brigade Headquarters move to VILLESELVE, and these get in touch with 109th and 61st Brigades,
6.15 p.m.	Message from 2nd Battalion, timed 6.0 p.m.- "Right flank driven in - 13th Gloster Regt. retired - My right company extending towards flank to get in touch with next Battalion on right.
6.25 p.m.	Message from 1st Battalion, timed 6.0 p.m. - "Stragglers of neighbouring unit have now returned and are now in line on my right."
6.25 p.m.	Collected all stragglers in VILLESELVE and sent them up under an Officer to left of CUGNY to get in touch with 2nd Battn.
7.0 p.m.	O.C. 1st Bn. reports on telephone that he is being attacked.
7.15.p.m.	O.C. 1st Bn. reports that he has repulsed the attack, but that he thinks they will attack again, he also reports that the troops on his left connecting him with the 2nd Bn. have retired
7.20 p.m.	Message from 2nd Battalion, timed 6.5 p.m. - "The enemy attack has ceased for the present. Line maintained.
7.21 p.m.	Message from 2nd Bn, timed 6.20 p.m.,- "Enemy cavalry working round left flank on other side of light railway."

March 23rd

7.23 p.m. Message from 2nd Bn., timed 7.10 p.m. - "Enemy about 600 yards away from our present line. He is attacking again."

7.24 p.m. Brigade Major proceeded to the line to ascertain the exact situation.

7.25 p.m. Message from 2nd Bn., timed 7.15 p.m. - "Our troops on both flanks have retired. Cannot regain touch."

7.45 p.m. O.C. 1st Bn. reports enemy attacking again, his left flank is being turned, and that the enemy are close up to him, and he thinks he will have to retire.

7.55 p.m. Message from Captain Miller, 15th R.Ir.Rif., who was commanding some details, states:- "Line back 1,000 yards S. of BROUCHY."

8.0 p.m. Brigade Intelligence Officer's report timed 7.50 p.m.:- "There is heavy M.G. fire on the CUGNY front and numerous white lights are being sent up, probably as signals and not for observation."

8.20 p.m. Situation report sent to Division.

8.30 p.m. Brigade Headquarters moved to BUILANCOURT, where we found Headquarters, 108th Brigade.

10.35 p.m. Brigade Intelligence Officer reports:- "Enemy is holding CUGNY and our line runs just outside the village with the exception of two slightly isolated houses we hold on the left of the road. The enemy shows no signs of further activity to-night."

11.45 p.m. Brigade Major returns from line and reports that the 2nd Bn. are holding a line from R.19.b.50.70. to R.20.c.20.30. with two Companies of 12th Kings on their right. The 1st Bn. have retired to higher ground in BEAULIEU.

12 midnight. Following order sent to Battalions:- 1st Bn. will take up a position from Q.30.d.50.99. to R.25.c.10.35. 2nd Bn. are holding a line from R.19.b.50.70.

March 23rd. 12.0 m.n. (Contd.) to R.20.c.20.30. Should the 2nd Bn. be forced to withdraw the 1st Battalion will cover their retirement to a position on the North side of the CUGNY - VILLESELVE Road in Q,30.b.

March 24th. 12.5 a.m. Situation report sent to Division.

2.50 a.m. Rations arrived and sent up to Battalions.

8.5 a.m. Situation wire of 61st Brigade states Enemy in BROUCHY, EAUCOURT and CUGNY.
61st Brigade Troops in area between EAUCOURT and OLLEZY.
109th Brigade South-East and South of BROUCHY.

8.50 a.m. Discovered that the 62nd and 89th Field Companies R.E. had retired from the line, ordered them to return and take up a position on the right of 1st Battalion R.Ir.Rif. from R.25.c.10.50. to R.31.a.80.75. (Division informed.)

9.0 a.m. G.O.C. 3rd Cavalry Division reports our line runs R.31.b. central R.32.central. - X.2. Central. He will send information about EAUCOURT and BROUCHY as soon as possible.

9.35 a.m. Situation by telephone to Division.

10.25 a.m. Situation report to Division. -
2nd Bn. R.Ir.Rif. and Kings. in R.19.b. and d.
1st Bn. R.Ir.Rif. in Q.30.b. and d.
108th and 109th Brigades - R.7.a., Q.18.central. - Q.17.c.70.00 Q.22.c.0.0. - Q.27.central. - Q.33.a.50.99. - Q.32.a.00.20. also Q.23.d.00.80., Q.24.c.00.70., Q.24.c.50.00., Our troops reported holding R.31.a.50.50.. R.32.central, X2. cent.

10.30 a.m. Brigade Intelligence Officers reports:-
"The enemy holds along main road running South CUGNY through R.26.central to R.32.central and has not apparently advanced on front of 2nd Bn. R.Ir.Rif.

12.10 p.m. G.O.C.Division came to Brigade Headquarters.

12.37 p.m. Cavalry report that 14th Division are falling back through French line. Report that our troops are falling back from Cugny and EAUCOURT. Enemy M.G. firing on them from CUGNY and BROUCHY.

March 24th
2.40 p.m. Brigade Intelligence Officer reports:-

"11.20 a.m. Our men are withdrawing from the railway N.E. of EAUCOURT. Another party has advanced to the West of Eaucourt. Some of our troops are taking up a line running North and South in Q.24.b.and d.

11.38 a.m. The enemy are taking up a position along the CUGNY - EAUCOURT Road. Troops from EAUCOURT are holding a line running from N. of MONTALMONT FARM in Q.23.d. to Q.24.d. central., others from EAUCOURT have crossed the VILLESELVE - BROUCHY Road, and are establishing themselves behind it. Everything quiet on the Brigade front.

2.40 p.m. Message from 1st Bn. R. Ir.Rifles, timed 2.10 p.m. - "The enemy have taken BROUCHY and all troops in that vicinity have retired with the exception of troops on my immediate left. These are retiring, or about to retire at the moment. The 2nd Bn. is being withdrawn. Troops have retired in a South-Westerly direction under heavy fire.

4.30 p.m. Message from 1st Bn. R. Ir.Rifles. states:-

"Almost surrounded and had to retire at 3.20 p.m., but now hold VILLESELVE front facing North-West. Commanding 1st R.Ir.Rifles and details of these units. 2nd R.Ir.Rif. are cut off and will not get away until dark."

4.35 p.m. Brigade Major returns from the line and reports:-

All troops are retiring in disorder except 1st and 2nd. R.Ir.Rifles. 2nd R.Ir.Rifles appear to be cut off, and it is doubtful if the 1st Battalion can get away as the troops on both flanks have retired."

Situation report sent to Division.

4.40 p.m. Brigade Major returned to line to assist in rallying men retiring on right. Staff Captain proceeded to VILLESELVE with ammunition

6.30 p.m. Proceeded to GUISCHARD to meet B.G.C. 108th Brigade, who had gone to the 62nd French Division for orders. Troops of all sorts were seen retiring on our right.

March 24th
7.0 p.m. After conference with B.G.C. 108th Brigade, the following message was sent to all Units of 36th Division:-

"If forced to retire try and form up Battalion along the ridge W.19, W.20., W.21., W.27., - Units too mixed to decide order of holding. Reorganise later. 107th on Right, 108th Centre, 109th Left. Get touch with Units on flanks. Brigade Headquarters V.30.d.0.0.

7.30 p.m. Troops retiring in all directions. B.Gs.C. 107th and 108th Brigades started for CRISOLLES to report situation to 14th Division. A message by a D.R. found on the road was sent with/situation report to 36th Division from Cross Roads about two miles South of GUISCHARD on NOYON Road by B.G.C. 108th Brigade. On arrival at CRISOLLES all units of 36th Division were collected on Eastern edge of the village. Situation was reported to G.O.C., 14th Division by B.G.C. 108th Brigade.

10.25 p.m. B.G.C. 108th Brigade reported situation to 36th Division.

11.0 p.m. All troops of 36th Division that could be collected moved to SERMAIZE, arriving 1.30 a.m. 25th.

March 25th
6.35 a.m. Units were re-organised as far as possible and rations issued.

8.0 a.m. Brigade moved to CATIGNY in accordance with Divisional Order G.B.13. An Officer of 107th Brigade and Interpreter of 108th Brigade rode on in advance to G.O.C. 62nd French Division at BEAULIEU under whose orders 36th Division had been placed. On arrival verbal orders were received from 62nd French Divisional Commander and 36th Division, that the Division was no longer required by the French Commander , and would move to the AVRICOURT area.

11.45 a.m. Received Divisional Order G.B.15 on road one mile S.E. of AVRICOURT.

1.35 p.m. Brigade in camp in wood $1^1/_8$ miles S.E. of I in AVRICOURT. (Division informed.)

March 25th
4.30 p.m. Orders received to march to GUERBIGNY.

6.5 p.m. Brigade marched from camp via TILLOY and ARMANCOURT to GUERBIGNY.

March 26th
1.30 a.m. Brigade Group in billets at GUERBIGNY

9.50 a.m. G.S.O.II of Division visited Brigade Headquarters and informed the B.G.C. that situation was unsatisfactory and all troops to stand to.

108th and 109th Brigades moved out of village and took up a line from ERCHES to AVRE RIVER in R.19.c., where French troops were on their right flank. 107th Brigade with 21st Entrenching Battalion, 121 Company, R.E. and 16th Bn. Royal Irish Rifles (P) to be in support.with eight M.Gs.

10.0 a.m. All troops ordered to stand to ready to move.

12.50 p.m. G.S.O.1 visited Brigade and stated that situation had not improved and that Brigade should move out of GUERBIGNY.

1.10 p.m. Situation worse. B.G.C. issued verbal orders to Commanding Officers to the effect that Brigade would take up the line Q.23.central. to Q.16.central. Order of battle from right to left 121 Coy. R.E., 1st R.Ir.Rifles, 2nd R.Ir.Rifles, 15th R.Ir.Rifles, 21st Entrenching Battalion, with 16th R.Ir.Rifles and 107th Trench Mortar Battery in Support. Trench Mortar Battery had no mortars. Owing to difficulty in communication it became impossible to issue orders to as many units as the Brigade now consisted of. Groups were therefore formed as follows:-

Colonel McCarthy-O'Leary's - 1st, 2nd, and 15th R.Ir.Rifles.

Major McCallum's - 21st Entrenching Battalion, 16th R.Ir.Rif. and 107th Trench Mortar Battery.

Major Lewen's - 121st Company, R.E.

1.20 p.m. Brigade Headquarters moved out of village to Q.22.b.central.

1.30 p.m. B.G.C. rode out to reconnoitre country between BOUCHOIR and GUERBIGNY.

March 26th
4.0 p.m. Verbal orders issued by B.G.C. to Commanding Officers to take up line ERCHES (inclusive) - BUCHOIR (exclusive) with Colonel McCarthy-O'Leary's Group on right, and Major McCallum's on Left: 121 Company R.E. to be in reserve. This was arranged in consultation with G.S.O. III, XVIII Corps, and B.G.C.108th Infy. Brigade, as there was a considerable gap on left of 108th Brigade

4.10 p.m. Division was informed of action taken and dispositions. Line running from K.29.d.10.90. to Q.10.d.50.60.

4.40 p.m. Brigade Headquarters moved to Q.2.b.8.3. B.G.C. visiting B.G.C. 108th Brigade at Q.9.c.

9.0 p.m. Orders received from Division to gain touch with 108th Bde. at Q.12.a.10.80. and hold the line from thence through Q.6.c.40.20 to Q.5.central to BOUCHOIR (exclusive.)

9.15 p.m. Orders ~~xxxxxxxxxxxxxxxxxxxx~~ issued in B.M.16 to the effect that a line would be established as follows:-

Colonel McCarthy-O'Leary's Group from Q.11.d.10.60. through Q.12.a.20.80. to wood in Q.6.c.40.20., where they will relieve 122nd Company R.E.

Major McCallum's Group from Q.6.c.40.20. to Q.5.a.40.80. thence to K.29.d.10.90.

9.20 p.m. Brigade Headquarters moved to QUARRY at Q.2.a.90.90.

9.30 p.m. Division Order G.B.26 acknowledged and Division asked to establish visual communication with Brigade O.P. at K.33.d.10.10. This communication was never established.

10.0 p.m. Brigade Major visited line to ascertain situation.

Brigade Major 108th Brigade came to Brigade Headquarters and reported that enemy patrol had attacked 108th Brigade Headquarter at about Q.15.a.2.3.. Staff Captain 107th Brigade, and Brigade Major, 108th Brigade, went to HANGEST and reported to 30th Division, as we had no touch with our Division at that time. D.R. being lost.

March 27th

3.10 a.m. Report received from 15th R.Ir.Rif., timed 12.10 a.m. stating that they were being heavily trench mortared from ERCHES.

121 Coy. R.E. report Light T.M. and M.G. firing from about Q.5.c.5.2.

A patrol of one Officer and two Other Ranks was sent out by the 121st Company, R.E., leaving Q.5.a.4.8. about 1.45 a.m. This patrol moved out to about 100 yards from QUESNOY - ERCHES Road, where it lay down and watched a large amount of enemy transport on this road, - wagons, limbers, about twenty cavalry, some straggling infantry, and one battery of Field Artillery. Nearly all this traffic was going into ERCHES. The Officer even spoke to a man marching on the road and states that there was no doubt that he was a German.

4.45 a.m. Brigade Major returned from the line, and Division were informed that the situation was as follows:-

About 9.30 p.m. O.C. 122 Coy.R.E. withdrew from the wood at Q.6.c.50.20. with the result that one Company of the 16th R.Ir.Rif. fell back from the trench running Q.6.c.40.50. to Q.5.a.40.70. By about 10.30 p.m. the enemy had occupied ERCHES in considerable strength and were firing on our trenches with T.Ms. and M.Gs. Patrols sent down the road towards GUERBIGNY met with enemy and suffered losses.

Our line runs from BOUCHOIR to Q.10.b.90.10. From all reports enemy seem to have advanced from QUESNOY South-westwards Large amount of transport being seen during night and early morning on QUESNOY - ERCHES and QUESNOY - ANDECHY Roads.

8.35 a.m. A gun at about Q.6.d. shelled our lines.

9.20 a.m. Division again informed of situation - that enemy were massing for an attack on our front, and our line was being heavily shelled.

9.30 a.m. Enemy attacked. Our line was driven in, and Staff Captain, who had gone up to front line, reported that at 11.50 a.m.

11.50 a.m. our line was as follows:-

March 27th
11.50 a.m. (Contd.) A thin line consisting of troops of 1st and 2nd R.Ir.Rif., 9th R.Ir.Fus., 107th Trench Mortar Battery and two guns of 'B' Company, 36th Divn. M.G.Battn. Left flank on high ground at Q.3.a.80.30., right flank at Q.3.b.90.80. A Lewis Gun covers left flank, and a M.G. right flank. Large numbers of enemy and transport are moving down ERCHES - GUERBIGNY Road and on towards DAVENESCOURT. No signs of a further frontal attack on our lines.

2.0 p.m. Owing to large numbers of enemy seen advancing towards DAVENESCOURT and disappearing in wooded country east of this village, our line was withdrawn by stages to S.E. of HANGEST. This withdrawal was carried out in an orderly manner and was complete by 5.0 p.m.

5.0 p.m. Troops were heavily shelled for five minutes just before reaching the line. Heavy guns firing from direction of ERCHES and light field guns from high ground E. of DAVENESCOURT.

6.0 p.m. Division notified that line now ran S.E. of HANGEST with Brigade Headquarters at J.28.b.

9.0 p.m. Instructions received through 30th Division, who had Hqrs. at HANGEST, that the Brigade was to move to HARGICOURT Area as soon as French troops had taken up their positions.

10.30 p.m. Corps Staff Officer informed B.G.C. that Brigade would withdraw to SOURDON.

March 28th.
12.30 a.m. French dispositions complete and withdrawal commenced. Brigade marching via HANGEST - PLESSIER - MOREUIL - MAILLY

6.0 a.m. to SOURDON, arriving 6.0 a.m.

1.30 a.m. Divisional Orders for above withdrawal received by Brigade Major on road near PLESSIER.

12.0 noon. G.O.C. sent for B.G.C. and verbally ordered Brigade to move to COULLEMELLE and form outpost line facing S.E. on S.E. side of village, as enemy had broken the French line at MESNIL ST. GEORGES.

March 28th
2.0 p.m. Brigade moved off.

5.0 p.m. Outpost line taken up from T.16.b.40.00 through T.10.d.60.00. to T.10.a.90.50. with 109th Brigade on right, and 108th Brigade in Reserve. Brigade Headquarters at T.9.b.99.40.

5.30 p.m. Division informed of situation.

March 29th
3.0 a.m. Patrols sent out to VILLERS TOURNELLE and BOIS des GLANDS and touch gained with French who state situation very satisfactory.

8.30 a.m. All troops withdrawn into the village of COULLEMELLE with the exception of six sentry posts and two advanced posts each with two M.Gs. and escort of Infantry to establish contact with French at VILLERS TOURNELLE.

12.0 noon. Orders received from 166th French Division to withdraw to CHAUSSOY - EPAGNY.

After this time the Brigade took no active part in fighting in this area.

2.0 p.m. Brigade left COULLEMELLE and marching via QUIRY - FOLLEVILLE - LA FALOISE - EPAGNY arrived at CHAUSSOY-EPAGNY at 5.30 p.m. Brigade was billetted in village and Brigade Headquarters were established at M.2.b.3.6.

6.0 p.m. Orders were received from Division for Brigade to move by road to WAILLY-VELENNES Area.

8.0 p.m. Brigade moved off. All transport being brigaded and marching in rear of Brigade Column. Some lorries were available about half-way through the march, and were used for the tired personnel of all units.

March 30th
9.0 a.m. Brigade all in billets at VELENNES.

11.0 a.m. Warning Order received from Division for Brigade to entrain night 30/31st for GAMACHES. All transport to go by road. Staging at ALLERY.

3.15 p.m. Divisional Order for move received. Brigade less transport to march to SALEUX, where it will entrain for GAMACHES.

5.0 p.m. Brigade marched from VELENNES via TAISNIL to SALEUX station.

March 30th
10.0 p.m. Brigade arrived at SALEUX Station and remained on the side of the road until 10.0 a.m.

March 31st
10.0 a.m. Brigade entrained and arrived at GAMACHES at 1.0 p.m.

4.0 p.m. Brigade arrived in billets in FEUQUIERES - MAISINIERES Arae. Brigade Headquarters in FEUQUIERES.

Appendix I

S E C R E T   Copy No ...9..........

107th Infantry Brigade Order No. 221.

Ref. Map GRUGIES.   3rd March 1918.
Edition 2A, 66C. N.W.I.

1. A raid will be carried out on the night 4/5th March 1918 by the 15th R.Ir.Rif.

2. INFORMATION.

Enemy posts have been located at B.7.b.55.45, at B.7.b.63.60, and at B.7.b.70.30. There are dugouts at B.7.b.65.50.

3. The post to be raided will be the oneat B.7.b.55.45.

4. OBJECT OF RAID.

To obtain an identification and to kill Germans. A prisoner alive or dead must be brought in.

5. METHOD OF CONDUCTING THE OPERATION.

The raiders, consisting of 4 Officers and 36 Other Ranks, will be divided into four parties as follows :-

Party "A"	1 Officer, ~~1 N.C.O.~~ and ~~6 men.~~ 1 Section
Party "B"	1 Officer, ~~2 N.C.Os~~ and ~~12 men.~~ 2 Sections
Party "C"	1 Officer, ~~1 N.C.O.~~ and ~~6 men.~~ 1 Section
Party "D"	1 Officer, ~~2 N.C.Os~~ and ~~6 men.~~ 1 Section

The point of departure from our own trenches will be B.7.b.25.35.

The point of entering enemy's trenches B.7.b.58.52.

At Zero Party "A" will leave the point of departure from our trenches and will cross enemy trench at B.7.b.58.52 and rush the post at B.7.b.55.45 from the rear. Guiding tape will be carried by this party and laid to the point of entrance to enemy trench.

Party "B" will follow Party "A" and deal with sentries over dugouts, etc. at B.7.b.65.50, and prevent interference with Party "A".

Party "C" will follow Party "B" and establish a block between the point of entry and enemy post at B.7.b.63.60, acting as a covering party to the operations.

Party "D" will follow up Party "C", take up a position outside point of entrance for the purpose of reserve, control, evacuation or withdrawal.

WITHDRAWAL.

Party "A" on completion of their task will return with their prisoners to O.C. Raid who will check the party and pass them on to point of departure from our trenches; Party "B" will follow carrying out same procedure, Party "C" will follow Party "B".

Party "D" will then withdraw, taking care to lift the tape, and report to Second-in-Command or Officer detailed, who will be in F.P.7, and who will check the party and send them down to Company Headquarters in A.18.d.

EQUIPMENT, ETC.

Box respirators will not be carried.

Officers and N.C.Os. will carry revolvers.

All Riflemen of Parties "C" & "D" will carry rifles and fixed swords.

Bayonet men of Parties "A" & "B" will carry rifles and fixed swords - remainder will carry clubs.

All ranks will carry 4 No.5 Mills Hand Grenades in their pockets.

Headdress - Cap comforter or cap with badge removed.

No orders, maps, letters, papers or A.B.64 will be carried.

Raid identity discs only will be worn.

Faces and hands will be blackened.

Watches will be synchronized.

The Second-in-Command or Officer detailed & the 107th Bde. Intelligence Officer will be in F.P.7, where a Fullerphone will be installed.

Zero hour will be notified later.

A C K N O W L E D G E.

E. Williams

Lieut.
A/Brigade Major.
107th Infantry Brigade.

Issued at ....8 pm......

Copy No. 1 to 15th R.Ir.Rif.
" " 2 to 109th Inf. Brigade.
" " 3 to 1st R. Innis. Fus.
" " 4 to 1st R.Ir.Rif.
" " 5 to 36th Div. M.G. Battn.
" " 6 to Left Group, R.F.A.
" " 7 to 36th Division "G"
" " 8 to War Diary.
" " 9 to War Diary.
" " 10 to File.

SECRET *Appendix II* Copy No ...23.........

107th Infantry Brigade Order No. 222

4th March 1918.

1. The following reliefs will be carried out on the night 6/7th March 1918. -

(a) The 2nd R.Ir.Rif. will relieve the 1st R.Ir.Rif. in the front system.
(b) The 15th R.Ir.Rif. will relieve the 2nd R.Ir.Rif. as garrison of the Battle Zone, Subsector "F", and will take over the dugouts in the Quarries in A.27.c.
(c) On relief the 1st R.Ir.Rif. will withdraw into Reserve and will take over the billets in SOMME Dugouts, HAMEL and GRAND SERAUCOURT, vacated by 15th R.Ir.Rif.

2. All details of relief, guides, etc. will be arranged between Commanding Officers concerned.

3. The relief of the 2nd R.Ir.Rif. by the 15th R.Ir.Rif. will be arranged in such a way that there is no interruption on the work in the Battle Zone. O.C. 15th R.Ir.Rif. will arrange that all ranks know their Battle Stations in Subsector "F".
The 1st R.Ir.Rif. will take over the various working parties supplied by the 15th R.Ir.Rif., these will begin work on the morning of 8th March.
1st R.Ir.Rif. will send a working party state to Brigade H.Qrs. by 9 a.m. on 7th Inst. giving working strength of each Company.

4. Relieving troops will not cross the Battle Zone till 4.0 p.m.

5. All trench stores, etc. will be handed over, and duplicate copies of receipts forwarded to Brigade Headquarters on 7th Inst.

6. Relief will be reported complete by wiring -

1st R.Ir.Rif.	S.C.
2nd R.Ir.Rif.	~~REINFORCE.~~ REINFORCE

1st R.Ir.Rif. and 15th R.Ir.Rif. will report arrival in new billets.

7. Acknowledge.

[signature]
Lieut.
a/Brigade Major.
107th Infantry Brigade.

Issued at 10 p.m.

Copy No. 1 to 1st R.Ir.Rif.	Copy No. 14 to 173 Bde R.F.A.
" " 2 to 2nd R.Ir.Rif.	" " 15 to 153 -do-
" " 3 to 15th R.Ir.Rif.	" " 16 to 36th Div "G"
" " 4 to 107th T.M.Bty.	" " 17 to 36th Div "Q"
" " 5 to Staff Capt.	" " 18 to C.R.A.
" " 6 to Bde Transport Offr.	" " 19 to C.R.E.
" " 7 to Bde Supply Officer.	" " 20 to A.D.M.S.
" " 8 to Bde Signal Officer.	" " 21 to 36th M.G. Bn.
" " 9 to 121 F. Coy. R.E.	" " 22 to A.D.V.S. XVIII Corps.
" " 10 to 150 -do-	
" " 11 to 110th F. Ambulance.	" " 23 to War Diary.
" " 12 to 108th Inf. Brigade.	" " 24 to -do-
" " 13 to 109th -do-	" " 25 to File.

Appendix III. War Diary

SECRET. Copy No 23

107th Infantry Brigade Order No. 225

12th March 1918.

1. The following reliefs will be carried out on the night 14/15th March 1918.:-

(a) The 15th R.Ir.Rif. will relieve the 2nd R.Ir.Rif. in the Front system.
(b) The 1st R.Ir.Rif. will relieve the 15th R.Ir.Rif. as garrison of the Battle Zone, Subsector "F", and will take over the dugouts in the Quarries in A.27.c.

(c) On relief the 2nd R.Ir.Rif. will withdraw into Reserve and will take over the billets in SOMME Dugouts, HAMEL and GRAND SERAUCOURT, vacated by 1st R.Ir.Rif.

2. All details of relief, guides, etc. will be arranged between Commanding Officers concerned.

3. The relief of the 15th R.Ir.Rif. by the 1st R.Ir.Rif. will be arranged in such a way that there is no interruption on the work in the Battle Zone (1st R.Ir.Rif. will commence work on Battle Zone on 14th Inst). O.C. 1st R.Ir.Rif. will arrange that all ranks know their Battle Stations in Subsector "F".

The 2nd R.Ir.Rif. will take over the various working parties supplied by the 1st R.Ir.Rif.; these will begin work on the morning of 16th March.

2nd R.Ir.Rif. will send a working party state to Brigade Headquarters by 9 a.m. on 15th Inst. giving working strength of each Company.

4. Relieving troops will not cross the Battle Zone till 5:0 p.m.

5. All trench stores, etc. will be handed over, and duplicate copies of receipts forwarded to Brigade H.Qrs. on 15th Inst.

6. Relief will be reported complete by wiring :-

15th R.Ir.Rif. "BOMBS"
1st R.Ir.Rif. "SHELLS"

2nd R.Ir.Rif. will report arrival in new billets.

7. Acknowledge.

A. G. Wilkins

Captain.
for Brigade Major,
107th Infantry Brigade.

Issued at 10 p.m.

Copy No. 1 to 1st R.Ir.Rif.
" " 2 to 2nd R.Ir.Rif.
" " 3 to 15th R.Ir.Rif.
" " 4 to 107th T.M.Bty.
" " 5 to Staff Capt.
" " 6 to Bde Transport Offr.
" " 7 to Bde Supply Officer.
" " 8 to Bde Signal Officer.
" " 9 to 121 Field Coy. R.E.
" " 10 to 150 -do-
" " 11 to 110th F. Ambulance.
" " 12 to 108th Inf. Bde.
" " 13 to 109th -do-

Copy No.14 to 173 Bde R.F.A.
" " 15 to 153 -do-
" " 16 to 36th Div "G"
" " 17 to 36th Div "Q"
" " 18 to C.R.A.
" " 19 to C.R.E.
" " 20 to A.D.M.S.
" " 21 to 36th M.G. Battn.
" " 22 to A.D.A.S. XVIII Corps.
" " 23 to War Diary.
" " 24 to -do-
" " 25 to File.

Appendix IV

S E C R E T

Copy No 23.........

107th Infantry Brigade Order No. 224

20th March 1918.

1. The following reliefs will be carried out on the night 22/23rd March 1918.
   (a) The 1st R.Ir.Rif. will relieve the 15th R.Ir.Rif. in the front system.
   (b) The 2nd R.Ir.Rif. will relieve the 1st R.Ir.Rif. as garrison of the Battle Zone, Subsector "F", and will take over the dugouts in the Quarries in L.27.c.
   (c) On relief the ~~1st~~ /15th R.Ir.Rif. will withdraw into Reserve and will take ov er the billets in SOMME Dugouts, HAMEL and GRAND SERAUCOURT, vacated by 2nd R.Ir.Rif.

2. All details of relief, guides, etc.will be arranged between Commanding Officers concerned.
   All details of working parties at present being supplied by 1st R.Ir.Rif.will be taken over by 2nd R.Ir.Rif.

3. The relief of the 1st R.Ir.Rif. by the 2nd R.Ir. Rifles will be arranged in such a way that there is no interruption in the work (2nd R.Ir.Rif. will commence work on Battle Zone on ~~21st~~ 22nd. Inst). O.C. 2nd R.Ir.Rif. will arrange that all ranks know their Battle Stations in Subsector "F".

4. Relieving troops will not cross the Battle Zone till 7.30 p.m.

5. All trench stores, etc. will be handed over, and duplicate receipt forwarded to Brigade H.Qrs. on 23rd Inst.

6. Relief will be reportd complete by wiring -

   1st R.Ir.Rif. "~~WIND~~" x Wind.
   2nd R.Ir.Rif. "WORK"

   15th R.Ir.Rif. will report arrival in new billets.

   Acknowledge.

C.J. Wilkins
Captain.
for Brigade Major.
107th Infantry Brigade.

Issued at 10 p.m.

Copy No. 1 to 1st R.Ir.Rif.	Copy No. 14 to 173 Bde. R.F.A.
" " 2 to 2nd R.Ir.Rif.	" " 15 to 153 -do-
" " 3 to 15th R.Ir.Rif.	" " 16 to 36th Div. "G"
" " 4 to 107th T.M.Bty.	" " 17 to 36th Div "Q"
" " 5 to Staff Capt.	" " 18 to C.R.A.
" " 6 to Bde Transport Offr.	" " 19 to C.R.E.
" " 7 to Bde Supply Offr.	" " 20 to A.D.M.S.
" " 8 to Bde Signal Officer.	" " 21 to 36th Div. M.G. Battn.
" " 9 to 121 F. Coy. R.E.	" " 22 to A.D.A.S. XVIII Corps.
" 10 to 150 -do-	" 23 to War Diary.
" " 110th F. Ambulance.	" " 24 to -do-
" 12 to 108th Brigade.	" " 25 to File.
" 13 to 109th -do-	

Appendix V

107th Brigade No. S.614.

SECRET   Copy No ..15......

War Diary

Herewith Copy No. 15 of 107th Infantry Brigade Defence Scheme.

Maps "A" and "B" have been issued already to those concerned.

Appendix on Signal Communications will follow.

Please acknowledge receipt.

Lieut.
A/Brigade Major,
107th Infantry Brigade.

Distribution -

Copy No. 1 to Brig.General Commanding.
" " 2 to 1st R.Ir.Rif.
" " 3 to 2nd R.Ir.Rif.
" " 4 to 15th R.Ir.Rif.
" " 5 to O.C. A. Coy. 36th M.G. Battalion.
" " 6 to 107th T.M. Battery.
" " 7 to Bde Signal Officer.
" " 8 to 108th Brigade.
" " 9 to 109th Brigade.
" " 10 to Right Group, R.F.A.
" " 11 to Centre Group, R.F.A.
" " 12 to C.R.A.
" " 13 to 36th Division "G"
" " 14 to D.M.G.O.
" " 15 to War Diary.
" " 16 to -do-
" " 17 to File.

SECRET

107th Infantry Brigade Defence Scheme

PART I.

FRONTAGE & BOUNDARIES.

1. The front held by the 107th Inf. Brigade extends from the junction of BORELLIER Trench with the ST QUENTIN - VENDEUIL Road (exclusive) (B.10.c.6.4) to the junction of JABAL Trench and Outpost Line (B.8.c.90.65).

2. The boundaries of the Brigade Sector are as follows -

(a) Southern Boundary

B.10.c.6.4 - B.15.a.7.0 - A.29.a.9.6 - G.4.Central.

(b) Northern Boundary.

B.8.c.90.65 - B.14.a.15.77 - A.16.c.1.0 - A.16.c.05.70.

PART II.

THE SYSTEM OF DEFENCE.

1. PRINCIPLE.

The main principle of the defence is distribution in depth. This is effected by successive zones of resistance, each organized in depth.

2. DEFINITIONS.

The organization in depth consists of successive defensive positions distributed chequerwise. In order to avoid confusion the following nomenclature will be adhered to -

STRONG POINT.

A strong point is a defended post organized for passive defence. It may or may not be wired all round. Its normal garrison is one platoon.

KEEP.

A Keep is a defended post wired all round, provided with rations, water, ammunition and bombs for 48 hours, and organized for protracted and passive defence. Its normal garrison is one platoon.

REDOUBT.

A redoubt is a glorified keep whose normal garrison is one Company.

DEFENDED LOCALITY.

A defended locality is a considerable area of ground defended by means of a number of strong points distributed chequerwise and in depth, combined with a network of wire obstacles and nests of machine guns. Its normal garrison is one Battalion.

PART II. Contd.

3. DEFENCE.

The defence of the front is organized in two zones -

(a) The Forward Zone
Sub-divided into -

(i) An Outpost Line.
(ii) A Line of Resistance.
(iii) A Counter-Attack Company.
(iv) A Line of Redoubts.

(b) The Battle Zone, organized in the same way as the Forward Zone.

4. GARRISON & DISPOSITIONS.

One Battalion will hold the Forward Zone, with two Companies in the Outpost Line and Line of Resistance, one Company for Counter-Attack, and one Company in the redoubt. The dispositions of the Battalion are shown in the attached Map "A".

One Battalion is allotted as garrison to the Battle Zone, Subsector "F", the limits and defences of the Battle Zone are shown on attached map "B".

This Battalion is billeted in the Quarries at A.27.c.

One Battalion is in Divisional Reserve and is billeted in SOMMEL DUGOUTS, HAMEL & GRAND SERAUCOURT.

5. POINTS OF TACTICAL IMPORTANCE.

The chief points in the Brigade area are -

In the forward system - The high ground South of PIEL AILLY, and on the Grid line between B.8.d. and B.14.b. and the plateau in B.15.b. & B.20.c.

In the Line of Redoubts - The neighbourhood of the railway cutting and the high ground in A.18.c.

In the Battle Zone - The high ground S.W. of CONTESCOURT.

6. The roles of the troops in different stations are as follows -

(a) The Outpost Line will keep the enemy's front line, No Man's Land and our own wire under constant observation by day and night, for this purpose they will patrol continually at night from their own post to the next behind their own wire. All outposts will be wired round and alternative positions for each outpost prepared and used at different times to prevent the possibility of surprise by the enemy. The purpose of the outposts is to give warning of any enemy attack and to disorganize it in such a way as to give time to man the line of resistance. They are responsible that the post is held against small raiding parties. In the case of an attack by large forces breaking through our line, they will fall back on their platoon in the line of resistance.

(b) The Line of Resistance will be held at all costs. Each Company will be divided into 4 strong points, garrisoned by a platoon each, less outposts. The strong points will be placed as shown on Map "A"

(c) The Counter-Attack Company's role in case of an enemy raid having effected a lodgement in our lines, is an immediate counter-attack by the two platoons nearest the point of lodgement.

But to enable them to resist in case of an enemy attack in force they will be organized in strong points, wired all round and prepared for all round defence.

6\. (c) continued.

Every Commander of Counter-Attack Platoons must have a clear idea of what he has to do and how he is going to do it. He must have a definite plan for the three following eventualities -

(a) Penetration of his front by the enemy.
(b) Penetration of his right.
(c) Penetration of his left.

The important point is that having made his decision, all ranks below him should know it and what it entails, and the route should be reconnoitred and marked and the actual movement rehearsed, at any rate by Platoon and Section Commanders, both by day and night.

(d) The Company in the Redoubt is for purposes of passive resistance. It will not be used for Counter-Attack or Reinforcement, but will hold out to the last in case of a general attack in order to give time for the Battle Zone to be manned. It will on no account retire until orders are received from higher authority.

(e) The Battle Zone is the zone which the Army Commander has chosen to give battle in case of a general enemy offensive.

7\. MACHINE GUNS.

In the Brigade Sector there are 10 Machine Guns in the Forward Zone and 6 in the Battle Zone. Their positions are shown on Maps "A" and "B" respectively.

There are 10 guns in Divisional Reserve.

The Machine Guns are so sited as to obtain the best field of fire over the sights.

8\. TRENCH MORTARS.

The Stokes Mortars are distributed as follows -

Front system.	2 mortars.
Redoubt.	2 "
Battle Zone	4 "

The location of the Stokes Mortars is also shewn in Maps "A" and "B".

9\. LIAISON.

Particular attention will be paid by all Commanders, down to Section Commanders, to the maintenance of close liaison with corresponding Units on their flanks. This liaison will be maintained by personal visits and the discussion of arrangements for mutual support and flank defence.

10\. OBSERVATION POSTS.

All Units consisting of a Company or more whether in support or reserve, and in special isolated platoons, will have their own O.Ps. from which they can obtain a good general view of the Brigade front. These O.Ps. will be manned continuously.

Brigade O.Ps. are being constructed at B.13.d.3.3 and A.18.d.05.10.

11. ALARM.

The warning in case of an attack will be sent from Brigade by wire -

"MAN BATTLE STATIONS"

On receipt of this wire all Units will "Stand To" in their Battle Positions, and report completion of the move to Brigade Headquarters.

(a) The Battalion detailed to man Subsector "F" of the Battle Zone will at once occupy the trenches and Keeps in accordance with Map "B".

Battalion H.Qrs. will move to ~~one of the Company H.Qrs or other suitable dugout in the zone~~ G.5.a.9.9, pending completion of the proper Battalion Headquarters.

(b) The Reserve Battalion will move from GRAND SERAUCOURT to the Quarries in A.27.c.

(c) The four Stokes Mortars will take up their positions in the Battle Zone.

(d) All working parties will rejoin their Units at once.

(e) The following personnel will be sent back to the Transport Lines -

33% of the Signallers, and Battalion Instructors in Lewis Gun, Musketry, Drill, Bombing and Gas.

All Visual and Fullerphone communications will be tested at once.

All Units will practise the manning of Battle Stations at least once by day and once by night during each tour

Lewis Guns ~~should~~ will be carried by platoons of the Battle Zone Battalions when they are forming working parties.

Each Battalion billeted in the Battle Zone area ~~should~~ will have one O.P. that is permanently manned.

Arrangements must be made to enable the troops to man their Battle Zone positions complete with at least 240 rounds of S.A.A., full water bottle, iron ration and S.O.S. Signals.

A scheme for the Counter-Attack Company will be drawn up at once on simple lines for the information of the whole Battalion. It should be based on the following -

The objective for the Counter-Attack Company.
The position of assembly for the Counter-Attack Company.
The method of reaching its objective.

Arrangements should be made for collecting Units at work, bathing, etc. in case of alarm.

Artillery formations must be adopted when moving to Battle positions.

R.O. Williams

Lieut.
A/Brigade Major.
107th Infantry Brigade.

1.3.18.

The following appendices are attached :-

Appendix "A"	Artillery Arrangements.		
" "B"	Battle Stragglers Post.		
" "C"	Signal Communications.	)	
" "D"	Medical Arrangements	)	Will follow.
" "E"	Location of Headquarters	)	
" "F"	Distribution of Ammunition	)	

Appendix II

ARTILLERY ARRANGEMENTS.

The Brigade front is covered by the Right Group, 36th Div. R.F.A. consisting of three 18-pdr batteries and one 4.5 Howitzer battery.

The normal S.O.S. lines on the Brigade front extend from B.10.a.50.00 - B.10.a.08.03 - B.9.b.67.06 - B.9.b.11.10 - B.9.a.42.16 - B.8.b.86.21 - B.8.b.45.24.

One 18-pdr gun covers a front of 60 yards, and six 4.5 Hows. fire on trench junctions and similar points.

In case of an attack confined to the Brigade front, this barrage will be reinforced by 3 additional batteries of 18-pdr. guns and one battery of 4.5 Howitzers.

S.O.S. SIGNAL.

This signal will normally be fired by the Officer on duty who will always carry the signal with him ready to fire at any time. Any other Officer may fire the Signal; in case there is no Officer in the trench the duty devolves upon the senior N.C.O.

The rates of fire of the Artillery in case the S.O.S. is sent up will be -

18-pdrs.	4	rounds per gun per	minute	for 5	minutes.
	3	-do-	-do-	5	"
	2	-do-	-do-	5	"
4.5 Hows.	2	-do-	-do-	10	"
	1	-do-	-do-	5	"

After 15 minutes fire will cease, unless another S.O.S. signal is made.

Further action will depend on the situation.

The Battalion in the Forward Zone will have a system of relay posts constantly manned who will report the S.O.S. Signal back as far as the Passive Resistance Company.

Artillery rocket guards are on duty night and day.

Appendix "P"

BATTLE STRAGGLERS' POSTS.

On receipt of the order "MAN BATTLE STATIONS", Divisional Stragglers Posts will be formed at G.12.a.2.6, G.3.d.1.1, A.27.c.9.4 and A.20.Central. These posts will be found by the M.M.P. and 16th R.Ir.Rif. (P).

There will be a Divisional Collecting Post at GRAND SERAUCOURT; the Reserve Battalion of each Brigade will detail 1 Officer, 1 N.C.O. and four men to report to this post for duty.

The 107th Brigade will have a Stragglers Post of 1 N.C.O. and four men, found by the Battalion Headquarters of the Battalion occupying the Forward Zone and stationed at A.24.b.2.2.

Stragglers Posts are found by the Right Brigade at B.25.b.8.8 and by the Left Brigade at A.18.b.3.4 and A.10.c.6.6

The post will have a copy of the attached orders, and the following supplies, for which the Staff Captain will arrange,

10 Spare Box Respirators.
2 Empty Grenade and S.A.A. Boxes.
25 First Field Dressings.
15 Preserved Rations, and 2 Petrol Tins of Water.
Note book and pencils, and a lamp (provided by A.P.M.)

Prisoners Cage will be at GRAND SERAUCOURT and the guard of one Officer, 2 N.C.Os and 15 men will be found by the Reserve Battalion of the 107th Brigade.

ORDERS FOR N.CO. i/c BRIGADE STRAGGLERS POST at A.24.b.2.2.

1. Stragglers are defined as -
   (a) men who leave the trenches ostensibly wounded but without Field Medical Card or other evidence of being wounded or gassed.
   (b) Superfluous assistants to wounded men.
   (c) Any other men who cannot give evidence of leaving the trenches on duty.

2. The N.C.O. i/c Post will stop all stragglers as above defined and will enter on a list the number, rank, name and regiment of all soldiers detained, and whether armed or unarmed. He will collect and pack in boxes all grenades and S.A.A. from wounded men and stragglers.

3. When a convenient number of stragglers has been collected he will forward them under escort, with the list mentioned in para.2 to the nearest Divisional Stragglers Post, or, if circumstances permit, he will send them back to their Units.

4. He will notify Brigade Headquarters if the number of stragglers appears likely to exceed the number with which his post can deal.

5. He will ensure that every man on the post knows the position of the following -
   (a) Brigade H.Qrs. at GRAND SERAUCOURT.
   (b) Nearest Divisional Stragglers Post at ESSIGNY Stn.
   (c) Nearest Field Ambulance Dressing Station at Cross Roads A.17.d.9.3.
   (d) Brigade Stragglers Post on Right flank at B.25.b.8.8.
   Brigade Stragglers Post on left flank at A.18.b.3.4.

36th Division.

B. H. Q.

107th INFANTRY BRIGADE

APRIL 1918.

Brigade Operation Orders & Defence Schemes attached

Instructions regarding War Diaries and Intelligence Summaries are contained in F. S. Regs., Part II. and the Staff Manual respectively. Title pages will be prepared in manuscript.

WAR DIARY
or
~~INTELLIGENCE SUMMARY.~~
(Erase heading not required.)

Army Form C. 2118.

April 1918 — H.Q's 107th Inf Brigade

Place	Date	Hour	Summary of Events and Information	Remarks and references to Appendices
	April			
FEUQUIÈRES	1st.		Bde in Billets in FEUQUIERE area. Bns reorganising and Lewis Gun Classes commenced	
"	2		Warning order received from DIV stating Bde would probably Entrain for the North on the 5th Inst. 21st and 23rd Entrenching Bns broken up and men of the Rifle Regiments distributed throughout the Brigade.	
"	3		Order No 225 issued re Entrainment of the Brigade see	App I
HOPITAL Fm	5th		Detrainment completed. Brigade in Billets in Hospital Fm Area	
			Order No 226 issued re Bde relieving 3rd Bde in front line. see	App II
~~ALBERTA~~	5th		Order No 227 issued re movement of troops to forward area by train see	App III
ALBERTA	7th		Relief complete 2.0 a.m.	
"	7-10th		Quiet time in line, slight T.M. and M.G activity by enemy.	
"	9th		Order No 226 issued re re-adjustment of Front. see	App. IV
"	11th		Redistribution completed 6.a.m. Reinforcements came up to battalions prior to redistribution.	
	11th		Order No 229 issued re relief by 109th Inf Bde	App V
	12th	10.5pm	1st and 2nd Rifles ordered to man Battle Zone on completion of relief. 9th Innis Fus withdrew to CANAL BANK and came under orders of B.G.C 107th Inf Bde	

T[illegible]B

2353 Wt. W2544/1454 700,000 5/15 D. D. & L. A.D.S.S./Forms/C. 2118.

Instructions regarding War Diaries and Intelligence Summaries are contained in F. S. Regs., Part II. and the Staff Manual respectively. Title Pages will be prepared in manuscript.

Army Form C. 2118.

WAR DIARY
or
~~INTELLIGENCE SUMMARY~~

(Erase heading not required.)

April 1918 — H.Qrs 107th Inf Bde

Place	Date	Hour	Summary of Events and Information	Remarks and references to Appendices
Ref Sheet 28 C.25 b.1.2	13	6am	All units reported in position. 1st and 2nd Rifles in Battle Zone right and left respectively. 15th Rifles and 9th Innis Fus in billets, 107th TMB at Hilltop Camp	
			During morning B.G.C. 107th Bde reconnoitres Reserve Line in Battle Zone and gives actual dispositions to O.C. 15th Rifles and 9th Innis Fus	
			All troops to work on their Battle Zone positions.	
	14th	9am	Order No 230 issued re Battle Zone dispositions see	App VI
			DIV Order issued ordering withdrawal of Division to the ~~outp~~ Battle Zone. 109th Bde to withdraw from present outpost line on morning of 16th inst and to take up positions in Battle Zone on right of 107th Bde	
	15th		Bde order No 231 issued on the above subject, and alterations in dispositions completed as far as they affected 107th Bde by 5pm. Work begun on new support line to the Battle Zone.	App VII
	16th		Morning passed quietly. In the afternoon the enemy was reported to be moving about in the neighbourhood of the old British outpost line and to be gradually moving forward.	
	17th		Bde order No 232 issued re relief by 4th Belgian Division of 2nd R.I. Rifles in the left subsector of the Brigade Front. Relief was completed by 1a.m 18th inst	See App VIII
			Brigade Defence Scheme issued	App IX
				T.M.B.

2449 Wt. W14957/M90 750,000 1/16 J.B.C. & A. Forms/C.2118/12.

Army Form C. 2118

Instructions regarding War Diaries and Intelligence Summaries are contained in F. S. Regs., Part II. and the Staff Manual respectively. Title Pages will be prepared in manuscript.

WAR DIARY
or
~~INTELLIGENCE SUMMARY~~
(Erase heading not required.)

April, 1918. Headquarters, 107th Infantry Brigade.

Place	Date	Hour	Summary of Events and Information	Remarks and references to Appendices
Ref. Sheet 28. C.25.b.1.2.	18th	11.30 a.m.	1st R. Ir. Rif. captured two enemy runners belonging to 458th Infantry Regt. On night 18th/19th patrol of 1st R. Ir. Rif. lost 3 O.R. killed and 6 wounded at C.12.d.35.40.	
(GLOUCESTER TERRACE, CANAL BANK EAST).	19th	—	15th R. Ir. Rif. relieved 1st R. Ir. Rif. in the line. Relief complete, 2.15 a.m., 20th April.	App. X
		10.15 p.m.	Patrol of 1st R. Ir. Rif. captured three prisoners (one wounded) of 458th Inf. Regt. about C.12.a.65.55.	
	20th		2nd R. Ir. Rif. relieved 1st Royal Irish Rifles in Reserve System, 1st R. Ir. Rif. withdrawing to SIEGE CAMP.	App. XI
C.25.d.2.5. (CANAL BANK WEST).	21st		Brigade Headquarters moved to CANAL BANK WEST. New Defence Scheme issued.	App. XII
	22nd		2nd R.I. Rifles relieved 15th RIR in the line, 15th withdrawing to Bde support	App XIII
"	23rd		1st R.I. Rifles relieved 15th R.I. Rifles in the Reserve Line at HILL TOP, 15th R.I.R withdrawing to SIEGE CAMP	App XIV
"	24th		The STEENBEEK was made into the line of Resistance.	App XV
"	25th		Quiet day.	
"	26/27		The line was withdrawn from the STEENBEEK to the line OBLONG FARM CALIBAN RESERVE. The 1st R.I. Rifles relieved the 2nd R.I. Rifles in the above line at 1 am the 2nd R.I. Rifles commenced withdrawing through the 1st R.I. Rifles. 15th R.I. Rifles moved from SIEGE CAMP and occupied the CANAL Defences. 2nd R.I. Rifles withdrew to the BRIELEN Line in the	Tau B.

1875 Wt. W593/826 1,000,000 4/15 J.B.C. & A. A.D.S.S./Forms/C. 2118.

Army Form C. 2118.

Instructions regarding War Diaries and Intelligence Summaries are contained in F. S. Regs., Part II. and the Staff Manual respectively. Title pages will be prepared in manuscript.

WAR DIARY
or
~~INTELLIGENCE~~ SUMMARY.
(Erase heading not required.)

April 1918 — HQ's 107th Inf Bde

Place	Date	Hour	Summary of Events and Information	Remarks and references to Appendices
			Vicinity of WAGRAM FARM. By 6 a.m all moves were complete. The 1st R.I.R established a post in CANOPUS Trench at C.17.A.40.55.	App XVI
			The enemy must have discovered our withdrawal early as at 11 a.m he was reported by the BELGIANS to be in the vicinity of GOLIET FARM.	
CANAL BANK West.	28/30th		These days all passed quietly.	

T. O. M. Buchan Capt
Brigade Major
107th Inf Bde.

(A7092). Wt. W12839/M1293. 750,000. 1/17. D. D. & L., Ltd. Forms/C.2118/14.

App I

S E C R E T.

Copy No. 25.

Ref. Map Sheets ABBEVILLE 1/100,000. HAZEBROUCK, 5A 1/100,000.

107TH INFANTRY BRIGADE ORDER, No.225.

3rd April, 1918.

1. The 107th Infantry Brigade Group (composed as under) will by strategical train to the II Corps Area on the 3rd and 4th April.

2. The Entraining Station will be FRESSENVILLE - FEUQUIERES and the Detraining Station, PROVEN.

3. Units will entrain as follows :-

Train No.	Time of Departure.	Units Entraining.
1	15 hours 3/4/18.	1st R.Ir.Fus and Hdqrs.21st Entrenching Battn.
2	18 hours 3/4/18.	107th Bde. Hqrs. Sig. Sect. 107th T.M.B'y. "A" Coy, 36th Div. M.G. Battn.
3	21 hours 3/4/18	2nd R.Ir.Fus. Hqrs. 23rd Entrenching Battn.
4	24 hours 3/4/18	15th R. Irish Rifles.
5	3 hours 4/4/18	121 Fld. Coy.R.E. No.2 Coy. 36th Div.Train.
6	6 hours 4/4/18	110th Fld. Amb. Mob.Vet.Sec.
7	9 hours 4/4/18	Div.Hqrs. No.1 Sec.Div.Sig. Coy. Hqrs.36th Div.M.G. Bn. Employment Coy.Salvage Coy.
8	12 hours 4/4/18	½ S.A.A. Sec. D.A.C. Loading Party, 15th R.I.R.

4. Transport and Supply Wagons will entrain with their respective Units; Supply Wagons will entrain full.

5. Personnel will arrive one hour before and Transport 3 hours before departure of their respective trains.

6. (a) 15th R. Irish Rifles will provide a loading party of 2 Officers and 150 O.R. This party will report at FEUQUIERES Station at 12 noon on 3/4/18 and will proceed by the last train on the 4th inst. They should bring Dixies and Rations for the 5th inst.
(b) 1st R. Irish Rifles will provide a similar unloading party to proceed by the first train to PROVEN.

7. Rations will be taken on the train for consumption the day after entraining as far as it is practicable.

8. The duration of the journey will be approximately 10 hours.

9. Captain COEY will be in charge of the entrainment. Each unit will send one Officer to report to him three hours before the time of departure of their trains.

10. Routes to entraining station as convenient.

11. Instructions with regard to billeting areas will be issued on arrival of trains at PROVEN.

12. Brigade Headquarters will close at [illegible] at 5 p.m. on 3.4.18.

ACKNOWLEDGE.

T. M. Bucknall[illegible]

Captain.

Brigade Major, 107th Inf. Brigade.

Issued at 7 a.m.

Copy No. 1 to Divl. Genl. Comdg.
" " 2 to 1st R. Ir. Rifles.
" " 3 to 2nd R. Ir. Rifles.
" " 4 to 15th R. Ir. Rifles.
" " 5 to 107th T. M. Btry.
" " 6 to 21st Entrenching Bn.
" " 7 to 23rd Entrenching Bn.
" " 8 to 36th Division "G".
" " 9 to 36th Division "Q".
" " 10 to 107th Bde. Sig. Sctn.
" " 11 to 107th Bde. Trans. Off.
" " 12 to 121 Field Coy., R.E.
" " 13 to No.2 Compy. 36th Div. Tr.
" " 14 to 110th Field Ambulance.
" " 15 to 48th Mobile Vet. Sect.
" " 16 to Campt Comdt. 36th Divn.
" " 17 to No.1 S. c. 36th Div. Sig. Coy.
" " 18 to 36th Div. Machine G. Battn.
" " 19 to Divl. Employment Company.
" " 20 to Divl. Salvage Company.
" " 21 to 36th D. [illegible] C.
" " 22 to Captain [illegible].
" " 23 to War Diary.
" " 24 to War Diary.
" " 25 to File.

App II

Addendum No.1 to 107th Inf. Brigade Order No. 226.

-------------------;-;-;-;-;-;-;-;-----------------

5th April, 1918.

1. On completion of relief the boundaries of the Brigade Area will be as follows :-

RIGHT BOUNDARY.

V.28.a.9.2 (approx.) - INCH HOUSES (D.3.b.0.9) exclusive - WELLINGTON (D.2.b.) inclusive - VALE HOUSE (D.8.a.0.8) exclusive - D.7 Central - C.12.d.8.0 - C.12.d.4.0 - BORDER HOUSE (C.18.b.0.3) inclusive - C.18.a.0.[illegible] - C.18.c.0.7 - VANHEULE FARM inclusive - C.17.c.0.3 - C.23.a.5.3 -.

LEFT BOUNDARY.

V.14 Central - V.19.a.1.0 - V.19.c.0.8 - DOG HOUSE exclusive - U.29.d.2.8 - U.29.d.1.0 - C.5.c.4.7 - C.10.b.0.2.

2. O.C., Battalions will forward as soon as possible after relief a Map showing their exact dispositions by Companies and Platoons.

3. Shrapnel Helmets must always be worn by all Ranks East of the CANAL.

4. The Western Boundaries of the Gas Zones are as follows :-

Alert Zone. WIELTJE - BOESINGHE - LIZERNE (all inclusive).

Ready Zone. DICKEBUSH - BRIELEN - ELVERDINGHE - WOESTEN (all inclusive).

T. M. Burke

Captain,
Brigade Major, 107th Infantry Brigade.

Issued to :-

Copy No. 1 to 1st R. Ir. Rif.
" No. 2 to 2nd -do-
" No. 3 to 15th -do-
" No. 4 to 9th R.Innis. F.
" No. 5 to 107th T.M. Bty.
" No.16 to 36th Division "G".
" No. 7 to 36th Division "Q".
" No. 8 to 1st Division "G".
" No. 9 to 3rd Inf. Brigade.
" No.10 to Bde.Transport Off.
" No.11 to Bde. Signal Offr.
" No.12 to War Diary.
" No.13 to War Diary.
" No.14 to File.

126

[illegible] INFANTRY BRIGADE ORDER NO. [illegible].

Ref. Sheet 28 NE. and NW. COPY NO:- 2

I/20000.

I. 107th. Inf. Bde. and 9th. Inniskilling Fusiliers will relieve 3rd. Inf. Brigade in the line on the night 6/7th. April in accordance with attached table "A".

2. (a) On completion of relief 107th. Inf. Brigade will have three Battalions in the front line and 9th Inniskilling Fusiliers in support.

(b) 3 Battalions in the front line will be disposed as follows:-

Right Battn. Ist. R. I. R. H. Qrs. HUBNER	From right Brigade boundary to left boundary of present centre company right Battn. (including WINCHESTER and WELLINGTON)
Centre Battn, 15th. R. I. R. H. Qrs. HUBNER	From left boundary of present centre C Right Battn. to left boundary right Company left Battn. (excluding Platoon in POELCAPPELLE) including BAV. ROISE.
Left Battn. 2nd. R. I. R. H. Qrs. NORFOLK HOUSE.	From left boundary R. Company left Battn. (including Platoon in POELCAPPELLE attached from right Company) to new left Brigade boundary including DELTA and ROSE.

3. Units will move up by rail; instructions for this move will be issued later.

4. Battalions of 3rd. Brigade will be responsible for guiding incoming units from railhead. Detailed arrangements of these guides will be made between C.O's concerned.

5. Units of 3rd. Brigade are leaving one Officer per Company in the line until standto on the morning of April 7th.

6. Units of 107th. Inf. Brigade will come under command of G.O.C. 3rd. Inf. Brigade on reaching Railhead and until completion of reliefs.

7. All trench stores, Aeroplane Photographs, I/10000 Maps, Defence schemes Etc., will be taken over.

8. O.C. 107th. T.M. Bty., will take over all Stokes Mortar Positions.

9. All Lewis Gun AA positions will be taken over and reciepts given for mountings. Units will forward a list showing locations of positions to Brigade Headquarters.

10. Completion of relief will be reported to 3rd Brigade H.Qrs. by the following code :-

I st. R. I. R. 10 Vacancies.
2nd. R. I. R. 15 Vacancies.
15th R. I. R. 20 Vcancies.
9th. Inns. Fus. 30 Vacancies.

II. G.O.C. 107th. Inf. Brigade will assume command of the line on completion of reliefs in the line at which hour Bde. H.Qrs. will open at [illegible].

[signature]

CAPTAIN.

Brigade Major 107th. Inf. Bde.

Issued at 12 noon.

Copy No. 1 to Brig.-General Commdg.
" No. 2 to Staff Captain.
" No. 3 to 1st R. Irish Rifles.
" No. 4 to 2nd R. Irish Rifles.
" No. 5 to 15th R. Irish Rifles.
" No. 6 to 107th [illegible]
" No. 7 to 107th Bde. Trans. O.C.
" No. 8 to 107th Bde. Signal O.C.
" No. 9 to 107th Bde. Intell. O.
" No. 10 to No. 2 Coy. 36th Div. [illegible]
" No. 11 to 110th Field Ambulance.
" No. 12 to 121 Field Coy. R.E.
" No. 13 to 3rd Inf. Brigade.
" No. 14 to 2nd Infantry Brigade.
" No. 15 to 36th Division "G".
" No. 16 to 36th Division "Q".
" No. 17 to 1st Division "G". 1st Div. G
" No. 18 to [illegible]
" No. 19 to 9th R. Irish Fusiliers.
" No. 20 to [illegible]
" No. 21 to C. R. A., 36th Divn.
" No. 22 to C. R. E., 36th Divn.
" No. 23 to A.D.M.S., 36th Divn.
" No. 24 to A. P. M., 36th Divn.
" No. 25 to 36th Divn. [illegible]

~~[illegible]~~
1st Div. Q.
109 Bde

TABLE "[illegible]".

Unit.	System.	Location.	Strength.	Relieving.
1st R.I.R.	Outpost System.	SOURD FARM.	1 Platoon.	
		BANFF	1 "	
		LEMIER	2 Platoons.	
		BERKS HOUSES	2 "	
	Main System.	VACHER & VACHER A	2 "	2nd Welch Regt.
		BURNS HOUSE	2 "	
	Rear System	WELLINGTON	1 Platoon.	
		WINCHESTER	2 Platoons.	1st S. W. B.
	Local Reserves	VACHER	1 Platoon.	
		BURNS HOUSE	1 "	2nd Welch Regt.
		GARELOCH	1 "	
5th R.I.R.	Outpost System.	SHAFT	1 "	
		ELLIOTS	2 Platoons.	2nd Welch Regt.
		TRACAS	2 Platoons.	
	Main System	OXFORD HOUSE	3 Platoons.	2nd Welch Regt.
		TEMPLIER	2 "	
		CROMBIE FARM	2 "	
		[illegible]	2 "	1st Glouc. R.
	Rear System	[illegible]	2 "	1st S. W. B.
	Local Reserve.	OXFORD HOUSE	1 Platoon	1st Glouc. R.
2nd R.I.R.	Outpost System.	[illegible]	2 Platoons	
		[illegible]	2 "	
		[illegible]	2 "	
	Main System.	[illegible]	2 "	1st Glouc. R.
		[illegible]	1 Platoon.	
		REAR DEFENCES [illegible]	3 Platoons.	
	Rear System	DELTA & ROAD	2 Platoons.	1st S. W. B.
	Local Reserves.	D.L.R. Shelters	2 Platoons.	1st Glouc. Regt.
9th R.Ir.F.	Support System Forward Zone.	All Posts.	2 Companies	1st S. W. B.
	Local Reserve	Coy. in [illegible] TRENCH.	2 Companies.	

SECRET.

app III

Copy No. ...

107TH INFANTRY BRIGADE ORDER NO.227.

5th April, 1918.

1. The 107th Infantry Brigade will move to the forward area by Train on the 6th instant as shewn on attached Table "A".

2. Troops will arrive at Entraining Station 30 minutes before departure of Trains.

3. One Officer per Unit will report at the Entraining Station 1 hour before the departure of each Train.

4. Guides from the 3rd Inf. Brigade will meet Units at the Detraining Station on arrival.

5. (a) Each Train on the narrow gauge consists of eleven trucks, each holding 30 men.
(b) In order to save time Troops must be told off into parties of 30 before reaching the Entraining Station.

Acknowledge.

T. [signature]

Captain.
Brigade Major, 107th Infantry Brigade.

Issued at 8 p.m.

Copy No. 1 to Brig-Genl. Commg.
" No. 2 to Staff Captain.
" No. 3 to 1st R. Ir. Rifles.
" No. 4 to 2nd R. Ir. Rifles.
" No. 5 to 15th R.Ir. Rifles.
" No. 6 to 107th T. M.Battery.
" No. 7 to Bde. Transport Off.
" No. 8 to Bde. Signal Officer.
" No. 9 to Bde. Intell.Officer.
" No.10 to No.2 Coy. 36th Div.Tr.
" No.11 to 110th Field Ambl.
" No.12 to 121 Field Comp'y. R.E.
" No.13 3rd Infantry Brigade.
" No.14 to 2nd Infantry Brigade.
" No.15 to 36th Division "G".
" No.16 to 36th Division "Q".
" No.17 to 1st Division "G".
" No.18 to Right Group, R.F.A.
" No.19 to 9th R. Innis. Fusl.
" No.20 to Right Railway Coy.
" No.21 to C.R.A., 36th Division.
" No.22 to C.R.E., 36th Division.
" No.23 to A.D.M.S., 36th Division.
" No.24 to A. P. M., 36th Division.
" No.25 to 36th Div. M. G. Battn.
" No.26 to 1st Division "Q".
" No.27 to 109th Inf. Brigade.

Copy No.28 to War Diary.
" No.29 to " "
" No.30 to File.

TABLE "A".

Train No.	Unit.	Entraining Station.	Detraining Station.	Depart.	Arrive.	Trucks allotted,
1.	1st R. Ir. Rif.	ELVERDINGHE. Marshalling Yard, B.15.b.0.5.	BROOKLYN. C.5.c.3.4.	6-30 p.m.	8-15 p.m.	11.
2.	1st R. Ir. Rif.	-do-	-do-	7-0 p.m.	8-45 p.m.	3.
	15th R.Ir. Rif.	-do-	-do-	-do-	-do-	8.
3.	15th R.Ir. Rif.	-do-	-do-	7-30 p.m.	9-15 p.m.	11.
4.	2nd R. Ir. Rif.	-do-	-do-	8-0 p.m.	9-45 p.m.	11.
5.	2nd R. Ir. Rif.	-do-	-do-	8-30 p.m.	10-15 p.m.	11.
1A	9th R.Ir. Fus.	DIRTY BUCKET CORNER. B.19.c.4.6.	WIELTJE. C.28.b.5.8.	6-0 p.m.	8-0 p.m.	450 men.
	107th Bde.H.Qrs.	-do-	-do-	-do-	-do-	70 men.
	107th T.M. Bty.	-do-	-do-	-do-	-do-	30 men.

SECRET. Aff. IV Copy No. 17.

107TH INFANTRY BRIGADE ORDER NO. 226.

Reference Sheets
28 N.W. and N.E.
1 - 20,000.

9:4:18

1. The 107th Infantry Brigade Front will be re-adjusted on the night of April XX 10/11 to a two Battalion front.

2. The Boundary between the Right and Left Sub-Sectors willl be the LEKKERBOTERBEEK.

3. (a) The 1st Bn. Royal Irish Rifles will relieve the 15th Bn. Royal Irish Rifles in the positions now held by them South of the LEKKERBOTERBEEK, and

   (b) The 2nd Bn. Royal Irish Rifles will relieve the 15th Bn. Royal Irish Rifles in all positions now held by them North of the LEKKERBOTERBEEK.

4. On relief by the 1st and 2nd Bns. Royal Irish Rifles, the 15th Bn. Royal Irish Rifles will relieve the 9th Royal Inniskilling Fusiliers in the positions now held by them.

5. On completion of the above reliefs the dispositions of Battns. of the 107th Infantry Brigade will be as laid down in the 'Warning Order' issued to units on the 8th inst.

6. The 9th Royal Inniskilling Fusiliers will withdraw after relief by the 15th Bn. Royal Irish Rifles to camp near CANAL, and come under the orders of the G.O.C., 109th Infantry Brigade.

7. All details of the above reliefs will be arranged between the Officers Commanding Units concerned.

8. Completion of reliefs will be reported to Brigade Headquarters by the code sentence -

   " B.M.L 103 Noted."

   Acknowledge by wire.

NOTE:- No movement of troops is to take place before 7.45 p.m.

T.Ohr. Buchanan
Captain,
Brigade Major,
107th Infy. Brigade.

Copies to:-

No.1 - 1st R.Ir.Rif.	No. 10 - 39th Bde.R.F.A.
2 - 2nd R.Ir.Rif.	11 - 36th M.G.Btn.
3 - 15th R.Ir.Rif.	12 - C.R.A., 1st Divn.
4 - 9th R.Innis.Fus.	13 - 36th Divn. "G".
5 - 107th T.M.Batty.	14 - " " "Q".
6 - 108th Brigade.	15 - 150 Coy. R.E.
7 - 109th Brigade.	16 - Bde. Sig. Offr.
8 - 88th Brigade.	17 - War Diary.
9 - 89th Brigade.	18 - [illegible] Diary.

19 - [illegible]

Issued at 7 p.m.

Secret.

App V

Copy No........

107TH INFANTRY BRIGADE ORDER NO.229.

Reference Sheets
B.3 - 1/10,000.
28 N.W. & N.E. 1/20,000.

---

1. The 107th Infantry Brigade will be relieved in the line on the night of April 12/13 by the 109th Infantry Bde. in accordance with the attached Table 'A'.

2. The 1st and 2nd Royal Inniskilling Fusiliers will send up advanced parties on the 11th inst. as laid down in 107th Brigade Warning Order, S.708, dated 11.4.1918.

These advanced parties, together with one Guide per Platoon from the 1st and 2nd Royal Irish Rifles, will meet their relieving units as shown in Table 'A'.

3. The 1st and 2nd Royal Irish Rifles will leave one Officer per Company and one N.C.O. per platoon in the line until "Stand-to" on the 13th inst.

4. Trains will be available to transport units out of the line as follows:-

1st R.Ir.Rifles.	1 Train.	2.0 a.m.
	1 Train.	2.30 a.m.
2nd R.Ir.Rifles.	1 Train.	3.0 a.m.

The 15th Royal Irish Rifles and the two Companies of the ~~1st~~ 2 Royal Irish Rifles going to BOSCH CASTLE and KEMPTON PARK will proceed by road.

Troops will entrain at BOSTON (C.17.b.60.70) and detrain at EXETER (C.25.b.50.80).

5. All Aeroplane Photographs, Defence Schemes, Defence Orders, trench stores, S.A.A., Bombs, S.O.S.Signals, Reserve Rations and water in the line will be handed over and receipts obtained.

6. Transport Lines of Units will remain unchanged.

7. Completion of reliefs will be reported to Brigade Hqrs. by the following code sentences:-

1st R.Ir.Rif.	-	3 Vacancies.
2nd R.Ir.Rif.	-	6 Vacancies.
15th R.Ir.Rif.	-	9 Vacancies.

Arrival in new camps will also be reported.

8. Brigade Headquarters will close at ALBERTA BUND on completion of reliefs and will open at C.25.b.1.2. at the same hour.

Acknowledge.

T. M. Buchan

Captain,
Brigade Major,
107th Infantry Brigade.

11.4.1918.

Issued at 7.0 p.m.

Table 'A'.

TABLE 'A' TO ACCOMPANY 107TH INFANTRY BRIGADE ORDER NO.229.

UNIT.	RELIEVED BY	GUIDES MEET INCOMING UNIT.	TIME.	MOVES TO	RELIEVING.	REMARKS.
1. 1st Bn. R.Ir.Rif.	2nd Bn. Royal Innis. Fus.	BROOKLYN Railhead. (C.6.c.30.20.	7.45 p.m.	CANAL BANK. C.25.d.3.7.	2nd Bn. Royal Innis. Fusiliers.	One Officer to be in charge of Battalion Guides.
2. 2nd Bn. R.Ir.Rif.	1st Bn.Royal Innis. Fus.	Hqrs. & 2 Coys. BROOKLYN Railhead. 2 Coys. Junc. GLOSTER AV. & POELCAPPELLE Rd. U.30.d.60.70.	7.45 p.m. 8.15 p.m.	2 Coys.& H.Q. CANAL BANK, C.25.a.6.7. 1 Coy. Kempton Pk. C.15.b.7.7. 1 Coy. BOSCH CASTLE,C.10.d.0.7.	1st Bn. Royal Innis. Fusiliers.	-do-
3.15th Bn. R.Ir.Rif.	9th Bn.Royal Innis.Fus.	To be arranged between C.Os. concerned.		C.19.d.9.7.	9th R.Innis.Fus.	
4. 107th T. M.Batty.	109th T.M.B.	-do-	-do-	Remain HILL TOP CAMP.		Guns to be handed over in the Line.

Copies to:-

No.1 - 1st Bn.R.Ir.Fus.
2 - 2nd " " "
3 - 15th " " "
4 - T.M.Batty.
5 - 107th Bde.Sig.Off.
6 - Staff Captain:
7 - 109th Brigade.
8 - 89th Brigade.
9 - 123rd Brigade.
10 - 39th Bde.,R.F.A.
11 - 36th M.G.Battn.

No. 12 - C.R.A.,1st Divn.
13 - C.R.E.,36th Divn.
14 - A.D.M.S.
15 - D.A.D.O.S.
16 - A.P.M.
17 - 150 Coy.R.E.
18 - 36th Div. "G".
19 - 36th Div. "Q".
20 - C.L.R.O.
21 - War Diary.
22 - War Diary.

No.23 - FILE.

----------:o0o:----------

SECRET.

1st Bn. Royal Irish Rifles.
2nd Bn. Royal Irish Rifles.
15th Bn. Royal Irish Rifles.
107th Trench Mortar Battery.
109th Infantry Brigade.
36th Division, 'G'.

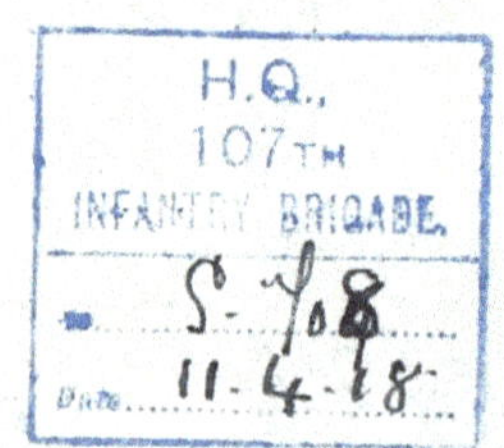

WARNING ORDER.

1. The 109th Infantry Brigade will relieve the 107th Infantry Brigade in the line on the night 12/13th April, 1918.

2. 2nd R.Innis.Fus. will relieve 1st R.Ir.Rif.
1st " " " " " 2nd " " "
9th " " " " " 15th " "

3. Advance parties of one Officer per Company and one N.C.O. per Platoon, Battalion Intelligence Officer and Battalion Signal Officer, from the 109th Infantry Brigade will come up to the Line to-night.

Guides will meet these parties and conduct them to Battalion Headquarters as follows:-

Right Sub-Sector - Under arrangements of C.Os.concerned.
Left Sub-Sector - At REGINA CROSS Roads, C.11.a.50.80. at 4.0 p.m.

4. 9th Bn. Royal Inniskilling Fusiliers will not send up advance parties to-night.

5. Battalions will be responsible for guiding incoming Units into the line, providing guides on a scale of 1 per Platoon and 1 for Battalion Headquarters.

Time and place where these guides will meet incoming Units will be notified in orders.

6. Orders will be issued this afternoon.

Acknowledge.

Captain,
Brigade Major,
107th Infantry Brigade.

11.4.1918.

SECRET. App VI

107TH INFANTRY BRIGADE ORDER
NO. 230.

Ref. Map-
ST. JULIEN, 1/10,000.

1. Owing to the situation in the South, the 41st, 36th, and 30th Divisions are hodling the BATTLE ZONE as the main line of resistance and the present front line as an outpost line.

2. The 1st and 2nd Bns. Royal Inniskilling Fusiliers, 109th Infantry Brigade, are holding the Outpost Line.

The 107th Infy. Brigade, with 9th Bn. R. Innis. Fus. and 109th Trench Mortar Battery attached, is holding the BATTLE ZONE? and is disposed as follows:-

1st Bn. R. Ir. Rif. - Right Sub-Sector, Hqrs. C.16.d.10.30.
2nd Bn. R. Ir. Rif. - Left Sub-Sector, Hqrs. BOCHCASTLE.
9th R? Innis. Fus. - CANAL BANK EAST (C.25.d.3.7.) detailed for defence of Right Sector of Reserve Line of BATTLE ZONE.
15th R. Ir. Rif. - JOFFRE CAMP (C.19.d.9.7.) detailed for defence of Left Sub-Sector of Reserve Line of BATTLE ZONE.

3. (a) 9th R. Innis. Fus. and 15th R. Ir. Rif. must be prepared to man the Reserve Line of the BATTLE ZONE ta short notice. All routes of approach must be thoroughly reconnoitred.

(b) The line runs approximately as follows:-
KEMPTON PARK - CANADIAN CAMP - FORWARD COTTAGES - C.22.a.03.00 C.28.a.05.56.
The Boundary between the two Sub-Sectors will be FORWARD COTTAGES - LA BELLE ALLIANCE - BURNT FME. - BRIDGE NO.4.

A map showing the dispositions of Coys is attacked (15th R. Ir. Rif. and 9th R. Innis. Fus. only).

Battalion Headquarters of 15th R. Ir. Rif. and 9th R. Innis. Fus. will be at LA BELLE ALLIANCE.

4. Coy. Hqrs. and Battn Hqrs. of the two Battalions occupying the BATTLE ZONE must establish O.Ps. which will be manned night and day.

5. Troops occupying the BATTLE ZONE will work on their defences improving them and diggingnnew defences where they are required. Attention must be paid to wiring.

6. The Reserve Line of the BATTLE ZONE is not dug. There is cover in old trenches and shell craters, old gun positions etc. which must be utilised. Work on these positions must be commenced at once by the 15th R. Ir. Rif. and the 9th R. Innis. Fus.

7. 1st and 2nd Bns. R. Ir. Rif. must establish liaison with the Battalions on their flanks.

8. Brigade Headquarters are at C.25.b,10.30.

Acknowledge.

T.B.M. Baker

Captain,
Brigade Major,
107th Infy. Brigade.

14.4.1918.

Issued at 9.0 a.m.

Copies to:-

No.1 - 1st R.Ir.Rif.
2 - 2nd R.Ir.Rif.
3 - 15th R.Ir.Rif.
4 - 107th T.M.B.
5 - 9th R.Innis.Fus.
6 - 109th Brigade.

No.7 - 122nd Brigade.
8 - Support Bde., 30th Div.
9 - 36th Div. 'G'.
10 - D.C.R.A., 1st Div.
11 - War Diary.
12 - War Diary.

No.13 - FILE.

SECRET.

Appendix VII

107TH INFANTRY BRIGADE

NO. 231.

Ref. Map:-
SH.28.N.W.2., 1/10,000.

1. The 41st, 36th and 30th Divisions are withdrawing to the BATTLE ZONE, with outposts on the left bank of the STEENBEEK, on the night of April 15/16th, 1918.

2. The 36th Division is extending its front and will hold the BATTLE ZONE with 109th Brigade on the right and 107th Bde. on the left.

3. (a) The Right Boundary of the 107th Brigade ~~[illegible]~~ will be:-

Junction of CANOPUS TRENCH and STEENBEEK at C.18.c.05.90. - V[illegible] FARM (exclusive) - CHEDDAR FARM (exclusive) - C.22.b.60.50. - CROSS ROADS C.22.c.60.75. - BUFFS ROAD to [illegible] Bridge No.4 (inclusive).

(b) The Northern Boundary of the Brigade will be FERDINAND FARM (inclusive) - thence along present Boundary to CANAL BRIDGE No.6 a (exclusive).

4. (a) The 1st and 2nd Bns. R.Ir.Rifles will continue to hold the Outpost Line on the STEENBEEK as at present.

(b) The Support Line of the BATTLE ZONE will be re-adjusted as follows:-

Trench from C.9.d.90.70 to C.10.c.25.75 - HURST PARK - BOCHCASTEL - OBLONG FM. - R of ROAD JUNCTION - CALIBAN RESERVE at C.16.d.45.00. to C.22.b.60.50.

(c) The Boundary between the Right and Left Sub-sectors will be STEENBEEK at C.11.b.20.80. - ALBERTA TRACK at C.11.c.00.00. - thence via ALBERTA TRACK to C.16.b.00.50. - OBLONG FARM (to left Sub-Sector) - C.16.c.60.50. - C.16.c.10.25.

5. (a) The 15th R.Ir.Rifles will remain at J[illegible] CAMP in Bde. Reserve ready to man the Reserve Line.

(b) The Reserve Line runs as formerly, but now extends to Cross Roads, C.22.c.60.75. The 15th R.Ir.Rif. will be prepared to hold this line with three Companies in front and one in support.

6. Work on constructing the Reserve and Support Line and on wiring must be commenced at once and pushed forward as quickly as possible.

7. (a) On the night 15/16th inst., the 1st and 2nd R.Innis.Fus., at present holding the original outpost line will withdraw through the front held by the 107th Brigade.

(b) The withdrawal will commence about 2.0 a.m. but the exact hour at which the outposts will be vacated will be notified later.

8. The 1st and 2nd R.Ir.Rifles will place posts on all tracks and roads crossing the STEENBEEK in their areas.
Each of these posts will be under the charge of an officer.
When the last man of the 109th Brigade has passed through our outpost line he will be followed by an officer who will report that everybody has passed through. From that time onwards all parties approaching our posts must be examined with the greatest precautions.

9. The Bridges over the STEENBEEK will be demolished by the R.E. after all men have passed over.

10. Before dawn on the 16th inst. the 1st and 2nd R.Ir.Rifles will send out patrols to the line GENOA - SLAB - STROOMBEEK - PHEASANT TRENCH locality. These patrols will take up positions from which they can observe the ground to their front. They will report at once any enemy movements and will take advantage of any opportunities of sniping the enemy.

They will only withdraw if the enemy appears in strength.

The 1st R.Ir.Rifles patrols will go to GENOA and SLAB, and the patrols of the 2nd R.Ir.Rifles to STROOMBEEK and PHEASANT.

Each patrol should consist of 1 Officer and 10 men.

11. The camouflage screening the roads from BOCHCASTEL to STEENBEEK and from VANHEULE FARM to STEENBEEK will be cut down by the 2nd and 1st Bns. R.Ir.Rifles respectively after dark to-night.

13. Brigade Headquarters will remain at C.25.b.20.10.

T. M. Buchan

Captain,
Brigade Major,
107th Infantry Brigade.

15.4.1918.

Copies to:-

No.1 - 1st R.Ir.Rif. ✓
2 - 2nd R.Ir.Rif. ✓
3 - 15th R.Ir.Rif. ✓
4 - 107th T.M.B. ✓
5 - 109th Bde. ✓
No.6 - 123rd Bde.
7 - 90th Bde.
8 - 36th Div. "G".
9 - 36th Div. "Q".
10 - 39th Bde. R.F.A.
No.11 - FILE.

Issued at 4.30 p.m.

SECRET. Appendix VIII

Copy No. 9...

107TH INFANTRY BRIGADE ORDER

No. 232.

Ref. Map.-
ST. JULIEN, 1/10,000.

1. The Fourth Belgian Division will relieve the 2nd Bn. Royal Irish Rifles in the Left Sub-Sector of the 107th Brigade Front on the night of the 17/18th inst.

2. The 1st and ~~2nd~~ 15th Bns. Royal Irish Rifles will remain in their present positions,

3. On completion of relief the Northern Boundary of the 107th Infantry Brigade Sector will be the present inter-Battalion Boundary, thence to FOCH FARM (inclusive) - JOFFRE CAMP (exclusive) then N.W. to CANAL at Bridge No.6a.

4. On completion of relief the 2nd Royal Irish Rifles will withdraw into the dug-outs in CANAL BANK EAST. Accomodation will be pointed out to Battalion Quartermaster, who has been instructed accordingly) by the Staff Captain to-morrow morning.

5. An Advance Party of two Machine gun Officers and twelve Infantry Officers from the Fourth Belgian Division will report at Brigade Headquarters at 9.0 a.m. 17th inst.

Officer Commanding, 2nd Bn. Royal Irish Rifles, will send one Officer and two Other Ranks to report at Brigade Headquarters at same hour to conduct the above party to Battalion Headquarters to reconnoitre the line.

6. The machine guns of the 36th Bn. M.G.C., occupying positions in the present Left Sub-Sector of the 107th Infantry Brigade will be relieved by ~~xx~~ equivalent guns of the Fourth Belgian Division.

7. Command of the Left Sub-Sector, 107th Infantry Brigade Front will pass to the Fourth Belgian Division at 8.0 a.m. on the 18th inst.

Acknowledge.

Captain,
Brigade Major,
107th Infy. Brigade.

17.4.1918.

Issued at 12.30 a.m.

Copies to.-

No.1 - 1st R.Ir.Rif.
2 - 2nd R.Ir.Rif.
3 - 15th R.Ir.Rif.
4 - 107th T.M.B.
No.5.- 36th Divn."G".
6 - 109th Infy.Bde.
7 - 90th Brigade.
8 - 4th Belgian Divn.
No.9 - FILE.

Appendix VIII

SECRET. COPY NO..........

ADDENDUM NO.2 TO 107TH INFY.BDE. ORDER No.232.

The following Addendum should be substituted for Addendum No.1 issued to Brigade Units to-day:-

1. (a) Two Companies of the 2nd Bn.18th Belgian Infantry Rgt., and two Companies of the 3rd Battalion will relieve the 2nd Bn. R.Ir.Rif. and two Coys. of the 15th Bn.R.Ir.Rif. North of new Brigade Boundary (see para.5) in the left Sub-Sector of the 107th Infy.Bde. Front on the night of 17/18th April, 1918.

(b) On completion of relief the disposition of the Belgians in the present left Sub-Sector will be:-

One Company, 2nd Battn. - Holding Outpost Line.
One Company, 2nd Battn. - Holding Support System.
Two Companies, 3rd Battn.- in CIVILISATION FARM - RACECOURSE FARM - [illegible] COT - NO MAN'S COT - CANADIAN CAMP Area.
2nd Battalion Headquarters - GOURNIER FARM.

2. All details of relief including guides will be arranged direct between Battalion Commanders concerned.

3. 2nd Bn.R.Ir.Rif. will arrange to leave one Officer per Company and one N.C.O. per platoon in the line until "stand-to" on morning of the 18th instant.

4. On completion of reliefs 2nd Bn.R.Ir.Rifles will withdraw to CANAL BANK EAST, and dispositions of 15th R.Ir.Rif. will be as follows:-

2 Coys. - RESERVE LINE.
1 Coy. - LA BELLE ALLIANCE & FOCH FARM.
1 Coy. - CANAL BANK.

5. On completion of reliefs the Northern Brigade Boundary will be as follows:-

C.11.b.2.8. - C.11.c.2.0. - C.17.a.0.5. - C.16.b.6.0. - C.16.c.0.0. - C.21.a.0.1. - C.20.Central. - B.23.Central.- B.22.d.2.9. - B.20.a.1.9. - B.14.c.0.5.

The Southern Boundary will remain the same as formerly.

6. 1st Bn.R.Ir.Rif. will establish International Posts with the 3rd Bn. 18th Belgian Regiment as follows:-

1 N.C.O. and four men to be sent to occupy the Outpost Position at C.11.a.68.36. in conjunction with the Belgian Post.

Same number of men to be sent to the post at C.16.b.55.20. in the main line of resistance.

The Belgians will send an N.C.O. and four men to the post ~~at~~ of the 1st Bn. R.Ir.Rif. at C.11.b.40.50.

Arrangements for these International Posts to be made direct by O.C. 1st Bn.R.Ir.Rif. with O.C. 2nd Bn., 18th Infy. Regiment.

The responsibility for the defence of the above Liaison Posts lies with the Unit in whose area the post is situated.

7. O.C. 107th T.M.Btty. will arrange to withdraw his two guns in the left Sub-Sector immediately after the Infantry relief is complete.

8. Command of the Sector will pass to the 18th Infantry Regt. on completion of relief.

9. Completion of reliefs will be reported by the code word "SHAKES."

Acknowledge.

[signature]
Captain,
Brigade Major,
107th Infy. Brigade.

17.4.1918.

8.15 p.m.
Issued at [illegible].

BRIGADE OFFICE
17 APR 1918
107th BRIGADE.

Copies to:-

No.1 - 1st Bn.R.Ir.Rif.
2 - 2nd Bn.R.Ir.Rif.
3 - 15th Bn.R.Ir.Rif.
4 - 107th T.M.Batty.
5 - 10th Belgian Inf.Rgt.
(c/o 36th Div. "G".)

No.6 - 36th Div. "G".
7 - Belgian Liaison Officer.
8 - 9th Brigade.
9 - 109th Brigade.
10 - 36th Div.R.F.A.

No.11 - File.

Appendix IX

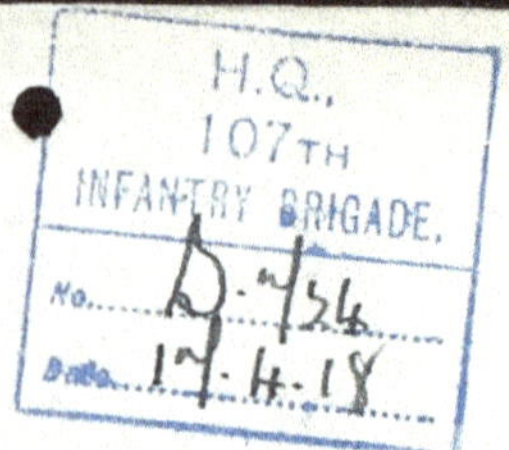

SECRET.

107TH INFANTRY BRIGADE.

DEFENCE SCHEME.

---

1. **FRONTAGE & BOUNDARIES.**

The 107th Infantry Brigade holds the left Sector of the 36th Div. Front.

The Brigade boundaries are as laid down in 107th Bde. Order No.231, dated 15.4.1918.

2. **DISPOSITIONS.**

The Brigade Front is divided into two Sub-Sectors, one Battalion holding the Outpost and Support Line in each Sub-Sector. One Battalion holds the Reserve Line.

The Boundary between the Right and Left Sub-Sectors is as follows:-

STEENBEEK at C.11.b.20.80. - ALBERTA TRACK at C.11.c.80.80) thence via ALBERTA TRACK to C.16.b.80.30. - OBLONG FARM (inclusive to Left Sub-Sector) - C.16.c.60.50. - C.16.c.10.25.

The Battalion holding the Right Sub-Sector is disposed as follows:-

Battalion Hqrs.	-	HILL TOP MINE, C.21.d.10.90.	
1 Coy. Hqrs.	-	C.17.b.40.20.	)
1 Platoon	-	-do-	)
1 Platoon	-	C.17.d.90.90.	) Outpost Company.
1 Platoon	-	C.18.a.15.80.	)
1 Platoon	-	C.11.d.95.10.	)
1 Coy. Hqrs.	-	ALBERTA.	)
1 Platoon	-	-do-	)
2 Platoons	-	C.11.b.40.52.	) Outpost Company.
1 Platoon	-	C.11.d.80.70.	)
1 Coy. Hqrs.	-	C.16.d.35.10.	)
2 Platoons	-	CALIBAN RESERVE.	
2 Sections	-	C.22.b.70.90.	
2 Sections	-	C.16.d.70.30.	
2 Sections	-	C.16.d.40.50.	
2 Sections	-	C.16.d.40.80.	
1 Coy. Hqrs.	-	HAMPSHIRE FARM.	
4 Platoons	-	HAMPSHIRE FARM Locality.	

The Battalion holding the Left Sub-Sector is disposed as follows:-

Battalion Hqrs.	-	HILL TOP MINE. C.21.d.10.90.	
1 Coy. Hqrs.	-	C.11.a.05.70.	)
1 Section	-	-do-	)
1 Section	-	C.5.c.10.45.	) Outpost Company.
2 Platoons	-	C.11.a.40.94.	)
1 Platoon	-	C.11.a.70.60.	)
1 Coy. Hqrs.	-	BOCHCASTEL.	
4 Platoons	-	MINTY TRENCH and CANDE TRENCH to C.10.d.00.53.	
1 Coy. Hqrs.	-	C.10.d.40.63.	
3 Platoons	-	CANDE TRENCH from C.10.d.00.53. to C.16.b.80.75	
2 Sections.	-	C.16.b.66.66.	
2 Sections	-	C.16.b.55.27.	
1 Coy. Hqrs.	-	CIVILIZATION FARM.	
3 Platoons	-	CALF RESERVE.	
1 Platoon	-	RACECOURSE.	

Battalion holding Reserve Line.

Battn Hqrs. - FOCH FARM.

1 Coy.
3 Platoons - From C.22.c.30.70. to C.22.c.00.80.
1 Platoon - C.21.d.85.80.

1 Coy.
1 Platoon - C.21.b.90.70.
1 Platoon - C.15.d.95.00.
1 Platoon. - C.15.d.70.40. C.21 B.75 40
1 Platoon - C.21.b.35.50.

1 Coy.
1 Platoon - HUNTER COT. 2 Platoons BELLE ALLIANCE
1 Platoon. - C.15.b.40.40. 2 " FOCH FARM
1 Platoon - C.15.b.80.00. 1 Coy CANAL BANK
1 Platoon - C.15.c.95.80.

1 Company - FOCH FARM. Brigade Reserve.

3. PRINCIPLES OF DEFENCE.

The Brigade Sector is divided into:-

(1) Outpost System.
(2) Support System.
(3) Reserve System.

~~Two Battalions~~ One Bn hold ~~the~~ Outpost and Support System and one Battalion the Reserve System.

~~In the~~
A. Outpost System.-

The Outpost line will do everything possible to prevent the enemy crossing the ~~xxxx~~ STEENBEEK. If forced to withdraw by superior enemy force, the Company at CORNER COT will retire to CALIBAN RESERVE in the Brigade Sector, the Company at ALBERTA will retire to the Support Line between CALIBAN RESERVE and OBLONG FARM; the Outpost Company of the Left Battalion will retire on MINTY TRENCH and CANDLE TRENCH.

In order to prevent confusion and to enable them to resist the Enemy step by step, supporting each other by fire, Os.C. Battalions will make it clear to platoon commanders the successive stages to which their platoons should move and the positions they should take up in order to support each other.

B. Support System.-

This is the main line of defence and will be held at all costs unless ordered to withdraw. Each Battalion in this System has one Company in Battalion Reserve which can be used by Battn. Commanders for counterattack or to reinforce the Support System.

C. Reserve System.-

The Reserve Line will become the main line should the enemy succeed in breaking through the Support System.

The troops in this System can also be used as a Brigade Reserve.

This Battalion has one Company in Reserve, at CANAL BANK ~~two platoons on the right of the line, and two platoons on the left of the line.~~

T.B.M. Buchan

Captain,
Brigade Major,
107th Infy. Brigade.

17.4.1918.

Appendix X

SECRET.

107th INFANTRY BRIGADE ORDER

No. 233.

Copy No. 11

---

1. The 15th Royal Irish Rifles will relieve the 1st Bn. Royal Irish Rifles in the line on the night of April 19/20th 1918.

2. On relief the 1st Bn.R.Ir.Rif. will withdraw into positions vacated by the 15th R.Ir.Rif.

3. No movement to commence before dusk East of HILL TOP FARM.

4. All details of relief to be arranged between Commanding Officers concerned.

5. All plans of work and defence and trench stores to be handed over and taken over.

6. Completion of reliefs to be reported by code word "LAMP."

Acknowledge.

T. M. Burham

Captain,
Brigade Major,
107th Infantry Brigade.

18.4.1918.

Issued at 12.0 pm

Copies to:-

No.1 - 1st Bn.R.Ir.Rif.	No.6 - 18th Belgian Inf.Rgt.
2 - 2nd Bn.R.Ir.Rif.	7 - Belgian Liaison Offr.
3 - 15th Bn.R.Ir.Rif.	8 - 39th Bde., R.F.A.
4 - 107th T.M.Batty.	9 - 36th Divn. "G".
5 - 109th Infy.Bde.	10 - FILE.

Copy No. 11 War Diary

Appendix XI

SECRET. Copy No. 8.....

107TH INFANTRY BRIGADE ORDER
NO. 234.

---

1. The 2nd Bn. Royal Irish Rifles will relieve the 1st Bn. Royal Irish Rifles in the Reserve System on the 20th April.

2. Relief to commence at 2.0 p.m. and to be complete before dark.

3. 500 yards distance will be observed between Companies West of the CANAL, and 200 yards between Platoons East of the CANAL.

4. 2nd Bn. Royal Irish Rifles will arrange to reconnoitre the defences of the reserve line carefully before relief, and all schemes of work and defence will be taken over.

5. 1st Bn. Royal Irish Rifles will withdraw on relief to SIEGE CAMP vacated by 2nd Bn. Royal Irish Rifles.

6. Completion of relief to be reported by code word 'PICK'.

Acknowledge.

Tom T Burke

Captain,
Brigade Major,
107th Infy. Brigade.

19.4.1918.

Copies to:-

No.1 - 1st Bn.R.Ir.Rif.
2 - 2nd R.Ir.Rifles.
3 - 15th R.Ir.Rif.
4 - 107th T.M.Btty.
No.5 - 25th Bde.R.F.A.
6 - 36th Divn. "G".
7 - Belgian Liaison Offr.
8 - FILE.

Issued at 8.0 p.m.

Appendix XII

SECRET.

1st Bn. Royal Irish Rifles.	109th Infantry Brigade.
2nd Bn. Royal Irish Rifles.	Belgian Liaison Officer.
15th Bn. Royal Irish Rifles.	25th Brigade, R.F.A.
107th Trench Mortar Battery.	36th Bn. M.G. Corps.
36th Division "G".	

Herewith pars. 1 to 6 of 107th Infantry Brigade Defence Scheme.

Please acknowledge.

21.4.1918.

Captain,
Brigade Major,
107th Brigade.

SECRET

107TH INFANTRY BRIGADE.

DEFENCE SCHEME.

This cancels my S.724, dated 17th instant.

1. **FRONTAGE & BOUNDARIES.** The 107th Infantry Brigade holds the left sector of the 36th Divisional Front.

The Brigade boundaries are as follows:-

Right Boundary -

C.18.c.12.93 - VENHEULE FARM (exclusive) - CHEDDAR VILLA (exclusive) - C.22.b.63.50. - C.22.c.60.80. - thence via BUFF ROAD to BRIDGE NO.4 (all inclusive).

Left Boundary -

STEENBEEK at C.11.b.20.80. - ALBERTA TRACK at C.11.c.80.80. thence via ALBERTA TRACK to C.16.b.80.30. - OBLONG FARM (exclusive) - C.16.c.60.50. - C.16.c.10.25. - C.21.a.45.15. FOCH FARM (inclusive) - C.19.a.10.00.

2. **DISPOSITIONS.**

The Battalion holding the Outpost Line and Main Line of Resistance is disposed as follows:-

Battalion Hqrs. - C.16.d.30.05.

1 Coy. Hqrs. - C.17.b.40.20.)
1 Platoon - -do-)
1 Platoon - C.17.d.90.90.) Outpost Company.
1 Platoon - C.18.a.15.80.)
1 Platoon - C.11.d.95.10.)

1 Coy. Hqrs. - ALBERTA.)
1 Platoon - -do-)
2 Platoons - C.11.b.40.52.) Outpost Company.
1 Platoon - C.11.d.80.70.)

1 Coy. Hqrs. - C.16.d.35.10.)
2 Platoons - CALIBAN RESERVE.
2 Sections - C.22.b.70.90.
2 Sections - C.16.d.70.30.
2 Sections - C.16.d.40.50.
2 Sections - C.16.d.40.80.

1 Coy. Hqrs. - HAMPSHIRE FARM.
4 Platoons - HAMPSHIRE FARM Locality.

Battalion holding Reserve Line.-

Battn. Hqrs. - FOCH FARM.

1 Coy.
3 Platoons - From C.22.c.30.70. to C.22.a.00.20.
1 Platoon - C.21.d.85.80.

1 Coy.
1 Platoon - C.21.b.75.40.
1 Platoon - C.21.b.90.70.
1 Platoon - C.15.d.95.00.
1 Platoon - C.21.b.35.50.

1 Coy.
2 Platoons - BELLE ALLIANCE.
2 Platoons - FOCH FARM.

1 Coy. - CANAL BANK.

3. PRINCIPLES OF DEFENCE.

The Brigade Sector is divided into:-

(1) Outpost System.
(2) Support System.
(3) Reserve System.

One Battalion holds the Outpost and Support System and one Battalion the Reserve System.

(a) Outpost System.-

The Outpost line will do everything possible to prevent the enemy crossing the STEENBEEK. If forced to withdraw by superior enemy force, the Company at CORNER COT will retire to CALIBAN RESERVE in the Brigade Sector, the Company at ALBERTA will retire to the Support Line between CALIBAN RESERVE and OBLONG FARM: the Outpost Company of the Left Battalion will retire on MINTY TRENCH and CANDE TRENCH.

In order to prevent confusion and to enable them to resist the enemy step by step, supporting each other by fire, Os.C. Battalions will make it clear to platoon commanders the successive stages to which their platoons should move and the positions they should take up in order to support each other.

(b) Support System.-

This is the main line of defence and will be held at all costs unless ordered to withdraw. Each Battalion in this System has one Company in Battalion Reserve which can be used by Battn. Commanders for counter-attack or to reinforce the Support System.

(c) Reserve System.-

The Reserve Line will become the main line should the enemy succeed in breaking through the Support System.

The troops in this System can also be used as a Brigade Reserve.

This Battalion has one Company in Reserve at CANAL BANK.

4. DIVISIONAL RESERVE BATTALION.

One Battalion is in Divisional Reserve at SIEGE CAMP. In the event of attack this Battalion will act under orders of 36th Division.

5. INTERNATIONAL POSTS.

There are international posts at the following places:-

C.11.a.68.60.
C.16.b.55.20.
C.11.b.40.50.

The responsibility for the defence of the above lies with the Unit in whose area the post is situated.

6. MACHINE GUNS.

Guns of the 36th M.G.Battalion are in position in the following places:-

C.11.c.95.80. - 2 Guns.
C.16.b.75.30. - 2 Guns.
OBLONG FARM - 2 Guns (Belgian).
C.17.c.62.10. - 2 Guns.
C.21.d.15.88. - 2 Guns.
C.21.c.10.67. - 2 Guns.
C.20.d.15.91. - 2 Guns.

MACHINE GUNS (CONTD.)

The following positions are prepared and will be manned in the event of an attack:-

C.16.d.20.25. - 2 Guns.
C.22.a.55.68. - 2 Guns.

Captain,
Brigade Major,
107th Brigade.

21.4.1918.

SECRET.

10TH INFANTRY BRIGADE

DEFENCE SCHEME (CONTD.)

---

7. NORTHERN FLANK DEFENCE.

Should the enemy attack the Brigade on our left and succeed in penetrating their line, the safety of our line would depend largely on the retention of the high ground about MULLER COT (C.18.b.05.45). Should the enemy, therefore, succeed in capturing MULLER COT it would be necessary to counter-attack with the Battalion in Brigade Reserve. In this eventuality it would probably be necessary to counter-attack with the whole Battalion.

All Officers of the Reserve Battalion must reconnoitre the ground about MULLER COT and the approaches thereto.

A scheme for counter-attack against an enemy holding MULLER COT must be prepared by Officer Commanding Battalion in Reserve Line and all Officers must be thoroughly acquainted with the scheme.

8. S.O.S. SIGNAL.

The S.O.S. Signal at present in force is a Rifle Grenade Rocket bursting into Stars RED
GREEN
YELLOW

This signal will be changed from time to time.

9. BATTLE STRAGGLERS' POSTS.

On receipt of the alarm, Stragglers' Posts, consisting of 1 N.C.O. and three men per post, will be established by the Battalion holding the Reserve System at the following positions:-

BRIDGE 4	-	C.19.c.80.00.
" 4A	-	C.19.c.60.25.
" 5	-	C.12.c.35.70.
RIGHT RAILWAY BRIDGE	-	C.19.a.23.05.

Appendix XIII

SECRET.

Copy No...16.....

107TH INFANTRY BRIGADE ORDER NO. 236.

1. The following reliefs will be carried out on the night of the 22/23rd April, 1918:-

(a) 1st Bn. Royal Irish Rifles will relieve the 2nd Bn. Royal Irish Rifles in the Reserve System.

(b) 2nd Bn. Royal Irish Rifles will relieve the 15th Bn. Royal Irish Rifles in the Front Line System.

(c) On completion of relief the 15th Bn. Royal Irish Rifles will withdraw to Divisional Reserve at SIEGE CAMP.

2. All details of relief will be arranged between Commanding Officers concerned.

3. All programmes of work and schemes of defence will be handed over.

4. Troops of the 1st Bn. R.Ir.Rif. will not cross the Canal before 8.30 p.m.

5. All movement West of Canal will be by Companies at 500 yards interval and East of Canal by Platoons at 300 yards interval.

6. Relief of 15th Bn. Royal Irish Rifles will not commence before 8.0 p.m.

7. All trench stores will be handed over and duplicate copies of receipts forwarded to Brigade Headquarters by 23rd instant.

8. Relief complete will be notified by wire:-

1st R.Ir.Rif. - S.C.1 Noted.
2nd -do- - S.C.2 Noted.
15th -do- - S.C.3 Noted.

Acknowledge.

T.Wm. Buchan

Captain,
Brigade Major,
107th Infy. Brigade.

21.4.1918.

Issued at 12.0 m.m.

Copies to:-

No.1 - 1st Bn. R.Ir.Rif.
2 - 2nd Bn.R.Ir.Rif.
3 - 15th Bn.R.Ir.Rif.
4 - 107th T.M.Batty.
5 - 36th Bn.M.G.C.
6 - Bde.Signal Offr.
7 - Staff Captain.
8 - 109th Bde.
9 - 18th Belgian Regt.
No.10 - Belgian Liaison Offr.
11 - 36th Divl.Arty.
12 - C.R.E., 36th Div.
13 - A.D.M.S.
14 - 36th Div. "G".
15 - 36th Div. "Q".
16 - War Diary.
17 - War Diary.
18 - FILE.

-------------:0:-------------

Appendix XIV

SECRET.

107TH INFANTRY BRIGADE ORDER NO. 237.

----

1. The following relief will take place on the 23rd instant.

1st Bn. Royal Irish Rifles, from Divisional Reserve, will relieve the 15th Bn. Royal Irish Rifles in the Reserve Line On relief the 15th Bn. Royal Irish Rifles will move to SIEGE CAMP and will become Divisional Reserve.

2. Relief to be complete by noon.

3. All movement West of CANAL will be by companies at 200 yards distance, and East of CANAL by platoons at 300 yards distance.

4. All programmes of work and schemes of defence will be handed over.

5. Completion of relief will be reported by code word "SHELL."

Acknowledge.

for Captain,
Brigade Major,
107th Brigade.

22.4.1918.

107th Brigade WAR DIARY

SECRET.

Appendix XV

107TH INFANTRY BRIGADE ORDER NO. 237.

Copy No. 10

1. The line of the STEENBEEK North of the point about point C.18.c.0.7. is to be the line of resistance.

2. The following alterations in dispositions will accordingly be made to-night, and will be complete by 12.0 midnight.

(a) 2nd Bn. Royal Irish Rifles will hold the line of the STEENBEEK with three companies and the Support Line with one Company.

1 Company of the 1st Bn.Royal Irish Rifles will move to HAMPSHIRE FARM, and will come under the orders of the O.C. 2nd Bn. R.Ir.Rifles. as Battalion Reserve.

(b) 1st Bn. R.Ir.Rifles will hold the Reserve Line as at present, one Company from the CANAL BANK being moved up for this purpose.

(c) O.C. 107th Trench Mortar Battery will move forward two guns to CORNER COT and two guns to HUGEL HOLLOW.

3. On completion of the above moves the dispositions of Battalions will be as shown on the attached map.

4. As soon as these dispositions are taken up the line of the STEENBEEK will become the main line of resistance. Should the enemy gain a footing in this line, he will be counter-attacked at once and driven out. The Company in the Support Line is at the disposal of the Commanding Officer of the Battalion in the line for this purpose, but if used it must be immediately replaced in the Support Line by the Company at HAMPSHIRE FARM in Battalion Reserve.

5. The outpost platoons East of the STEENBEEK will be maintained as at present. They will be found from the Support Platoons of the Right and Centre Front Companies. These outposts will be relieved every 24 hours.

6. Completion of the above moves will be reported to Brigade Headquarters by code -

1st Bn. R.Ir.Rif. - SHOES.
2nd Bn. R.Ir.Rif. - LACES.
107th T.M.Batty. - SOLES.

Acknowledge.

J.C. Coey Lt
for Captain,
Brigade Major,
107th Brigade.

24.4.1918.

Issued at 12.0 noon.

Copies to:-

No.1 - 1st Bn. R.Ir.Rif.
2 - 2nd Bn. R.Ir.Rif.
3 - 15th Bn.R.Ir.Rif.
4 - 107th T.M.Batty.
5 - 36th Bn. M.G.C.
6 - 36th Div. 'G'.
No. 7 - OLDHAMS Group.
8 - 66th D.A.
9 - Belgian Liaison Offr.
10 - War Diary. ✓
11 - War Diary.
12 - FILE.

----------;00:----------

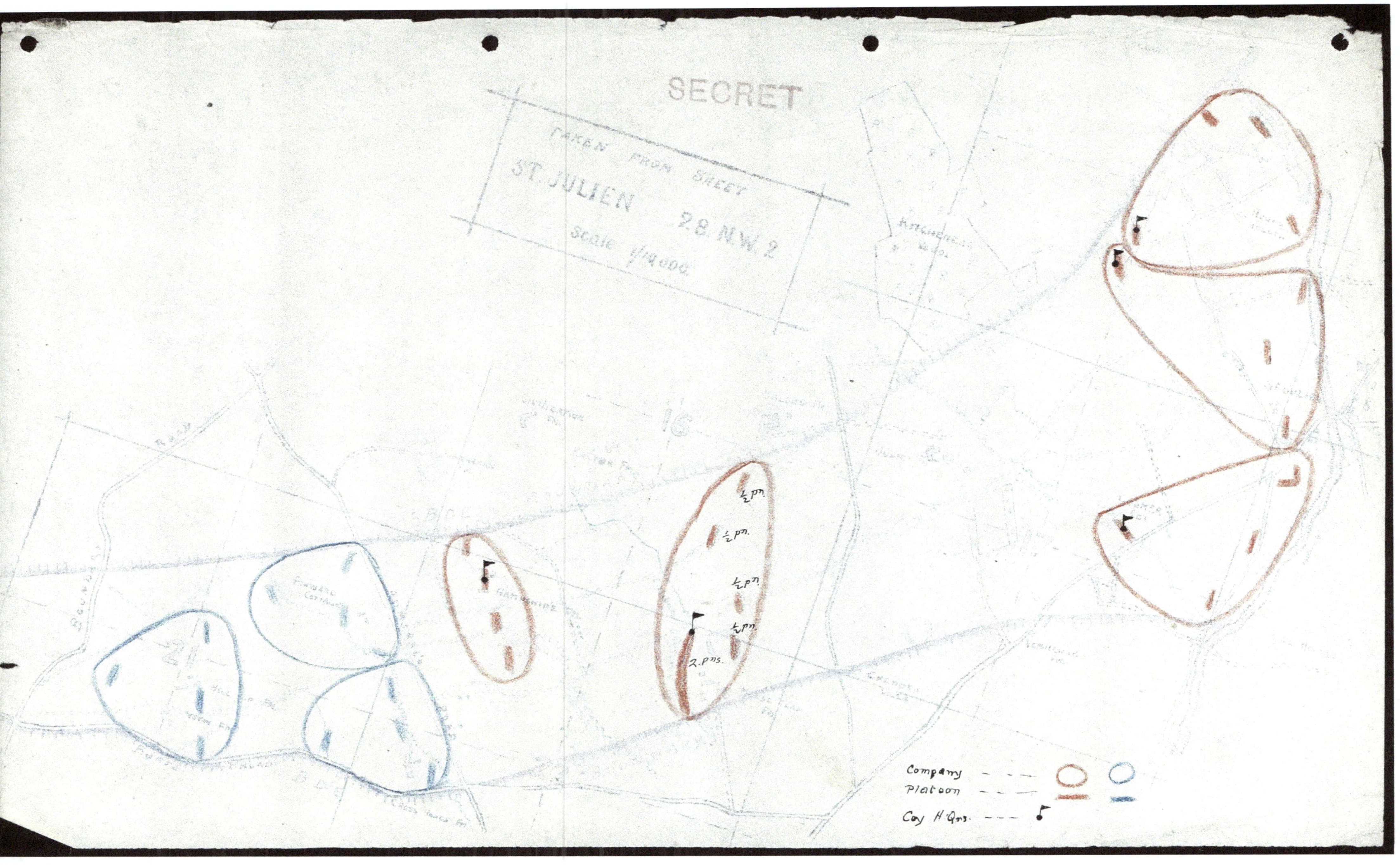

SECRET
TAKEN FROM SHEET
ST. JULIEN 28 N.W. 2
Scale 1/10,000
½ pn.
½ pn.
½ pn.
½ pn.
2 pns.
Company
Platoon
Coy H.Qrs.

Appendix XVI

SECRET.

107TH INFANTRY BRIGADE NO. 240.

1. At 4.0 a.m. on the 27th April, the Support Line from OBLONG FARM to R. of CALIBAN RESERVE, and the present Reserve Line will become the Outpost System.
The CANAL will become the main line of resistance.

2. The outpost system will be held by the 1st Bn.R.Ir.Rif. with two Companies in the present Support Line from OBLONG FARM to R. of CALIBAN RESERVE, and two Companies in the Reserve Line from C.22.c.30.85 to C.21.b.60.99. Battalion Hqrs. HILL TOP MILL.

3. The above dispositions will be carried out as follows:-

(a) 1st Bn. R.Ir.Rif. will relieve 1 Company of 2nd Bn.R.Ir.Rif. in the present Support Line with two Companies, and will keep two Companies in the present Reserve Line.

(b) 15th Bn. R.Ir.Rif. will take up the line of the CANAL with two Companies on each Bank.

(c) At 1.0 a.m. 2nd Bn. R.Ir.Rif. will commence to withdraw through the 1st and 15th Bns. R.Ir.Rif. and will move to ~~[illegible]~~ WAGRAM FARM B.23 and trenches running from B.23.a.90.20 to B.23.a.60.70

4. The withdrawal of the 2nd Bn. Royal Irish Rifles must be carried out by alternate platoons, each platoon leaving Section and Platoon Headquarters behind until the remainder are at least 500 yards clear.
FARM ~~B.23 and trenches running from B.23.a.90.20 to B.23.a.60.70~~

5. The 1st Bn.R.Ir.Rif. will establish examining posts on MOUSETRAP and ALBERTA TRACKS, and O.C. 2nd Bn.R.Ir.Rif. will ensure that these posts are informed immediately the last man of his Battalion has come past.

6. There must be no decrease in Lewis Gun and sniping activity until the last post has left the front line.

7. (a) O.C. 1st BN. R.Ir.Rif. will ensure that all bombs, S.A.A., S.O.S. Signals, are withdrawn from the front line.

(b) Buried cables at Signal Stations should if possible be destroyed.

(c) All remains of Bridges over the STEENBEEK must be pulled down.

Companies must keep close touch with Companies on their flanks.

8. (a) O.C. 107th T.M. Batty. will withdraw his guns from the front line to positions in the CANAL BANK WEST, as indicated to him by the Brigadier General Commanding.

(b) All T.M. ammunition must be brought back to-night.

9. The above moves must be completed by 4.0 a.m.

10. Completion of moves will be reported by code word 'BOTHER'.

Acknowledge.

Captain,
Brigade Major,
107th Brigade.

26.4.1918.

Issued at 8.0 p.m.

Copies to:-

No.1 - 1st Bn.R.Ir.Rif.	No.6 - 36th Divn. 'Q'.
2 - 2nd Bn. R.Ir.Rif.	7 - 36th M.G.Bn.
3 - 15th Bn.R.Ir.Rif.	8 - 153rd Bde.R.F.A.
4 - 107th T.M.B.	9 - War Diary.
5 - Rear Headquarters.	10 - War Diary.

No.11 - FILE.

107th Bde.No. 8889.

Headquarters,
36th Division 'G'.

In reply to your G.B.342 of the 19th instant, the required report is forwarded herewith.

G Thorpe

Brig-General,
Commdg. 107th Infy. Brigade.

21. 5. 1918.

107TH INFANTRY BRIGADE.

Narrative of Operations during Month of April, 1918.

April 7th to 12th

From 7th April to 12th April the 107th Infantry Brigade held the line from V.28.a.90.20. to V.14.Central, with two Battalions in the Line and one Battalion in Support.

Brigade Headquarters at ALBERTA BUND.

April 12th

On April 12th the Brigade was in process of relief by the 109th Infantry Brigade, when, about 11.0 p.m., orders were received from 36th Division that instead of withdrawing to Camps in the neighbourhood of the CANAL BANK, the 107th Infantry Brigade would man the BATTLE ZONE.

The relief had already commenced and instructions were issued for the 15th Bn. Royal Irish Rifles to move to JOFFRE CAMP, the 1st Bn. Royal Irish Rifles to man the BATTLE ZONE in the Right Sub-Sector, and the 2nd Bn. Royal Irish Rifles to man the BATTLE ZONE in the Left Sub-Sector.

April 13th

The 9th Bn. Royal Inniskilling Fusiliers (109th Infantry Brigade), located in the CANAL BANK EAST, were placed under the orders of the G.O.C. 107th Infantry Brigade, and this Battalion, together with the 15th Bn. Royal Irish Rifles, was detailed for the defence of the Reserve Line to the BATTLE ZONE. This line had not yet been constructed, and work was commenced on it on the morning of the 13th April. The site for the Reserve Line to the BATTLE ZONE was reconnoitred by the G.O.C. 107th Infantry Brigade and ran approximately as follows:-

KEMPTON PARK - CANADIAN CAMP - FORWARD COTTAGES - C.22.a.03.00. - C.23.a.05.56.

The dividing line between the Right and Left Sub-Sectors being FORWARD COTTAGES.

The Battalion Headquarters of the two Battalions holding these two lines to be at LA BELLE ALLIANCE MINE.

April 13/14.

The POELCAPPELLE Line was held by the 109th Infantry Brigade as an Outpost Line, and the BATTLE ZONE by the 107th Infantry Brigade as the Main Line of Resistance.

April 14th.

On the 14th instant, orders were received from the Division that on the 16th April, the line of the STEENBEEK would become the Outpost Line, and the line BOCHCASTEL - OBLONG FARM - CALIBAN RESERVE, would become the Main Line of Resistance. On that date the 109th Infantry Brigade would withdraw from the POELCAPPELLE Line, and would man the BATTLE ZONE on the right of the 107th Infantry Brigade.

The Boundary between the 109th and the 107th Infantry Brigades would run as follows:-

STEENBEEK at C.18.a.30.70. - VANHEULE FARM - CHEDDAR VILLA (both inclusive to 109th Brigade) - 'R' of CALIBAN RESERVE - CROSS ROADS - BUFFS ROAD (inclusive to 107th Infantry Brigade) - to CANAL at Bridge No.4.

April 15th

On the morning of the 15th inst. the G.O.C. 107th

April 15th (Contd.) Infantry Brigade reconnoitred the new line running from CANOPUS TRENCH, immediately East of OBLONG FARM to CALIBAN RESERVE, and sited new posts to connect these two trenches. Work on these ~~xxx~~ posts was commenced at once.

By 5.0 p.m. the dispositions of the 107th Infantry Brigade had been completed in accordance with the new scheme, and the 9th Royal Inniskilling Fusiliers came under the orders of the G.O.C. 109th Infantry Brigade. During the night the 109th Infantry Brigade withdrew from the POELCAPPELLE LINE to the BATTLE ZONE in the Right Sector of the Divisional Front.

April 16th. The morning passed quietly. In the afternoon the enemy were reported to be moving about in the neighbourhood of the old British Outpost Line and to be gradually dribbling forward.

Standing patrols which had been left out at GENOA, SLAB and KEERSALARE did not come into touch with the enemy. On the night of the 16/17th these posts were re-adjusted, and one established at SPRINGFIELD and the other at MON/DU HIBOU.

April 17th. On the morning of the 17th inst. the enemy was pushing forward, and the post at SPRINGFIELD was accordingly withdrawn to C.12.d.60.50., after inflicting casualties on the enemy patrols.

April 17/18 On the night of the 17/18th the Fourth Belgian Division took over the Left Sub-Sector of the 107th Infantry Brigade Front, i.e. up to OBLONG FARM (inclusive.) thereby relieving the 2nd Bn. Royal Irish Rifles, who withdrew to CANAL BANK EAST. The Belgians did not take over the standing patrol at MON DU HIBOU, which position was consequently evacuated.

Northern Boundary of the 107th Infantry Brigade then became OBLONG FARM (exclusive) - C.16.c.00.00. - C.21.a.40.35.

April 18th to 23rd. From 18th to 23rd April the situation remained unchanged. The enemy appeared to be making his Outpost Line on the line - MON-DU HIBOU - TRIANGLE - ARBRE RIDGE.

Two standing patrols were kept out - one at C.12.a.60.50. and one at C.12.c.65.25.

During this period these posts captured five prisoners of the 458th Infantry Regiment. On the 23rd inst. orders were received to make the STEENBEEK into the Main Line of Resistance.

April 23/24. On the night 23/24th Instant, the B.G.C. 107th Infantry Brigade, reconnoitred the line of the STEENBEEK and sited new posts with the above object in view.

April 24th Line of the STEENBEEK made into the Main Line of Resistance.

April 26/27. In accordance with orders from Division the line was withdrawn from the STEENBEEK to the line OBLONG FARM (Exclusive) - CALIBAN RESERVE.

This line, together with the old reserve line became the Outpost System. The CANAL Line became the Main Line of Resistance.

April 26/27 (Contd.)

The 1st Bn. Royal Irish Rifles took over the new outpost system and the 15th Bn. Royal Irish Rifles moved from SIEGE CAMP to the CANAL Line.

April 27th.

At 1.0 a.m. on the 27th inst. the 2nd Bn. Royal Irish Rifles withdrew from the old Outpost Line on the STEENBEEK to the BRIELEN DEFENCES at WAGRAM FARM.

By 6.0 a.m. all moves were completed. A post of the 1st Bn. Royal Irish Rifles was left in CANOPUS TRENCH.

April 27th to 30th

No alteration in our lines took place. The German Outposts were apparently established on the following line:-

CANOPUS TRENCH at C.17.a.70.40. - CALIFORNIA DRIVE - CHEDDAR VILLA.

-----------:oOo:-----------

Instructions regarding War Diaries and Intelligence Summaries are contained in F. S. Regs., Part II. and the Staff Manual respectively. Title pages will be prepared in manuscript.

WAR DIARY
or
~~INTELLIGENCE SUMMARY.~~
(*Erase heading not required.*)

Army Form C. 2118.

May 1918 — H.Q's 107th Inf Bde — Vol 31

Place	Date	Hour	Summary of Events and Information	Remarks and references to Appendices
CANAL BANK WEST.	1st		~~Bns [illegible] [illegible] have [illegible] [illegible] [illegible] the [illegible] Div at 6 H.Q.~~	
	1st		15th R.I.Rifles relieved 1st R.I.Rifles who withdrew to WAGRAM FARM 2nd R.I.Rifles moved to CANAL BANK	
	2/3		No change. Enemy artillery moderately active. Our artillery firing Counter preparations morning and evening.	
	2/5		No change.	
	6/7		2nd R.I.R relieved 15th R.I.R who withdrew to WAGRAM FARM. 1st RIR moved to CANAL BANK.	
	7/10		No change. Enemy artillery showed slightly increased activity, especially in shelling the forward area and CALIBAN RESERVE.	
	10/11		The Brigade extended its front taking over the front of the 109th Bde. 1st R.I.R relieved 1st R. Inniskilling Fusiliers in 109th Bde Sector. 15th R.I.R moved to CANAL	
	11/12th		15th R.I.R relieved 2nd R.I.R in left subsector. Prior to relief 2nd R.I.R took over line 1st R.I.R down to BUFFS Road inclusive which became Inter Bde Boundary. The Post in CANOPUS Trench was withdrawn after being filled in	
	13th		Div orders for Relief of 107th Bde by 108th Bde on 17/18th inst Received. Fairly Quiet day	T. [illegible]

(A7092). Wt. W12839/M1293. 750,000. 1/17. D. D. & L., Ltd. Forms/C.2118/14.

Army Form C. 2118.

WAR DIARY
or
~~INTELLIGENCE~~ SUMMARY.
(Erase heading not required.)

Instructions regarding War Diaries and Intelligence Summaries are contained in F. S. Regs., Part II. and the Staff Manual respectively. Title pages will be prepared in manuscript.

May 1918 — H.Q's 107th Inf Bde.

Place	Date	Hour	Summary of Events and Information	Remarks and references to Appendices
CANAL BANK	May 14th		Slight increase in enemy artillery activity and aerial activity. No change.	
"	15th		Constant shelling of area immediately East of CANAL.	
"	16th		No change. Hostile artillery active in the morning. Bde Order 246 issued re relief of 107th Bde by 108th Bde.	
"	17th/18th		Quiet day. At 4 pm Division stated that there was possibility of enemy attack on our right. Units warned to take extra vigilance. Reliefs were completed by 2.30 a.m. Bde HQs moved to A.22.B.50.50.	
A.22 B.55				
"	19/28th		Brigade remained in Divl Reserve. One Bn trained each day and two Bns worked on the GREEN LINE under R.E. Coy R.C. Bde Order No 247 issued for relief of 108th Brigade in the line.	
	29th		Brigade H.Qs moved to the CANAL BANK at 4 pm.	
CANAL BANK	30th		Reliefs completed by 2.55 a.m.	
	31st		Quiet day.	

T. Om Buchan Capt
Brigade Major
107th Bde

(A7092). Wt. W12839/M1293. 750,000. 1/17. D. D. & L., Ltd. Forms/C.2118/14.

Army Form C. 2118.

WAR DIARY
or
INTELLIGENCE SUMMARY.
(*Erase heading not required.*)

Instructions regarding War Diaries and Intelligence Summaries are contained in F. S. Regs., Part II. and the Staff Manual respectively. Title pages will be prepared in manuscript.

June 1918. H.Q's 107th Inf Bde

Place	Date	Hour	Summary of Events and Information	Remarks and references to Appendices
CANAL BANK	June 1st		Order No 249 issued for Relief of 15th R.I.R by 1st R.I.R. Warning order received from the Division for the probable Relief of the Brigade on 4/5th inst by two Regiments of a Belgian Division	App. I
"	1/4		The period passed quietly. The enemy shelled artillery was inactive. Each day advanced parties from the Belgians came up to visit the line.	
"	5th		The 1st Grenadier Regt (3rd & 1st Bns) and the CARABINEER REGT (3 and 2nd Bns) relieved the Brigade. Relief was completed by 1.25 a.m 6/6/18.	App II
F25.d. JAN TER BIEZEN	6th		Brigade H.Qs opened at JAN TER BIEZEN at 4 A.M. Bde was all in Billets by 8 A.M.	
"	7/12		Brigade all in ROAD CAMP. Four days allotted for reorganization Bathing and cleaning up. On 10th June Brigade was paraded for Corps Commanders inspection. At last moment Parade was cancelled owing to wet. The Corps Commander interviewed all officers only.	
PROVEN	12th		Brigade moved to PROVEN Area taking over Camps and working parties from 108th Bde	App III
			5 [illegible]	

T.O.M.B.

(A7092). Wt. W12839/M1293. 750,000. 1/17. D. D. & L., Ltd. Forms/C.2118/14.

Army Form C. 2118.

WAR DIARY
or
INTELLIGENCE SUMMARY.
(*Erase heading not required.*)

Instructions regarding War Diaries and Intelligence Summaries are contained in F. S. Regs., Part II. and the Staff Manual respectively. Title pages will be prepared in manuscript.

June 1918 H.Q's 107th Inf Bde

Place	Date	Hour	Summary of Events and Information	Remarks and references to Appendices
PROVEN	June 14/20		The whole Brigade provided working parties daily for work on the EAST POPERINGHE LINE. Only small Bn classes of instruction were kept back. Schemes were prepared for the occupation of the Blue Line	See App IV
			Brigade Order 253 for the move to TUNNELLING CAMP issued on 18th	See App V
			Brigade Order 254 giving moves of units for period June 22nd July 2nd	See App VI
TUNNELLERS CAMP	21		Brigade moved to TUNNELLERS CAMP	
"	22		1st Bn The Royal Irish Rifles moved to BOIS ST ACAIRE and T.M.B to XXII Corps School for 4 days practice in firing	
"	24/28		2nd Bn The Royal Irish Rifles moved to CASSEL and ROUBRUCK and returned on the 28th. During this period all Bns concentrated chiefly on musketry having the use of short ranges.	
"	29		Brigade Order 255 issued for the move of the Brigade to the CORMETTE Musketry Camp. At 10 pm in the evening orders were received from the Division cancelling the move and for the 1st R.I.Rifles to return to TUNNELLING CAMP.	App VII
				TBm B

(A7092). Wt. W12839/M1293. 750,000. 1/17. D. D. & L., Ltd. Forms/C.2118/14

Appendix I

SECRET. Copy No. 13 ......

107th INFANTRY BRIGADE ORDER NO. 249.

1. The 1st Bn. Royal Irish Rifles will relieve the 15th Bn. Royal Irish Rifles in the left subsector of the Brigade Front on the night 1/2nd June, 1918.

2. On relief the 15th Bn. Royal Irish Rifles will withdraw to Brigade Reserve and take up the positions vacated by the 1st Bn. Royal Irish Rifles.

3. Details of relief will be arranged direct between Commanding Officers concerned.

4. All aeroplane photos, defence schemes, programmes of work, A.A. Lewis Gun mountings and trench stores will be handed over and receipts forwarded to Brigade Headquarters by 6.0 p.m. 2nd June.

5. No movement E. of HAMMOND'S CORNER will take place before 9.0 p.m.

6. Completion of reliefs will be reported to Brigade Headquarters by the code word "KITTENS."

Acknowledge.

T. Om. Bucka

Captain,
Brigade Major,
107th Brigade.

Issued at 6.0 a.m.
1.6.1918.

Copies to:-

No.1 - 1st R.Ir.Rif.
2 - 2nd R.Ir.Rif.
3 - 15th R.Ir.Rif.
4 - 107th T.M.By.
5 - 'B' Coy. 36th M.G.C.
6 - Belgian Liaison.
7 - 173 Bde. R.F.A.
No. 8 - 36th Divn. 'G'.
9 - X 36th T.M.B.
10.- 109th Infy. Bde.
11 - Rear Hqrs.
12 - Bde. Sig. Offr.
13 - War Diary.
14 - War Diary.
No. 15 - FILE.

Army Form C. 2118.

WAR DIARY
or
~~INTELLIGENCE SUMMARY.~~
(Erase heading not required.)

Instructions regarding War Diaries and Intelligence Summaries are contained in F. S. Regs., Part II. and the Staff Manual respectively. Title pages will be prepared in manuscript.

June 1918. H.Q. 107th Inf Bde

Place	Date	Hour	Summary of Events and Information	Remarks and references to Appendices
TUNNELLING CAMP	July 30th		1st R.I.Rifles returned to TUNNELLING CAMP. Fresh scheme issued for the occupation of the EAST POPERINGHE LINE	App VIII
			T.om Buchan Capt Brigade Major 107th Inf Bde	

(A7092). Wt. W12839/M1293. 750,000. 1/17. D. D. & L., Ltd. Forms/C.2118/14.

19

Army Form C. 2118.

Vol 33

WAR DIARY
or
INTELLIGENCE SUMMARY.

(Erase heading not required.)

Instructions regarding War Diaries and Intelligence Summaries are contained in F. S. Regs., Part II. and the Staff Manual respectively. Title pages will be prepared in manuscript.

JULY 1918. Headquarters, 107th Infantry Brigade.

Place	Date	Hour	Summary of Events and Information	Remarks and references to Appendices
TUNNELLERS CAMP.	JULY 1st		Warning Order received for the move of the Division to the area of the XVIth French Corps.	
	2nd		Order 256 and Administrative for the move issued.	App. I.
ST. MARIE CAPPEL.	3rd		Brigade moved to ST. MARIE CAPPEL Area, arriving about 11.0 a.m. Orders issued for the occupation of the 2nd Line, XVI Corps Area in the event of attack.	
	4th		At a conference of Brigade Majors, G.S.O.1 gave details for the relief of the 41st French Divn.	
	5th		B.G.C. visited French Regiments in the line and arranged details of relief.	
	6th		Brigade Order No. 257 issued for the relief of the French. 2nd and 15th Bns. Royal Irish Rifles moved up to the line, 2nd R.Ir.Rif. into Support and 15th R.Ir.Rif. into reserve.. Reliefs completed by 2.30 a.m., 7th inst. Captain J.T.DUFFIN, M.C. proceeded to 47th Division. Duties of Staff Captain taken over by Captain C.M.CASTLE, M.C.	App. II
	7th		1st Bn. R.Ir.Rif. moved up into Support in LA MANCHE Area, relieving a Battalion of French, 42nd Regiment. 15th Bn. R.Ir.Rif. moved up into line between BENEDICT CROSS ROADS and SALVO FARM, relieving 1st Bn. 128th French Regiment. Brigade Headquarters and 107th Light Mortar Battery moved to R.33, between PIEBROUCK and FONTAINE HOUCK. Relief complete about 4.0 a.m. 8th July.	
Sh. 27. R.33.b.5.1.	8th		Staff of 128th French Regiment left 5.30 a.m. Captain T.O.M. BUCHAN, M.C., Brigade Major, proceeded to 56th Division as G.S.O. (2). Duties taken over by Captain J.H.A. PATTON.	
	9th		Situation quiet.	
	10th		Captain H.D.C. CRAIG, HIGHLAND LIGHT INFANTRY, took over appointment as Brigade Major. 2nd Bn. R.Ir.Rifles commenced work on new trench on extreme right of Brigade Front, connecting right sap to trench dug by Brigade on right to BENEDICT CROSS ROADS - POE CROSS Road.	
	11th		Work on new trench continued during night.	
	12th		Uneventful day. Very wet weather.	
	13th		Very quiet day.	
	14th		Brigade Headquarters moved back to PIEBROUCK (Sheet 27, R.27.a.10.95.)	
PIEBROUCK.	15th	[illegible]	1st R.Ir.Rif. relieved 15th R.Ir.Rif. in line, the latter withdrawing into reserve.	App. III.

(A7092). Wt. W12839/M1293. 750,000. 1/17. D. D. & L., Ltd. Forms/C.2118/14.

Army Form C. 2118.

WAR DIARY
or
INTELLIGENCE SUMMARY.
(Erase heading not required.)

Instructions regarding War Diaries and Intelligence Summaries are contained in F. S. Regs., Part II. and the Staff Manual respectively. Title pages will be prepared in manuscript.

JULY, 1918. Headquarters, 107th Infantry Brigade.

Place	Date	Hour	Summary of Events and Information	Remarks and references to Appendices
PIEBROUCK.	JULY 16th	a.m. 5.30	Heavy thunderstorm. Water broke into dugouts containing clerks' and Brigade Major's Offices, running in from above. Many papers, etc. destroyed.	
			Dispositions of 1st R.Ir.Rif. altered during night 16/17th.	
	17th	a.m. 2.40	Heavy artillery and trench mortar bombardment of front of Brigade on our left, extending to our extreme left. Lewis Gun in our left post destroyed by heavy T.M.bomb.	
		11.0	20 High Velocity Gun shells close to Brigade Headquarters (fired at working party of 30th Divn.)	
	18th		Usual patrol activity.	
	19th	a.m. 7.55	9th Division (on our right flank) attacked and took METEREN, with over 200 prisoners.	
		8.15	Two platoons attempted to raid enemy lines opposite our right flank but failed owing to enemy barrage.	
		p.m. 4 - 5	Heavy shelling of ST. JANS CAPPEL and KOPJE FARM AREAS. 1st Bn. R.Ir.Rif. captured one O.R. of 4th Coy., 88th Infantry Regiment, 56th Division (Normal) who was wandering in No Man's Land.	
	20th	a.m. 2 - 3	Gas shelling round KOPJE FARM. Usual patrol activity during 24 hours.	
	21st	a.m. 12.45	Gas shelling round KOPJE FARM.	
	22nd		PELMAN HOUSE and ST. JANS CAPPEL heavily shelled during the day.	
	23rd		Front line heavily shelled by 77-m.m. guns during night. 2nd Bn. R.Ir.Rif. relieved 1st Bn. R.Ir.Rif. in the line and 15th Bn.R.Ir.Rif. relieved 2nd Bn.R.Ir.Rif. in Support during night 23/24th. 1st Bn.R.Ir.Rif. withdrew into Reserve.	App. IV.
	24th		Headquarters of 1st Bn. R.Ir.Rif. in RIFLE RANGE WOOD, (R.33.central) shelled by 210-m.m. howitzer (13 rounds). Patrols active. Brigade Defence Scheme issued.	App. V.
	25th		Visibility very good. R.33. and 3.4., X.3. and 4. heavily shelled by 210-m.m. and 150-m.m. howitzers during afternoon.	
	26th		Visibility good. X.4.a. received about 90 shells of various calibres. Enemy infantry opposite our front unusually quiet.	
	27th		Weather very wet. Artillery on both sides quiet. Patrols active.	
	28th		Artillery quieter than usual. No.2 Special Coy. R.E. arranged to project gas at MURAL FARM at midnight. Operation postponed on account of weather.	

(A7092). Wt. W12839/M1293. 750,000. 1/17. D. D. & L., Ltd. Forms/C.2118/14.

Army Form C. 2118.

WAR DIARY
or
INTELLIGENCE SUMMARY.

Instructions regarding War Diaries and Intelligence Summaries are contained in F. S. Regs., Part II. and the Staff Manual respectively. Title pages will be prepared in manuscript.

JULY 1918. (*Erase heading not required.*) Headquarters, 107th Infantry Brigade.

Place	Date	Hour	Summary of Events and Information	Remarks and references to Appendices
PIEBROUCK	JULY 29th	a.m. 4.40	Enemy aeroplane over our lines at 4.40 a.m., driven off by Light Mortar, Lewis Gun and Rifle Fire.	
		p.m. 7.0	Patrol under Lieut. D.B.WALKINGTON and 2nd Lieut. J.N.G.STEWART, 2nd Bn. Royal Irish Rifles, (2 Officers and 4 Other Ranks), encountered enemy post at X.12.c.01.24., killed or wounded 8 of the enemy and brought in two unwounded prisoners of 10th Company, 3rd Battalion, 88th Infantry Regiment, 56th Division (Normal.)	
	30th	a.m. 11.30	Operation Order No. 260 issued.	App. VI.
		p.m. 4.0	HAUTE PORTE FARM, X.11.c.70.90. heavily shelled. Cellars blown in and several casualties caused. Our artillery bombarded enemy communications during ~~xxxxxxxxx~~ night on account of suspected enemy relief.	
	31st		Enemy replied with bombardment of our front and support lines and roads in forward area just before dawn. 15th Bn.R.Ir.Rif. moved into line, relieving 2nd Bn. R.Ir.Rif. who withdrew into Reserve. 1st Bn. R.Ir.Rif. moved from Reserve to Support.	App.VII.
		p.m. 10.50.	Four Aeroplane Bombs dropped near Brigade Headquarters. From 8th July until 31st July, Brigade Transport Lines were at Q.23.c.35.05.	
			Map Sheet 27 (Scale 1/40,000) and Combined Sheet 27 S.E. and 28 S.W. (parts of) (1/20,000) are attached for reference.	App.VIII. App. IX.
			Statement of casualties is attached.	App. X.

E. Thorpe Brig-General,
Commanding 107th Infantry Brigade.

A5834 Wt. W4973 M687 750,000 8/16 D. D. & L. Ltd. Forms/C.2118/13.

Instructions regarding War Diaries and Intelligence Summaries are contained in F. S. Regs., Part II. and the Staff Manual respectively. Title pages will be prepared in manuscript.

WAR DIARY
or
INTELLIGENCE SUMMARY.
(*Erase heading not required.*)

107th Inf. Brigade H.Q.

Army Form C. 2118.

Place	Date	Hour	Summary of Events and Information	Remarks and references to Appendices
PIEBROUCK. (Sh. 27, R.27.a.10.95)	August 1st		Brigade Transport Lines at Q.23.c.35.05.	
			11.0 a.m. till 4.0 p.m. - Promiscuous shelling of forward area. Night quiet.	
	2nd	a.m. 3.15	Enemy aeroplane flew along our Front Line dropping flares. Very wet day.	
		p.m. 8.0	Warning order No.262 issued.	App. I.
	3rd		G.O.C. X Corps visited Brigade Headquarters. Operation Order No.263 issued.	App. II
	4th		Operation Order No. 263 cancelled. Daylight patrol reported houses in S.7.b.central unoccupied.	
	5th		SENLAC FARM shelled all day. Enemy inter-battalion relief suspected during night.	
	6th		Daylight patrol of 15th Bn.R.Ir.Rif. reconnoitred WIRRAL FARM, S.7.d.75.95. and found it occupied. Patrol was bombed, casualties 2 Officers and 1 N.C.O. wounded.	
	7th		O.P. established at MEULEHOUCK, S.2.a.25.80. Brigade Hqrs. shelled in evening.	
	8th		Posts established in farm and orchard S.7.b.60.40. early in morning.	
		a.m. 8.0	Operation Order 265 issued.	App. III.
	9th		1st R.Ir.Rif. relieved 15th R.Ir.Rif. in line early in morning, the latter withdrawing into Reserve. 2nd R.Ir.Rif. moved into support.	App. IV.
			Operation Order No. 266 issued, and Operation Order No.260 amended.	App. V.& VI.
			Projector discharge on MURAL FARM carried out at 12.0 midnight by "L" Special Company, R.E. (see Appendix V.) R.27. bombarded by 105 m.m. and 150 m.m. howitzers all day.	
	10th	a.m. 2.15	Patrols of 1st R.Ir.Rif. went out to report on Gas Discharge. Posts at X.17.b.10,80. and X.11.d.15.15. were found unoccupied. Patrols penetrated without opposition to within 70 yards of MURAL FARM, but were held up there by guns firing on MURAL FARM. No casualties. Visibility particularly good during day.	

(A9175) Wt W2358/P360 600,000 12/17 D. D. & L. Sch. 52a. Forms/C2118/15.

Instructions regarding War Diaries and Intelligence Summaries are contained in F. S. Regs., Part II. and the Staff Manual respectively. Title pages will be prepared in manuscript.

WAR DIARY
or
INTELLIGENCE SUMMARY.
(Erase heading not required.)

Army Form C. 2118.

Place	Date	Hour	Summary of Events and Information	Remarks and references to Appendices
PIEBROUCK, (Sheet 27, R.27.a.10.95)	August 11th		Active patrolling in neighbourhood of MURAL FARM. Visibility particularly good during the day. Brig-General E.I.de S.THORPE proceeded on leave. Command of Brigade taken over by Lieut-Col. R.C.SMYTHE, D.S.O. Royal Inniskilling Fusiliers, attached 15th Bn. Royal Irish Rifles.	
	12th		Patrols active. Gas shelling round Brigade Headquarters early in morning.	
	13th	p.m. 9.30	SCHAEXKEN and LA MANCHE heavily gas-shelled, 9.30 p.m. - 12.0 midnight. About 35 casualties.	
		m.n. 12.0	Brigade Order No. 268 issued.	App. VII.
	14th		Quiet day. Patrols active at night.	
	15th	a.m. 2.0	One of our patrols (1st R.Ir.Rif.) encountered enemy post at X.17.a.80.80. Casualties were inflicted on the enemy. Patrol lost 1 Officer and 2 O.R. wounded and one O.R. missing.	
	16th		Inter-Battalion Relief carried out. 1st R.Ir.Rif. went into Support, 2nd R.Ir.Rif. into Line in Left Brigade Sector (Right Subsector), relieving 9th R.Ir.Fusiliersm and coming under orders of G.O.C., 108th Infy. Brigade. 15th R.Ir.Rif. went into Line, and 12th R.Ir.Rif. from Support in 108th Brigade Area, came into Reserve to 107th Infy. Bde. Lieut-Col.J.P.HUNT, D.S.O., commanding 1st R.Ir.Rifles, was wounded during relief. Brigade Commander reconnoitred Right Sub-sector, 108th Infy. Brigade during the night.	App.VII.
	17th	p.m. 10.0	Brigade Order No.269 issued. Front Line was heavily shelled 3.0 - 4.0 a.m. in reply to wire-cutting by Divl. Artillery near WIRRAL FARM.	App.VIII.
	18th		Active patrolling. Our Front shelled about 11.0 a.m. Bde. Order No.270 issued.	App.IX.
	19th		Brigade Orders 271 and 272 issued.	App.X. & XI.
	20th	a.m. 2.20	Party of 15th R.Ir.Rif. attempted to rush WIRRAL FARM, but failed, enemy being very alert. One Officer wounded.	
	21st	a.m. 2.0	"Chinese Attack" on WIRRAL FARM. Divl.Artillery fired barrage on farm and Battalion in line	

(A9175) Wt W2358/P360 600,000 12/17 D. D. & L. Sch 52a. Forms/C2118/15

Instructions regarding War Diaries and Intelligence Summaries are contained in F. S. Regs., Part II. and the Staff Manual respectively. Title pages will be prepared in manuscript.

WAR DIARY
or
INTELLIGENCE SUMMARY.
(Erase heading not required.)

Army Form C. 2118.

Place	Date	Hour	Summary of Events and Information	Remarks and references to Appendices
PIEBROUCK.	August 21st (contd)		threw smoke cases into No Man's Land. Enemy retaliation feeble. Orders received for attack on 22nd.	
	22nd	a.m. 12.30	15th R.Ir.Rif. attacked and took line X.17.a.50.25 - MURAL FARM - WIRRAL FARM (See special report). 1st R.Ir.Rif. (Support) changed places with 2nd R.Ir.Rif. in Right Sector, 108th Infy. Bde. Front.	App. XII. XIII and XIV.
	22nd	p.m. 11.0	Enemy counter-attacked our new line in dense formations up roads etc. Attack broken up by rifle and Lewis Gun fire. Relief of 15th R.Ir.Rif. by 12th Bn.R.Ir.Rif. was in progress at the time Our casualties slight.	App XV.
	23rd		16th R.Ir.Rif.(P). sent two Companies to assist in digging continuous front line during night. Line completed from X.17.a.50.25. to MURAL FARM.	
	24th	a.m. 7.0	In co-operation with enterprise on left by 108th Infy. Bde., we established post at S.8.c.10.75 Operation successful by 7.30 a.m. Three prisoners taken. of 186th Infantry Regiment (one wounded.)	App.XVI.
		p.m. 7.0	Enemy, after heavy bombardment, counter-attacked on front of our left platoon, and on portion of 108th Infy. Bde. front. Attack was completely repulsed. Men of 186th Infy.Regt. were killed in front of our left posts. During the night $2\frac{1}{2}$ Coys., 16th R.Ir.Rif.(P). and 1 Coy. 2nd R.Ir.Rif. continued the consolidation of our new line. Enemy's artillery and M.Gs. were very active.	
	25th		Two Companies of 2nd R.Ir.Rif. carried on with digging of new front line during night. First instructions re relief of Brigade received. 12th R.Ir.Rif. re-adjusted garrison of front line system during night, leaving three Companies in line, each with two platoons in front, one in support and one in reserve in our old front line. 27 German dead were buried by this date, killed in the recent attack and counter-attacks. Digging of new front line completed by 2nd and 12th Bns. R.Ir.Rifles.	
	26th		Quiet day. Arrangements for relief completed. Nucleus garrisons in BLUE LINE relieved.	App. XVI (a)

Instructions regarding War Diaries and Intelligence Summaries are contained in F. S. Regs., Part II. and the Staff Manual respectively. Title pages will be prepared in manuscript.

WAR DIARY
or
INTELLIGENCE SUMMARY.
(Erase heading not required.)

Army Form C. 2118.

Place	Date	Hour	Summary of Events and Information	Remarks and references to Appendices
PIEBROUCK.	August 27th		Relief by 31st Divn. commenced at dusk. Details will be found in Bde. Order No.279. The first train to leave GODEWAERSVELDE was stopped $\frac{1}{4}$ mile off by enemy shelling, which broke the line, and all troops had to march to ST. MARIE CAPPEL AREA. About 9.0 p.m. three deserters of 88th Infantry Regiment were captured in S.12. by 12th R.Ir.Rif. Relief was complete by 1.30 a.m. Brig-General E.I. de S.THORPE, D.S.O. rejoined from leave and Captain J.H.COOLING, Royal Sussex Regiment joined as Staff Captain, vice Major J.T.DUFFIN, M.C., appointed D.A.A.G.,47th Divn.	App.XVII.
ST. MARIE CAPPEL.	28th		Brigade in rest.	
	29th		Brigade resting.	
	30th		Training commenced. In evening news of enemy withdrawal from BAILLEUL was received.	
	31st		X Corps Horse-Show. 1st R.Ir.Rif. took first prize for turn-out of 2 limbers, 1 water cart, 1 cooker and 2 pack-animals.	
BUDGET COPSE (MONT NOIR)		p.m. 1.0	Brigade moved to BUDGET COPSE, MONT NOIR. Hqrs. in old Brigade Headquarters of 108th and 109th Brigades. Battalions at MONT NOIR CHATEAU, WOLFHOEK and MONT KOKEREELE. Transport Lines moved to BERTHEN.	App.XVIII.
			Summary of Casualties during month is attached.	App.XIX
			Map Sheet, 27 S.E. and 28 S.W. Combined Sheet, is attached for reference.	App.XX.

E. Thorpe
Brig-General,
Commanding 107th Infantry Brigade.

(A9175) Wt W2358/P360 600,000 12/17 D. D. & L. Sch 52a. Forms/C2118/15

Army Form C. 2118.

Instructions regarding War Diaries and Intelligence Summaries are contained in F. S. Regs., Part II, and the Staff Manual respectively. Title pages will be prepared in manuscript.

WAR DIARY
or
INTELLIGENCE SUMMARY.
(Erase heading not required.)

SEPTEMBER, 1918. 107TH INFANTRY BRIGADE.

Place	Date	Hour	Summary of Events and Information	Remarks and references to Appendices
BUDGET COPSE MONT NOIR.	Sept. 1st		Brigade awaiting orders, in Divisional Reserve. Transport Lines at BERTHEN.	
		p.m. 10.0	Brigade Headquarters closed at BUDGET COPSE and opened at ST. JANS CAPPEL Chateau. Battalions moved to area between BAILLEUL and KEERSEBROM, relieving units of 108th Infantry Brigade, who went into line at NEUVE EGLISE, 109th Infantry Brigade moving back to Divisional Reserve.	Appendix I
ST. JANS CAPPEL Ch Chateau (M.32.a.00.20)	2nd		Brigade in Divisional Support.	
		a.m. 9.0	Brigade Headquarters moved to ASYLUM at BAILLEUL. Headquarters in cellars which were very dirty.	
S.18.a. 50.65.	3rd	p.m. 8.30	Brigade Headquarters moved to S.18.a.50.65. Battalions in area S.12., S.18., T.13., T.19., still in Divisional ~~xxxxxxx~~. Support.	
	4th		Brigade did not move.	
	5th	a.m. 11.0	Brigade received warning orders re taking over line from 108th Infantry B rigade.	
			Brigade took over from 108th Inf.Bde. in Front Line, LA PLUS DOUVE FARM Sector. Front Line ran just by BRISTOL CASTLE. Relief complete, 3.15 a.m. 6th September. Orders for attack on 6th September received about 9.30 p.m. Brigade Headquarters at T.19.b.90.90. was severely gas-shelled during the night, several casualties being caused.	Appendix II
T.19.b. 90.90.	6th		Brigade Commander visited 2nd Bn. R.Ir.Rif. in line at 6.0 a.m.	
		p.m. 3.0	Brigade Headquarters moved temporarily to UGBROOKE FARM (T.10.central).	
		4.0	Barrage for attack opened. Heavy rain commenced a few minutes before.	
		4.14	2nd Bn. Royal Irish Rifles report by 'phone that attack seems to have started off well. "A lot of heavy stuff being put in valley behind our lines, where there in no one."	Appendices III and IV
		4.20	2nd Bn. R.Ir.Rif. report message received from front line stating 200 yards already gained and all going well.	
		4.21	Above passed to Division 'G' by 'phone.	
		4.29	Front Line reports 500 yards gained.	
		4.35	Situation reported to Division and flank Brigades. 2nd R.Ir.Rif. 'phone, "Well in touch on the right."	
		4.49	2nd R.Ir.Rif. report casualties rather heavy, but troops appear to be getting on all right.	
		4.59	2nd R.Ir.Rif. report nothing new.	
		5.6	2nd R.Ir.Rif. report a wounded man returning states troops within 100 yards of objective and M.G. fire heavy. Statement not very reliable.	

(A9175) Wt W2358/P360 600,000 12/17 D. D. & L. Sch 52a. Forms/C2118/15

Army Form C. 2118.

Instructions regarding War Diaries and Intelligence Summaries are contained in F. S. Regs., Part II, and the Staff Manual respectively. Title pages will be prepared in manuscript.

WAR DIARY
or
INTELLIGENCE SUMMARY.

SEPTEMBER, 1918. *(Erase heading not required.)* 107TH INFANTRY BRIGADE.

Place	Date	Hour	Summary of Events and Information	Remarks and references to Appendices
T.19.b.90.90.	SEPT. 6th (Contd	p.m. 5.10	Wire says "VOQI H.Q. moved from T.6.c.6.5. to T.6.d.4.7.".	
		5.11	Above message cancelled.	
		5.12	VOQI states by 'phone attack held up on left.	
		5.14	'Phone message states Lieut-Colonel BRIDCUTT slightly gassed.	
		5.16	Enemy reported to be using gas shell freely. Attack held up at BOYLE'S FARM.	
		5.20	Reported to Division 'G' by telephone.	
		5.20	2nd R.Ir.Rif. report objective on right appears to be gained. 5 prisoners reported,	
		5.24	Division 'G' state that O.Ps. report enemy guns firing on BOYLE'S FARM.	
		5.32	Centre Company reported on objective, also right Company. Left Company held up. HANBURY SUPPORT in good condition but has no fire-steps.	
		5.35	Situation reported to all concerned.	
		5.42	Contact aeroplane went over.	
		6.10	Report from O.C. 2nd R.Ir.Rif. from reliable sources objective taken except BOYLES FARM, a crater near which he is dealing with. Enemy machine gun and snipers troubling from CRATER, ONTARIO FARM. Arrangements made with Artillery to deal with them.	
		6.30	So far 6 O.R. prisoners of 12th Company, 72nd Infantry Regiment, and 3 of 12th Company, 22nd Infantry Regiment, (both normal).	
		6.50	Situation reported to Division and Flank Brigades.	
		6.53	Written report from 2nd R.Ir.Rif. "Fight appears to have gone well." Only slight casualties except on left flank, where left company is reported to have suffered severely from M.G. fire. Enemy now putting down heavy gas barrage along valley T.5.b.and d. and T.11.b. and d. Little doubt that objectives are gained.	
		7.10	Aeroplane report received. It places troops slightly forward of our information. Sent on to Battalion in line.	
		8.50	News that enemy is attempting to push in between us and Brigade on our left. 2nd R.Ir.Rif. informed and one Company of 1st R.Ir.Rif. pushed up to restore situation. 2nd R.Ir.Rif. asked for artillery fire North and East of ONTARIO FARM every half hour.	
		9.40	2nd R.Ir.Rif. report situation satisfactory. All objectives secure.	
		10.0	Reported situation to all concerned.	
		10.20	94th Infantry Brigade (on right) report all objectives taken.	
		10.30	Reported trouble on left due to a few enemy stragglers. All quiet.	
			Result of operation :- 19 unwounded prisoners of 22nd and 72nd Inf.Regts.; 8 M.Gs.; 2 T.Ms. Many enemy dead, estimated at 50.	

(A9175) Wt W2358/P360 600,000 12/17 D. D. & L. Sch 52a. Forms/C2118/15

Army Form C. 2118.

Instructions regarding War Diaries and Intelligence Summaries are contained in F. S. Regs., Part II. and the Staff Manual respectively. Title pages will be prepared in manuscript.

WAR DIARY
or
INTELLIGENCE SUMMARY.

SEPTEMBER 1918. *(Erase heading not required.)* 107TH INFANTRY BRIGADE.

Place	Date	Hour	Summary of Events and Information	Remarks and references to Appendices.
T.19.b. 90.90.	Sept. 6th (Contd)	p.m. 11.30	Brigade Headquarters re-opened at T.19.b.90.90.	
			Lieut-Colonel R.C.SMYTHE, D.S.O., and several of Battalion Headquarters, 15th R.Ir.Rif. were gassed in NEUVE EGLISE early on morning of 6th September. Captain H.D.C.CRAIG, Brigade Major and Lieut. H. ORMANDY, M.C., Brigade Signal Officer were also slightly gassed and went to hospital, the former on the night of 6th Sept., the latter on the morning of 7th Sept.	
	7th		Warning orders received for "side-slip" to right. B.G.C. visited 94th Inf.Bde. to make arrangements. Quiet day. Afternoon wet.	
	8th		Relief of 2nd R.Ir.Rif. (less 1 Platoon on right) by a Battalion of 89th Inf.Bde., 30th Divn.; relief of 1 Platoon on right of 2nd R.Ir.Rif. and 24th R.Welsh Fus., 94th Inf.Bde., 31st Divn., by 1st R.Ir.Rif. 15th R.Ir.Rif. relieved 1st R.Ir.Rif. in Support, also 2 Coys. of 12th Norfolk Regt., 94th Inf.Bde. 2nd R.Ir.Rif. came in to Reserve. These moves resulted in Brigade taking over the HILL 63 Sector with one Battalion.	Appendix V
		a.m. 5.0	Enemy put down a heavy bombardment on our front, and attacked our left at 5.30 a.m. Attack was of a half-hearted nature. Two "groups" penetrated our front line, but were satisfactorily dealy with. Two prisoners of 3rd Company, 72nd Inf.Regt., 8th Division, were taken, one wounded. Our line remained intact.	
			Message of congratulation on success of our operation on 6th September, was received from Army Corps and Divisional Commanders.	
	9th		Detachment of Xth Corps Cyclists Battalion attached to Brigade, left to rejoin their Hqrs., 10.0 a.m.	
		p.m. 9.30	Two prisoners (one a Sergeant) of 2nd Coy., 72nd Inf.Regt., 8th Divn., were taken at GOOSEBERRY FARM by 1st Bn. R.Ir.Rif.	
	10th		Very wet day. Site for new Brigade Headquarters at T.14.c.80.80. was selected.	
	11th		NEUVE EGLISE shelled all forenoon. Very wet morning.	
	12th		Very wet day. Enemy artillery quiet during forenoon, but active during rest of day and night. 15th Bn.R.Ir.Rif. went into Front Line, relieving 1st R.Ir.Rif., who moved in Reserve. 2nd R.Ir.Rif. went from Reserve to Support. Relief complete 2.15 a.m.	Appendix VI
	13th		Orders received for relief by 109th Inf.Bde. Brigade Major, 109th Brigade visited Brigade Headquarters. Divisional Commander went round line in the evening. Brig-General E.I. de S. THORPE, was wounded in front line about 11.0 p.m. Preliminary Defence Scheme for HILL 63 Sector issued.	
	14th		Lieut-Colonel M.A MacKENZIE, M.C. (C.R.E. 36th Division) reported to take over Brigade temporarily.	

WAR DIARY
or
INTELLIGENCE SUMMARY.

Army Form C. 2118.

Instructions regarding War Diaries and Intelligence Summaries are contained in F. S. Regs., Part II. and the Staff Manual respectively. Title pages will be prepared in manuscript.

SEPTEMBER, 1918. *(Erase heading not required.)* 107TH INFANTRY BRIGADE.

Place	Date	Hour	Summary of Events and Information	Remarks and references to Appendices
T.19.b. 90.90.	Sept. 14th (Contd)	p.m. 11.30	15th Bn. R.Ir.Rifles captured one O.R. of 4th Company, 6th Pioneer Battalion, 11th Reserve Division.	
			During night, enemy made two unsuccessful raids on left Company of 15th R.Ir.Rif. Both were driven off by rifle and Lewis Gun fire. NEUVE EGLISE Line was heavily gas-shelled during the night. 250 yards of new Front line was dug by Companies of 2nd R.Ir.Rif. on our left Company Front during the night. *Brigade side-slipped 200 yds. to the right during the night*	*Appendix VII*
	15th		Heavy gas shelling after dark all over the area.	
			109th Inf.Bde. relieved 107th Bde. during the night. 107th Bde. withdrew into Divisional Reserve in the BERTHEN - PIEBROUCK Area. Relief was completed without incident at 11.55 p.m.	
			107th Bde. retained command of the Sector until 10.0 a.m. 16th September.	
			Prisoner captured on 14th September gave much valuable information.	
			Two O.R. of Brigade Headquarters Intelligence Section were slightly gassed during the night.	
MONT DES CATS.	16th	a.m. 10.0	Brigade Headquarters closed at T.19.d.90.90. and opened at MONT DES CATS at same hour. No work done by Units, but day devoted to rest and cleaning up. Conference of Commanding Officers at Brigade Headquarters, 6.0 p.m., to settle details of training etc.	*Appendix VIII*
	17th		Day devoted to rest and cleaning up, except by 107th Light Mortar Battery. Light Mortar demonstration at BERTHEN, 5.30 p.m.	
	18th		Training commenced. Mayor of EALING visited Brigade Headquarters.	
			Orders received for move on 19th September.	
			It is definitely established that Brig-General THORPE was wounded by a sentry of 15th R.Ir.Rif. whose post he approached without responding to a challenge.	
P.24.a. 70.40.	19th		Brigade moved by march route to STEENVOORDE Area. Brigade Headquarters at P.24.a.70.40. (Sheet 27.)	*Appendix IX*
	20th		Brigade remained at P.24.a.70.40. (Sheet 27) STEENVOORDE AREA.	
ESQUELBECQ.	21st		Brigade made night march to ESQUELBECQ Area. Headquarters - ESQUELBECQ Chateau. March completed by 1.0 a.m. Troops stood the march well.	*Appendix X*
	22nd		Brigade remained at ESQUELBECQ.	
			Notification received that Brig-General H.J.BROCK, C.M.G., D.S.O., R.A., (from C.R.A., 36th Division) to command the Brigade.	
	23rd		Brig-General H.J.BROCK, C.M.G., D.S.O., R.A., took over command of Brigade from Lieut-Colonel M.A.MacKENZIE, M.C., R.E.	
			Platoon Training. Party of 3 Officers (including Brigade Major) paid a visit to the Fleet at DUNKERQUE.	

(A9475) Wt W2358/P360 600,000 12/17 D. D. & L. Sch. 52a. Forms/C2118/15

WAR DIARY
or
INTELLIGENCE SUMMARY.

Army Form C. 2118.

Instructions regarding War Diaries and Intelligence Summaries are contained in F. S. Regs., Part II. and the Staff Manual respectively. Title pages will be prepared in manuscript.

SEPTEMBER, 1918. *(Erase heading not required.)* 107TH INFANTRY BRIGADE.

Place	Date	Hour	Summary of Events and Information	Remarks and references to Appendices
ESQUELBECQ	Sept 24th		Platoon Training. Weather fine.	
	25th		Divisional Commander inspected Battalions of Brigade and presented Medal Ribbons. In the afternoon Battalions carried out training with No.36 and No.37 Rifle Grenades.	
	26th		Orders received from Division for move of Brigade on night 26/27th by march route to TUNNELLING CAMP, South of PROVEN. Moved to TUNNELLING CAMP by march route.	Appendix XI
TUNNELLING CAMP.	27th		Brigade moved from TUNNELLING CAMP to 'P', 'F', and 'X' CAMPS AREA (Sh.28/A.15. and 16.) by march route.	Appendix XII
'P' CAMP.	28th		Moved by light railway from 'P' CAMP to WHITE CHATEAU, YPRES -MENIN ROAD.	Appendix XIII
WHITE CHATEAU	29th		Transport Lines established at WHITE CHATEAU. Brigade moved to WESTHOEK by march route. In Divisional Reserve.	
WESTHOEK.	30th		Moved from WESTHOEK to TERHAND - BECELAERE Area and came into Divisional Support.	Appendix XIV
			Statement of Casualties for month attach.	App. XV.
			Map, Belgium and France, Sheet 28, 1/40,000 is attached for reference.	App. XVI.

H. J. Brock
Brig-General,
Commanding 107th Infantry Brigade.

(A9175) Wt W2358/P360 600,000 12/17 D. D. & L. Sch 52a. Forms/C2118/15

Instructions regarding War Diaries and Intelligence Summaries are contained in F. S. Regs., Part II, and the Staff Manual respectively. Title pages will be prepared in manuscript.

WAR DIARY
or
INTELLIGENCE SUMMARY.

(Erase heading not required.)

Army Form C. 2118.

OCTOBER, 1918. 107th INF. BRIGADE. Vol

Place	Date	Hour	Summary of Events and Information	Remarks and references to Appendices
TERHAND	Oct. 1.		2nd R.Ir.Rif. with objective as HEULE, G.17., BISSEGHEM, G.35., and COURTRAI, attack at 6.15 a.m. 1st R.Ir.Rif. in Support, 15th R.Ir.Rif. in Reserve. Attack held up by enemy machine guns. 1st R.Ir.Rif. relieve 2nd R.Ir.Rif. in ~~Support~~ front; 15th R.Ir.Rif. relieve 1st R.Ir.Rif. in Support; 2nd R.Ir.Rif. withdraw to Brigade Reserve.	App I.
TERHAND.	2nd		An attempt at 7.30 a.m. to push forward our positions in 24.c. and 30.a. resulted in our reaching DIBSLAND FARM, K.24.d.60.05. Heavy machine gun fire encountered. Line runs K.29.a.93.53. - K.30.a.20.70. - K.24.c.55.30. - K.24.b.00.20. Headquarters TERHAND.	App II
	3rd		A quiet day. One prisoner belonging to the 172nd Inf. Regt. captured while he was collecting wounded about K.30.c.0.7.	
	4th		Fairly quiet day. 15th R.Ir.Rif. from Support relieved 1st R.Ir.Rif. in front line, who withdrew to Brigade Reserve. 2nd R.Ir.Rif. moved from Reserve to Support.	
	5th		Quiet day. Brigade relieved by 104th and 105th Infantry Brigades, 35th Division. 15th and 2nd Bns. R.Ir.Rif. on relief withdrew to billets in J.10. and 11, and Northern half of J.16. and 17. 1st R.Ir.Rif. and Brigade Headquarters did not move.	App III " III (a)
			Regarding the period of past week under review, the Brigade came into the attack when the enemy defence was thickening and becoming organized. Owing to the bad weather and extensive crater area from YPRES to BECELAERE it had not been possible to bring up more than, at first, 18-pdrs. The supply of artillery ammunition was very limited owing to difficulty of carriage by pack on long and almost impassable roads. The limited roads that existed were blocked with transport and troops (including a French Cavalry Division) for long periods. Certain wagons of Brigade Headquarters took 36 hours to get from WHITE CHATEAU, YPRES to TERHAND. Opposite the Brigade Sector was 172nd Inf.Regt., 1st Bavarian Division. From evidence of prisoners their Battalion strength was only 100, but they had nine light machine guns per Company. With these well ensconced in concrete pill-boxes, the Infantry, unsupported by Tanks and with very little artillery support - practically no smoke shells being available - could make very little progress without suffering considerable losses. The supply of S.A.A. and rifle grenades, Nos.36 and 37, was difficult; this was met by the Royal Air Force who dropped in two days 36,000 rounds of S.A.A. including some boxes of bombs in the Brigade Sector. While it was important to push towards COURTRAI, and further, out-flank the enemy defensive	

(A9175) Wt W2358/P360 600,000 12/17 D. D. & L. Sch. 52a. Forms/C2118/15

Army Form C. 2118.

WAR DIARY
or
INTELLIGENCE SUMMARY.

Instructions regarding War Diaries and Intelligence Summaries are contained in F. S. Regs., Part II. and the Staff Manual respectively. Title pages will be prepared in manuscript.

OCTOBER, 1918. *(Erase heading not required.)* 107TH INF. BRIGADE.

Place	Date	Hour	Summary of Events and Information	Remarks and references to Appendices
	Oct.		lines protecting LILLE, the losses suffered by troops (in good spirits though tired) decided in favour of a policy of waiting until our guns and supplies came up, ~~and~~ before undertaking an advance again on a big scale. The enemy was well supplied with artillery which he used freely. He relied on his artillery and machine guns to defend the sector. Without this support it/is doubtful whether his Infantry would have put up any fight.	
	6th		Quiet day, except for some field gun and field howitzer shelling.	
	7th		TERHAND Cross-roads heavily shelled at intervals throughout the 24 hours.. 1st R.Ir.Rif. moved to J.11.a. in the afternoon.	
J.11.d. 10.20.	8th	a.m. 9.45	Brigade Headquarters closed at TERHAND and opened at J.11.d.10.20. Capt. H.D.C.CRAIG, Brigade Major, was admitted to Hospital, his duties being taken over by Capt. E.A.GODSON,M.C., 9th Bn. Royal Irish Fusiliers.	
POLYGONNE BUTT.	9th		Brigade Headquarters moved to POLYGONNE BUTT Captain J.H.COOLING, Staff Captain, rejoined from leave.	
	10th		Quiet day. Three observation balloons brought down by enemy aeroplanes close to Brigade Headquarte rs.	
	11th		Captain W.J.MENAUL, M.C., 9th Bn. Royal Irish Fusiliers, Assistant Staff Captain, returned to 108th Inf.Bde., and Captain A. WALLACE, 2nd Bn. R.Ir.Rif. rejoined from 108th Inf.Bde. as Assistant Staff Captain.	
	12th		Nothing of note. Wet day.	
	13th		Final operations for attack . In evening Brigade moved by march route to assembly positions. 15th R.Ir.Rif. assembled in trenches just dug by 16th R.Ir.Rif. (P) and 122nd Field Company,R?E. Guiding tapes were laid out by Brigade Intelligence Section in advance of this line. 1st and 2nd R.Ir.Rif. assembled in areas west of out front line. Assembly complete about 01.00 on 14th October.	App IV
GUINNESS FARM.	14th	04.40 05.00	- Enemy counter-preparation bombardment on our assembly areas. Very few casualties caused, assembly having taken place in positions seldom shelled.	
		05.32 05.35	Barrage for attack opened. 'H' hour. Attack commenced. Fairly heavy enemy reply to our barrage. Fine morning, just dawning. Heavy ground mist!	

(A9175) Wt W2353/P360 600,000 12/17 D. D. & L. Sch 52a. Forms/C2118/15

WAR DIARY
or
INTELLIGENCE SUMMARY.
(Erase heading not required.)

Army Form C. 2118.

Instructions regarding War Diaries and Intelligence Summaries are contained in F. S. Regs., Part II, and the Staff Manual respectively. Title pages will be prepared in manuscript.

OCTOBER, 1918. 107TH INFY. BRIGADE.

Place	Date	Hour	Summary of Events and Information	Remarks and references to Appendices
GUINNESS FARM.	Oct. 14th (Contd)	06.00	Mist continued. Enemy artillery quieter.	
		06.25	15th R.Ir.Rif. report move forward of their Headquarters and report prisoners of 1st R.I.R., 1st Bavarian Division.	
		06.30	Several prisoners of 1st R.I.R. passed Brigade Headquarters. Prisoners state attack was not expected.	
		07.13	Following by runner from 15th R.Ir.Rif.? "Advance apparently proceeding satisfactorily, but no news yet from Companies." Timed 6.35 a.m.	
		09.00	No further news from our troops. Visibility much better, about 400 yards. Not much hostile shelling.	
		09.25	Captain PATTON, with advance party from 107th and 109th Brigades and 153rd and 173rd Bdes.R.F.A. went forward to open advanced Headquarters at ASHMORE FARM. On way very few dead were seen. Enemy artillery quiet.	
		09.30	Orders sent out to watch right flank carefully, as 35th Division appear to be checked there.	
		09.30	Order from Division received, ordering 108th Brigade (Divl. Reserve) to move forward.	
		10.00	Divn. wire that flares were seen on line L.17.a.5.9. - L.17.a.3.6. - L.23.c.1.1. - L.21.b.6.7. - L.28.b.5.5.	
		10.33	Division report that our troops were seen entering MOORSEELE.	
		11.05	Report that 15th R.Ir.Rif. are consolidating on line just East of MOORSEELE, and 1st R.Ir.Rif. passing through them. Timed 09.45.	
ASHMORE FARM.		12.00	Brigade Headquarters moved to ASHMORE FARM.	
		13.00	Brigade Headquarters arrived complete at ASHMORE FARM. Lieut. McCAULL, 107th L.M.Battery, went forward to reconnoitre.	
		12.40	1st R.Ir.Rif. line approximately G.19.b. and d. 15th R.Ir.Rif. report MOORSEELE cleared.	
		13.25	1st R.Ir.Rif. report line G.20.c.50.70. North to G.14.a.80.00. 109th Inf.Bde. reported to be digging in North of this.	
		13.25	1st R.Ir.Rif. report 104th Bde. (on right) getting on. 1st R.Ir.Rif. sending a party to turn GULLEGHEM from South.	
		13.30	1st R.Ir.Rif. report troops still moving forward under heavy machine gun fire from GULLEGHEM.	
		17.00	1st R.Ir.Rif. still checked before GULLEGHEM. Verbal instructions were given to O.C. Motor Machine Gun Battery, and O.C. Platoon of II Corps Cyclists sent up by Division, that they were to attempt to turn GULLEGHEM from the South.	
		17.08	1st R.Ir.Rif. informed of above. They state they believe our troops are already in GULLEGHEM.	
		16.00	British aeroplane crashed at Windmill East of MOORSEELE. Both pilot and observer killed.	
		22.55	Divn. order Motor Machine Battery and Corps Cyclists, who had as yet not moved off, to revert to Divisional reserve.	

Army Form C. 2118.

WAR DIARY
or
INTELLIGENCE SUMMARY.
(Erase heading not required.)

Instructions regarding War Diaries and Intelligence Summaries are contained in F. S. Regs., Part II. and the Staff Manual respectively. Title pages will be prepared in manuscript.

OCTOBER, 1918. 107TH INF. BRIGADE.

Place	Date	Hour	Summary of Events and Information	Remarks and references to Appendices
ASHMORE FARM.	Oct. 14th (contd)	16.00	Enemy aeroplane shot down by Lewis gun fire at G.19.d.50.50.; one officer and one "Gefreiter" of 16th Flieger Abteilung taken prisoners.	
			The following message was received from G.O.C.II Corps and forwarded to units :-	
			"The Army Commander wishes me to convey to you and all commanders and troops engaged to-day "his congratulations on the successful results achieved on what has been a long and arduous "day."	
			Numerous enemy prisoners were taken during the day, mainly of 1st Bavarian Reserve Inf.Regt., 1st Bavarian Res. Divn. A number of civilians were found in MOORSEELE and the outskirts of GULLEGHEM and evacuated to the rear. MOORSEELE was heavily gas-shelled at dusk, otherwise there was little enemy artillery fire after 10.00.	
	15th		The situation at midnight, 14/15th October, was :-	
			1st R.Ir.Rifles - In position 300 yards West of GULLEGHEM, in touch with units on both flanks.	
			2nd R.Ir.Rifles - In support just East of MOORSEELE.	
			15th R.Ir.Rifles - In reserve about MOORSEELE.	
		00.30	Orders were issued for an attack at 09.00. 1st R.Ir.Rif. were to attack at that hour under a creeping barrage and take GULLEGHEM, halting on a line East of the village; 2nd R.Ir.Rif. were then to pass through and proceed to the "Corps 1st Objective". 15th R.Ir.Rif. were to follow up and consolidate a line between the two streets running S.E. and S.W. from the centre of GULLEGHEM.	
		04.20	1st R.Ir.Rif. report situation quiet. MOORSEELE was being gas-shelled.	
		07.20	2nd R.Ir.Rif. Headquarters at buildings S. of BARLEY CORNER.	
		09.00	Attack opened.	
		09.30	Attack progressing satisfactorily	
		10.00	Position as follows :-	
			1st R.Ir.Rifles - On objective East of GULLEGHEM, but owing to 1st R.Ir.Rif. having "lost the barrage" by proceeding too slowly through the heavy wire just West of GULLEGHEM and through that village, 2nd R.Ir.Rif. were unable to pass through them on the first objective.	
			2nd R.Ir.Rifles were therefore halted in the street running S.E. from the centre of GULLEGHEM.	
			15th R.Ir.Rifles consolidating line as ordered.	
		11.00	Prisoners arriving at Brigade Headquarters from GULLEGHEM. They belonged mainly to the 2nd and 3rd Bns. 181st Inf.Regt., 40th (Saxon) Division. A few belonged to 9th Ulahnen Regt., 6th Cavalry Division. Enemy shelling GULLEGHEM.	
		14.10	Arrangements made with Divl. Artillery to fire on machine guns holding up 2nd R.Ir.Rif. at 15.30. 2nd R.Ir.Rif. are then to advance and gain "Corps 1st Objective."	

WAR DIARY
or
INTELLIGENCE SUMMARY.

Army Form C. 2118.

Instructions regarding War Diaries and Intelligence Summaries are contained in F. S. Regs., Part II. and the Staff Manual respectively. Title pages will be prepared in manuscript.

OCTOBER, 1918. (*Erase heading not required.*) 107TH INF. BRIGADE.

Place	Date	Hour	Summary of Events and Information	Remarks and references to Appendices
ASHMORE FARM.	Oct. 15th (Contd)	14.30	109th Inf.Bde. on our left reported through HEULE.	
		16.10	2nd R.Ir.Rif. report advance proceeding satisfactorily.	
		17.20	2nd R.Ir.Rif. at G.23.d.2.4. and advancing.	
		19.10	2nd R.Ir.Rif. report objective reached.and touch with Brigade on left. B.G.C. instructed 2nd R.Ir.Rif. by 'phone to push on ~~xxx~~ LYS.	
		16.59	15th R.Ir.Rif. (Reserve Battalion) report touch with leading Battalion of Brigade on right (19th Durham Light Infantry) at G.27.a.60.60. The latter are stationary and have an outpost line 150 yards forward of this point.	
		20.15	1st R.Ir.Rif. instructed to form a defensive flank from G.22.d.00.30. to G.23.d.30.20.	
	16th		During the night 15/16th October, all troops of this Brigade which had passed beyond the "Corps first Objective", i.e. practically all of 2nd R.Ir.Rif. fell back on that line, under orders received from Division.	
			108th Inf. Bde. formed up on this line and attacked under a barrage at 05.30 proceeding as far aa the LYS at COURTRAI. This was done in ignorance of the fact that a patrol of 2nd R.Ir. Rifles had penetrated to the LYS through COURTRAI during the night. This patrol under Lieut. F. ADAMS, a native of COURTRAI, failed to send back reports of its whereabouts, and remained in COURTRAI until involved in our own barrage, returning later with five prisoners.	
		09.00	Brigade Headquarters moved to farm at G.14.c.60.20.	
G.14.c. 60.20.		11.00	Orders were received for the Brigade to move back to billets in the ROLLEGHEM CAPPELLE Area. Many civilians passed to the rear during day.	
L.3.b.45.75.		13.30	Brigade moved to ROLLEGHEM CAPELLE Area via KOH-I-NOR Cross Roads. Brigade Headquarters moved to L.3.b.45.75. near POET'S CORNER. Very wet afternoon.	
	17th		Brigade at rest.	
	18th		B.G.C. visited units in the morning and addressed troops on parade. In the afternoon, Brigade marched to LENDELEDE via WINKEL ST. ELOI, and remained in billets in LENDELEDE Area during the night.	app. V
B.13.a. 20.40.	19th		Brigade Headquarters at B.13.a.20.40. Officers of all units reconnoitred forward area between BAVICHOVE and OYGHEM, held by 109th Inf. Bde. G.O.C. 36th Division inspected Battalions on parade in the afternoon.	
		16.30	Conference of C.Os. at Brigade Headquarters to discuss orders received for attack next day.	app VI
		21.00	Brigade Headquarters moved to old enemy ammunition dump at B.17.central. Units moved to their assembly positions during the night. Very wet night.	app VI (a)

WAR DIARY or INTELLIGENCE SUMMARY.

Army Form C. 2118.

Instructions regarding War Diaries and Intelligence Summaries are contained in F. S. Regs., Part II, and the Staff Manual respectively. Title pages will be prepared in manuscript.

OCTOBER, 1918. (*Erase heading not required.*) 107TH INF. BRIGADE.

Place	Date	Hour	Summary of Events and Information	Remarks and references to Appendices
B.17.cent.	Oct. 20th	02.00	15th and 1st R.Ir.Rif. moved off and crossed the LYS by bridge just completed at C.19.a.50.20. forming up just N.W. of the HARLEBEKE - VIVE ST. ELOI Road, and relieving a Battalion of 109th Inf.Brigade, which had reached that line after an attack opening at 02.00.	
		05.55	Telephone through to 15th R.Ir.Rif., who state they are 300 - 400 yards behind main road, 109th Inf.Bde. not having reached their objective.	
		06.00	Barrage opened and attack commenced, 15th R.Ir.Rif. leading, followed by 1st R.Ir.Rif. Morning very misty. Dawn commenced about 05.30. Heavy enemy machine gun fire audible at Brigade Headquarters.	
		07.24	15th R.Ir.Rif. report by 'phone that troops are keeping well up to the barrage.	
		09.25	Report from Captain J.H.A. PATTON states line reported checked at I.10.central.	
		09.52	Following from Captain PATTON at C.20.c.30.40., "15th Bn. message timed 09.15 states Battalion going on well. Line believed near objective.	
		10.00	Brigade Headquarters moved to C.20.c.30.40.	
~~C.20.c.~~ 30.40.		11.40	Message from 15th R.Ir.Rif. giving approximate line as I.10.d.40.10. - I.10.b.99.01. - I.5.c.70.20. Advance checked by machine gun fire from several places. Arrangements made for artillery to deal with these places.	
		12.35	15th R.Ir.Rif. checked by machine gun fire from Mill at I.5.d.01.10. Lieut-Colonel B.J.JONES, D.S.O., commanding 15th R.Ir.Rifles, reported killed.	
		13.33	Mill at I.5.d.01.10. reported cleared. 15th R.Ir.Rif. line runs about 200 yards North-West of the GAVERBEEK.	
			During the evening 15th R.Ir.Rif. advanced slightly and reached and crossed the GAVERBEEK. About 80 enemy prisoners were taken during the day, including six officers.	← Not borne out by unit diaries
	21st	07.30	1st R.Ir.Rif. attacked, 2nd R.Ir.Rif. moving in support.	
		11.20	1st R.Ir.Rif. report Left Company checked at I.18.b.20.20. by machine gun fire. They have no touch with 108th Inf.Bde. on left.	
		11.33	1st R.Ir.Rif. report centre Company line from J.11.c.30.70. to I.18.d.60.00.	?
I ?		13.00	1st R.Ir.Rif. on line I.18.d.50.00., I.18.d.60.10., I.18.b.10.40., I.18.a.70.10. Progress during day was slow. At dusk the line was approximately I.24.a.60.50. - I.24.a.99.99. I.18.d.80.10. - L.5.central, the left flank portion of this being held by one Company each of 2nd and 15th Bns. R.Ir.Rif. with one Company of 1st R.Ir.Rif., and the remainder of the line by two Companies of 1st R.Ir.Rif., one Company of 1st R.Ir.Rif. being in Battalion Reserve. A few prisoners of 40th Division were taken.	
	22nd		During the night 21/22nd there was considerable enemy shelling, the whole Brigade area receiving a general sprinkling of H.E. and gas-shell. Enemy M.Gs. were very active.	

Army Form C. 2118.

WAR DIARY
or
INTELLIGENCE SUMMARY.
(Erase heading not required.)

Instructions regarding War Diaries and Intelligence Summaries are contained in F. S. Regs., Part II, and the Staff Manual respectively. Title pages will be prepared in manuscript.

OCTOBER, 1918. 107th INF. BRIGADE.

Place	Date	Hour	Summary of Events and Information	Remarks and references to Appendices
C.20.c. 30.40.	Oct. 22nd	09.00	2nd R.Ir.Rif. advanced and took the line J.26.a.80.20. - J.20.a.60.10. - J.20.a.10.75. - J.19.b.80.90. Considerable trouble was caused by enemy machine guns in the Mill at J.20.a.40.00. and by the exposure of our left flank due to the 108th Inf.Bde. being much behind us.	App VII
		14.55	2nd R.Ir.Rif. report enemy counter-attack pushing back their left and centre Companies. Artillery informed. 2nd R.Ir.Rif. send four platoons (two from reserve Company and two from attached Company of 15th R.Ir.Rif.) to restore situation. Brigade Commander orders two Companies of 1st R.Ir.Rif. to KNOCK to support 2nd R.Ir.Rif. Situation was completely restored before the arrival of these two Companies, and original line re-established. Reports from prisoners taken next night indicate that this counter-attack, which was a dertermined effort to turn the KIIJTBERG Ridge position from the North, was carried out by a Prussian Assault Battalion sent up for the purpose. About 60 prisoners taken during day.	
		19.55	Division order positions now held to be consolidated, as advance is to cease temporarily. Orders issued; 2nd R.Ir.Rif. to hold front, and 15th R.Ir.Rif.left flank positions.	App VIII
		23.50	2nd R.Ir.Rif. report a prisoner of 104th Inf.Regt., a runner, with orders carried by him ordering a withdrawal of his Battalion in an Easterly direction, distance not stated. Prisoner had lost his way and been captured by a patrol.	
	23rd	01.15	Prisoner about-mentioned arrived at Brigade Headquarters. Information wired to Division and flank Brigades, and 2nd and 15th R.Ir.Rif. ordered to send out patrols to maintain touch with the enemy.	App IX
		10.17	Verbal instructions sent by 'phone to 1st R.Ir.Rif. to detail two Companies as Advanced Guard, to move towards L'ESCAUT at TENHOVE. Remainder of Brigade to stand in readiness to follow, except Machine Gun Company attached to Brigade, which was ordered to take over the defence of the left flank. 108th Inf.Bde. on left have instructions to move also. A wounded prisoner of 104th Inf.Regt. taken by 2nd R.Ir.Rif. corroborates withdrawal of his Company, but does not know how far they are moving.	
		11.10	Captain DESNOYERS, Commanding 3rd Squadron, 28th Regt. de Dragons, French Army, reported to Brigade Commander. He was instructed to proceed towards TENHOVE, to try to seize KLEINEBERG and BERGWIJK and bridge over L'ESCAUT.	
		14.05	Situation:- Enemy holding HEINWEG and HUISBOSCH, also SCHEIDHOEK and INGOYGHEM. Remainder of 1st R.Ir.Rif. about J.19.central, 15th R.Ir.Rif. following 1500 yards behind. 2nd R.Ir.Rif. standing ready to move. French Cavalry unable to proceed beyond J.19.central owing to long-range machine gun fire. 4th Motor Machine Gun Battery supporting Cavalry, also halted.	

(A9175) Wt W2358/P360 600,000 12/17 D. D. & L. Sch. 52a. Forms/C2118/15

Army Form C. 2118.

WAR DIARY
or
INTELLIGENCE SUMMARY.
(Erase heading not required.)

Instructions regarding War Diaries and Intelligence Summaries are contained in F. S. Regs., Part II. and the Staff Manual respectively. Title pages will be prepared in manuscript.

OCTOBER, 1918. 107TH INF. BRIGADE.

Place	Date	Hour	Summary of Events and Information	Remarks and references to Appendices
C.20.c. 30.40.	Oct. 23rd (Contd)	19.00	Situation :- 1st R.Ir.Rif. on line J.26.d.05.40. - J.26.d.80.80. - J.26.b.55.90. - J.20.d.40.50 - J.20.b.90.60, in touch with 27th Inf. Bde. on right and 108th Inf.Bde. on left. 15th R.Ir. Rifles in support and 2nd R.Ir.Rif. in reserve. 4th M.M.G.Battery assisting in defence, also 'C' Coy., 36th Bn. M.G.C. French Cavalry withdrawn.	
			During the night 109th Inf.Bde. relieved 107th Inf.Bde. 107th Inf.Bde. withdrew to Divl. Reserve in the area HULSTE - OYGHEM - DESSELGHEM. Command of sector passed to 109th Bde. at 24.00 on completion of relief.	App X
			Capt. H.D.C.CRAIG, Brigade Major, rejoined from Hospital and took over duties from Capt. A.E.GODSON, M.C.	
			Two congratulatory messages were received, one from Marechal FOCH, commanding the Allied Armies, and one from G.O.C., II Corps. (Copies are attached.)	App XI
~~XXXXXXXXX XX~~.	24th	10.00	Brigade Headquarters closed at I.3.b.30.70. and opened at C.20.a.40.30. Brigade resting. Weather fine.	
C.20.a.40.30.	25th		The Brigade, less Brigade Headquarters and 1st Bn. Royal Irish Rifles, moves into position in close Divisional Support. ~~XXXXXXXXXXXXX~~	App XI (A)
	26th		107th Infantry Brigade plus 36th Bn. Machine Gun Corps moved to Area LENDELEDE, Square B.13. and B.14.	App XII
LENDELEDE.	27th		Brigade Group moved from LENDELEDE to BELLEGHEM Area. Brigade Headquarters located at N.29.c.10.80.	App XIII
N.29.c.10. 80.	28th		Belleghem. Battalions Training.	
	29th		BELLEGHEM. Battalions Training.	
	30th		BELLEGHEM. Battalions Training.	
	31st		BELLEGHEM. Battalions Training.	App XIV Reinforcements & Casualties during month.

C Becher.
Lieut-Colonel,
for Brig-General,
Commanding 107th Infantry Brigade.

107TH INFANTRY BRIGADE

Narrative of Operations carried out by the 107th Inf.Bde.
28.9.1918. to 28.10.1918.

++++++++++++++++++++

Ref. Sheets 28 N.W. and 28 N.E. 1/20,000.

Sept.28th On afternoon of this date Brigade moved by Light Railway from 'P' Camp Area, A.15., to Camp in neighbourhood of B.27. On arrival in this Area orders were received from Corps that the attack delivered on the YPRES Front that morning had progressed so favourably that the Brigade was not to detrain, but to move on to accommodation in the Trench Systems just East of YPRES. Brigade detrained at HELL FIRE CORNER, I.10.d. at about 23.00. Brigade Headquarters for the night 28/29th was in the Ramparts, YPRES.

Sept.29th The Brigade (in Divisional Reserve) moved by march route to WESTHOEK, J.7.b.

Sept.30th On night 29/30th the situation was roughly as follows :-

109th Inf.Bde. on the Divisional Front had reached a line just West of TERHAND.
108th Inf.Bde. were in support, and 107th Inf.Bde. in Reserve.at WESTHOEK.
Orders were received on the night 29/30th for 108th Inf. Bde. to pass through the 109th Inf.Bde., and for the 107th Inf.Bde. to follow in support of the 108th Inf.Bde. The line troops of 107th Inf.Bde. to be on a North and South line through BECELAERE by 07.00 on the 30th. The Brigade moved accordingly, Brigade Headquarters moving to POLYGON BUTTS, J.10.a.6.8, conforming with the advance made by the 108th Infantry Brigade. The Brigade again moved forward at 11.00; the xxxxxRxIrxRix. 2nd R.Ir.Rif. proceeding to the outskirts of TERHAND; 1st and 15th Bns.R.Ir.Rif. to the neighbourhood of MOLENHOEK, K.7.d. Brigade Headquarters was established with Headquarters of 108th Inf.Bde. at Cross Roads, TERHAND. On the afternoon of the 30th situation was as follows :-

29th Division, on right of 36th Division, were on the outskirts of GHELUWE, which was offering strong resistance.
The 88th Inf.Bde. were taking the village.
108th Inf.Bde, were advancing through 9th Divn. (on left of 36th Divn.) between L.13.central and KLEPHOEK.
9th Division were on the general line L.13.central - F.19.d.

At 13.55 orders were issued for 2nd R.Ir.Rif. to move South-East from TERHAND to K.29.c. to deploy in that area and attack on a 800 yards front due East, with centre on KLYTHOEK, L.26.d. - ~~KISSEGHEM~~ POESELHOEK, L.25.d. - KISSEGHEM - G.25. The 1st R.Ir.Rif. to move in Support 1000 yards in rear of 2nd R.Ir.Rif. 15th R.Ir.Rif. to move to Western outskirts of TERHAND. At 17.50 2nd R.Ir.Rif. deployed on line astride TURNBULL FARM, K.28.b.9.3. and attacked at 18.00. The attack reached a general line K.29.central - CARTON HOUSE, K.30.a.; troops being held up by strong uncut wire in front of enemy trench system in this area. They were also met by extremely heavy machine gun fire.

Oct. 1st At 06.15 the 2nd R.Ir.Rif. attacked with extended frontage K.29.central - VIJFWEGEN; 1st R.Ir.Rif. in support, 15th R.Ir. Rifles in reserve.

Owing to machine guns fire from pill-boxes, particularly on the right flank, the attack did not meet with much success. Lieut-Colonel J.H.BRIDCOTT, D.S.O., Commanding 2nd R.Ir.Rifles, was killed whilst attempting to re-organise two of his Companies which had lost direction owing to the mist and darkness, in the neighbourhood of CARTON HOUSE. 1st R.Ir.Rif. relieved 2nd R.Ir.Rif. in front line on the evening of the 1/2nd October, 1918.

Oct. 2nd At 07.30 an attempt was made to push forward our positions in K.24.c. and K.30.a. The attack met with no success.on right, but on the left one platoon succeeded in reaching DIBSLAND FARM, K.24.d.60.05. This platoon was not however, able to hold the farm. Heavy machine gun fire was again encountered.

The line then ran as follows :-

K.29.a.95.53. - K.30.a.20.70. - K.24.c.55.30. - K.24.b.00.20.
Brigade Headquarters - TERHAND.

Oct. 3rd A quiet day. One prisoner belonging to the 172nd Inf. Regt. captured while he was collecting wounded about K.30.c.0.7.

Oct. 4th Fairly quiet day. 15th R.Ir.Rif. from Support relieved 1st R.Ir.Rif. in front line, who withdrew to Brigade Reserve. 2nd R.Ir.Rif. moved from Reserve to Support.

Oct. 5th Quiet day. Brigade relieved by 104th and 105th Infantry Brigades, 35th Division. 15th and 2nd Bns. R.Ir.Rif. on relief withdrew to billets in J.10. and 11. and Northern half of J.16. and J.17. 1st R.Ir.Rif. and Brigade Headquarters did not move.

Regarding the period of past week under review, the Brigade came into the attack when the enemy defence was thickening and becoming organised. Owing to the bad weather and extensive crater area from YPRES to BECELAERE it had not been possible to bring up more than, at first, 18-pdrs. The supply of artillery ammunition was very limited owing to difficulty of carriage by pack on long and almost impassable roads. The limited roads that existed were blocked with transport and troops (including a French Cavalry Division) for long periods. Certain wagons of Brigade Headquarters took 36 hours to get from WHITE CHATEAU, YPRES, to TERHAND.

Opposite the Brigade Sector was 172nd Inf.Regt., 1st Bavarian Division. From evidence of prisoners their Battalion strength was only 100, but they had nine light machine guns per Company. With these well ensconced in concrete pill-boxes, our Infantry, unsupported by Tanks and with very little artillery support - practically no smoke shells being available - could make very little progress without sufferring considerable losses. The supply of S.A.A. and rifle grenades, Nos.36 and 37, was difficult; this was met by the Royal Air Force who dropped in two days 36,000 rounds of S.A.A. including some boxes of bombs in the Brigade Sector.

While it was important to push towards COURTRAI, and further, out-flank the enemy defensive lines protecting LILLE, the losses suffered by troops (in good spirits though tired) decided in favour of a policy of waiting until our guns and supplies came up, and before undertaking an advance again on a big scale. The enemy was well supplied with artillery which he used freely. He relied on his artillery and machine guns to defend the sector. Without this support it is

Oct. 5th (Contd) doubtful whether his Infantry would have put up any fight.

Oct. 6th to 13th. From 6.10.1918. to 13.10.1918. Brigade in Divisional Reserve in Area POLYGON WOOD and POLYGONE BUTTE. These dates spent in training and re-organisation and preparation for continuation of operations.

Oct. 12th Orders issued for attack on morning of the 14th Oct.

Oct.13th On evening of 13th Brigade moved to positions of assembly. 15th R.Ir.Rif. forming up in trenches newly dug by 16th Bn. R.Ir.Rif. (P) and 122nd Field Company, R.E. in Sh. 28/N.E./29 N.W. L.19. (GREEN Line). 1st R.Ir.Rif. assembling N., W., and S. of WORTHINGTON FARM. 2nd R.Ir.Rif. in area K.16.d.6.8. Assembly complete about 01.00, 14th October. Casualties slight. Brigade H.Q. established GUINNES FARM, K.17.d.

Oct. 14th On 14th Oct, at 04.40 enemy put down counter-preparation barrage on assembly area. Very few casualties caused as choice of assembly area was made after careful reconnaissance.

05.32. Barrage for attack opened. Enemy reply heavy.

05.35, Attack commenced - 15th R.Ir.Rif. leading; 1st R.Ir.Rif. in Support; and 2nd R.Ir.Rif. in reserve. On the right of Brigade the 104th Inf.Bde., 35th Division, and on the left the 109th Inf.Bde., 36th Division.

A dense fog made keeping of direction very difficult for the Infantry but no serious loss of same occurred. Attack made rapid progress.

10.35. 15th R.Ir.Rif. had taken MOORSELE and were consolidating East of that place - 1st R.Ir.Rif. passing through them.

12.00. Brigade Headquarters moved to ASHMORE FARM (L.15.c.)

104th Inf.Bde, on right, previously temporarily checked have now moved forward.

13.25. Line - G.20.c.50.70. North to G.14.a.80.00. 1st R.Ir.Rif. had encountered three belts of wire West of outskirts of GULLEGHEM and endeavoured to out-flank the village from the South in co-operation with attempt by 109th Inf.Bde. to do the same from the North. Both attempts failed, (the fog having disappeared), under heavy machine gun fire.

23.59. At midnight 14/15th October position was -

1st R.Ir.Rif. dug in 300 yards West of GULLEGHEM, in touch with Units on both flanks.

2nd R.Ir.Rif. in support East of MOORSELE,

15th R.Ir.Rif. in reserve about MOORSELE.

Oct. 15th

09.00. 1st R.Ir.Rif. under a barrage captured GULLEGHEM and at 10.00. were consolidating their objective East of the village.

14.30. 109th Inf.Bde. on left were reported through HEULE at 14.30.

19.10. 2nd R.Ir.Rif., having passed through 1st R.Ir.Rif. have reached objective and in touch with 109th Inf.Bde. Brigade on right not in line, but in touch with 15th R.Ir.Rif. in Brigade Reserve at G.27.a.60.60.

Patrol of 2nd R.Ir.Rif. under Lieut. F. ADAMS entered COURTRAI during the night.

Oct. 16th Brigade in rest ROLLEGHEM-CAPPELLE Area 16/17th Oct.

Oct. 19th Moved to LENDELEDE on 19th October, on which date orders were issued for attack on following day.

Units of Brigade moved to assembly area 29 N.W./B.17.cent. Very wet night.

Oct. 20th

02.00. 15th and 1st Bns. R.Ir.Rif. crossed the River LYS by bridges just erected at C.19.a.50.20. and formed up N.W. of HARLEBEKE - VIVE ST. ELOI Road, under intermittent shell-fire.

Oct. 20th (Contd) 06.00. Attack commenced and by 09.52 15th R.Ir.Rif. were reported nearing objective. This Battalion was later checked on line I.10.d.40.10. - I.10.b.99.01. - I.5.c.70.20. by heavy machine gun fire. Lieut-Colonel B.J.JONES, D.S.O., Commanding the Battalion, being killed. Principal opposition was from MILL at I.5.d.01.10. This MILL cleared by a Platoon of 1st Bn. R.Ir.Rif.

13.33. Situation at 13.33 :-

15th R.Ir.Rif. line about 200 yards N.W. of River GAVERBEEK.

During night 1st R.Ir.Rif. crossed GAVERBEEK.

Oct. 21st 07.30. 1st R.Ir.Rif. attacked. Progress was slow, considerable opposition being met.

Line at close of day - I.24.a.60.50. - I.24.a.99.99. - I.18.d.80.10. - L.5.central.

Heavy gas shelling and machine gun fire during night.

Oct. 22nd 09.00. 2nd R.Ir.Rif. attacked and took line J.26.a.80.20. - J.20.a.60.10. - J.20.a.10.75. - J.19.b.80.90. Left flank exposed owing to 108th Inf.Bde. on left not being in line. Enemy counter-attacked this flank at 14.55 and succeeded in pushing back our left and centre Companies. The counter-attack was determinedly made by a Prussian Assault Battalion sent up for the purpose. The situation was however completely restored. Prisoners captured during night with orders for withdrawal of his Battalion.

Oct. 23rd 1st R.Ir.Rif. sent two Companies as Advance Guard with orders to move towards L'ESCAUT at ZEMROVE.

3rd squadron, 28th Regt. de Dragoons, French Army, moved up in rear of Advance Guard, with instructions to move towards ZEMROVE.

Advance Guard found enemy holding HEIRWEG and HUISBOSCH, SCHELDHOEK and INGOYGHEM. Cavalry unable to proceed beyond J.19.central owing to long range machine gun fire.

19.00. Situation at 19.00 - 1st R.Ir.Rif. on line J.26.d.05.40. - J.26.d.80.80. - J.26.b.55.90. - J.20.d.40.50. - J.20.b.90.60. in touch with 27th Inf.Bde. on right and 108th Inf.Bde. on left. 15th R.Ir.Rif. in support and 2nd R.Ir. Rifles. inreserve. 4th Motor Machine Gun Battery and 'C' Company, 36th Bn. Machine Gun Corps, assisting in defence. French Cavalry withdrawn.

The Brigade were relieved during the night by the 109th Inf.Bde. and withdrew into Divisional Reserve in Area HULSTE - OYGHEM - DESSELGHEM.

Oct. 25th The Brigade moved South to Xth Corps Area, staging at LENDELEDE and arriving at BELLEGHEM 28th October, 1918.

At the close of operations under review, congratulatory messages were received, one from MARECHAL FOCH and the other from G.O.C., IInd Corps.

The operations were of a trying and exhausting nature. Opposition chiefly met was machine gun fire, against which our Infantry showed courage and fighting qualities of a high order.

The constant movement, entailing 'digging in' in many cases, was a test of endurance of a severe nature, and all ranks 'carried on' in a manner indicative of a high morale and confidence in our superiority over the enemy.

C Becher
Lieut-Colonel,

8.11.1918. Commanding 107th Infantry Brigade.

Army Form C. 2118.

Instructions regarding War Diaries and Intelligence Summaries are contained in F. S. Regs., Part II. and the Staff Manual respectively. Title pages will be prepared in manuscript.

WAR DIARY
or
INTELLIGENCE SUMMARY.
(Erase heading not required.)

NOVEMBER, 1918. 107TH INFANTRY BRIGADE HQRS.

Place	Date	Hour	Summary of Events and Information	Remarks and references to Appendices
	1918 Nov.			
BELLEGHEM.	1st		107th Infantry Brigade Group, including 36th Bn. M.G.Corps. and No.2 Coy., 36th Div. Train, moved from BELLEGHEM Area to Area RECKEM (R.29), CROISE (R.36), DRONKARD (R.35.) Sheet 28. Brigade Headquarters at RECKEM.	App. I
			Capt. J.H.COOLING, Staff Captain, admitted to Hospital. Duties of Staff Captain taken over by Captain A. WALLACE, 2nd Bn. Royal Irish Rifles.	
RECKEM.	2nd		Uneventful day.	
	3rd		107th Infantry Brigade Group, including 36th Bn. M.G.Corps and 121st Fd. Coy., R.E., moved to Western Area of MOUSCRON.	App. II
MOUSCRON.	4th		Brigade Boxing Competition held in the Theatre, Tourcoing Street, MOUSCRON. Brig-Gen. H.J.BROCK, C.M.G., D.S.O., proceeded to Officers' Rest ~~xxxxx~~ Hostel, HARDELOT PLAGE. Lieut-Colonel C.M.L.BECHER, D.S.O., assumed temporary Command of the Brigade.	
	5th		Battalions Training.	
	6th		Very wet day. Sports Meeting held at Brigade Headquarters. 107th L.M.Battery moved to HEESTEERT for duty with 30th Division.	
	7th		Uneventful. Brigade Sports postponed owing to inclement weather.	
	8th		Brigade Sports held under favourable conditions. 107th L.M.Battery rejoined from 30th Division and billetted in MOUSCRON.	
	9th		Battalions Training.	
	10th		-do-	
	11th		Receipt of official notification that Hostilities would cease at 11.00 hours. Brig-Gen. H.J.BROCK, C.M.G., D.S.O., rejoined from Officers' Rest Hostel.	
	12th		Brigade Parade. Rehearsal for inspection by Divisional Commander.	
	13th		Brigade inspected, and Medal Ribbons presented by the Divisional Commander.	

(A9175) Wt W2358/P360 500,000 12/17 D. D. & L. Sch 52a. Forms/C2118/15

Army Form C. 2118.

WAR DIARY
or
INTELLIGENCE SUMMARY.

(Erase heading not required.)

Instructions regarding War Diaries and Intelligence Summaries are contained in F. S. Regs., Part II. and the Staff Manual respectively. Title pages will be prepared in manuscript.

NOVEMBER, 1918. 107TH INFANTRY BRIGADE HQRS.

Place	Date	Hour	Summary of Events and Information	Remarks and references to Appendices
	1918 Nov.			
MOUSCRON.	14th		Brigade Route March carried out.	APP. III
	15th		Battalions Training.	
	16th		-do-	
	17th		-do-	
	18th		-do-	
	19th		-do-	
	20th		Brigade practice concentration march carried out.	APP. IV
			Brig-Gen. H.J.BROCK, C.M.G., D.S.O., admitted to Hospital. Lieut-Colonel C.M.L.BECHER, D.S.O., 2nd Bn. Royal Irish Rifles, assumed command of the Brigade.	
	21st		B attalions Training.	
	22nd		Brigade Advanced Guard Scheme carried out.	APP. V
	23rd		Battalions Training.	
	24th		-do-	
	25th		-do-	
	26th		Repetition of "Advanced Guard Scheme" carried out on 22nd.	APP. VI
	27th		Battalions Training.	
	28th		-do-	
	29th		-do-	
	30th		Brigade Advanced Guard Scheme carried out.	APP. VII

C.Becher.
Lieut-Colonel,
Commanding 107th Infantry Brigade.

1

Instructions regarding War Diaries and Intelligence Summaries are contained in F. S. Regs., Part II, and the Staff Manual respectively. Title pages will be prepared in manuscript.

WAR DIARY
or
~~INTELLIGENCE SUMMARY.~~
(Erase heading not required.)

Army Form C. 2118.

December 1918 — H.Q. 107th Infantry Brigade

VR 38

Place	Date	Hour	Summary of Events and Information	Remarks and references to Appendices
MOUSCRON	1/12/18	-	Battalions Training. Capt H.D.C. Craig, Brigade Major, proceeded on leave to United Kingdom. Lieut R.D. Williams, No 1 15 R. Ir Rif assumed duties of Brigade Major.	
"	2/12/18	-	Practice Ceremonial Parade by all Units of the Brigade.	
"	3/12/18	-	Route marches carried out under Battalion arrangements.	
"	4/12/18	-	Battalions Training.	
"	5/12/18	-	-do- -do-	
"	6/12/18	-	Brigade participated in Divisional Ceremonial Parade	App I
"	7/12/18	-	Battalions Training Brigade H.Q. moved from Tourcoing Street to No 1. Grande Place.	
"	8/12/18	-	Church Parades 15th R. Irish Rifles moved from RISQUONS TOUT to MOUSCRON, to billets vacated by Brigade H.Q. The award of the French Croix de Guerre to the following of Brigade H.Q., was announced:- T/Capt. A Wallace R. Ir Rif — a l'Ordre Corps (Golden Star) 9/14927 Sergt J Hooks, R. Ir. Rif — a l'Ordre Regt (Bronze Star) 57840 " W.J. Quinn, R.E. — a l'Ordre Brigade (Bronze Star)	

(A9475) Wt W2358/P360 600,000 12/17 D. D. & L. Sch. 52a. Forms/C2118/15.

(2)

WAR DIARY

or

~~INTELLIGENCE SUMMARY~~.

(Erase heading not required.)

Army Form C. 2118.

Instructions regarding War Diaries and Intelligence Summaries are contained in F. S. Regs., Part II, and the Staff Manual respectively. Title pages will be prepared in manuscript.

December 1918 — HQ 107th Infantry Brigade

Place	Date	Hour	Summary of Events and Information	Remarks and references to Appendices
MOUSCRON.	9/12/18	-	Battalions Training. Brigade Sports Meeting held at Bde. H.Q.	
"	10/12/18	-	-do- -do-	
"	11/12/18	-	-do- -do-	
"	12/12/18	-	Inspection by Corps Commander postponed owing to inclement weather. Capt. C.C. Titchmarsh arrived and assumed duties of Staff. Captain.	
"	13/12/18	-	Route marches carried out by all Units of the Brigade under their own arrangements.	
"	14/12/18	-	Battalions Training.	
"	15/12/18	-	Church Parades.	
"	16/12/18	-	Brigade took part in Divisional Parade for inspection by Corps Commander.	App II.
"	17/12/18	-	Battalions Training. Lt Col (T/Brig. Gen) P. Leveson Gower, CMG - DSO, Notts & Derby Regt. arrived and took over command of the Brigade from Lt. Col CMJ Becher DSO, 2nd Bn R. Ir. Rif., vice Lt Col (T/Brig. Genl) H J Brock, CMG, DSO, RA, evacuated to England.	

(A9475) Wt W2358/P360 600,000 12/17 D. D. & L. Sch. 52a. Forms/C2118/15.

(3)

Army Form C. 2118.

WAR DIARY
or
INTELLIGENCE ~~SUMMARY~~.
(Erase heading not required.)

Instructions regarding War Diaries and Intelligence Summaries are contained in F. S. Regs., Part II, and the Staff Manual respectively. Title pages will be prepared in manuscript. December 1918

HQ 107 Infantry Brigade

Place	Date	Hour	Summary of Events and Information	Remarks and references to Appendices
MOUSCRON	18/12/18	-	Battalions Training.	
"	19/12/18	-	-do- -do- Capt HDC Craig, Bde major, rejoined from leave.	
"	20/12/18	-	Battalions Training. Final of the Brigade Football Competition. 15 R. Ir. Rif 2 goals v 2 R. Ir. Rif Nil	
"	21/12/18	-	Battalions Training. Brigade Boxing Competition held	App. III
"	22/12/18	-	Church Parades.	
"	23/12/18	-	Battalions Training. 2nd Lieut E.C. Happold, R.E. arrived and assumed duties of Brigade Signal Officer vice Lt H Ormandy MC RE	
"	24/12/18	.	Battalions Training	
"	25/12/18	.	Church Parades. Holiday.	
"	26/12/18	.	Holiday	
"	27/12/18	.	Battalions Training.	
"	28/12/18	.	-do- -do-	
"	29/12/18	.	Church Parades.	
"	30/12/18	.	Battalions Training	

(A9475) Wt W2358/P360 600,000 12/17 D. D. & L. Sch. 52a. Forms/C2118/15.

(4)

Instructions regarding War Diaries and Intelligence Summaries are contained in F. S. Regs., Part II, and the Staff Manual respectively. Title pages will be prepared in manuscript.

WAR DIARY
or
~~INTELLIGENCE SUMMARY~~
(Erase heading not required.)

Army Form C. 2118.

December 1918 — HQ 107th Infantry Brigade

Place	Date	Hour	Summary of Events and Information	Remarks and references to Appendices
MOUSCRON	31/12/18	-	Battalions Training	
			<u>General</u> A feature of the work of the Brigade during the month under review has been the success of the Education scheme throughout the Brigade and the Units affiliated to it for this purpose. Although the subject is voluntary the men took it up with whole-hearted enthusiasm; officers and NCO's coming forward willingly to give their services as teachers.	
			Very marked progress was made in each of the very large range of subjects taken up; this was especially noticed in those who formerly could neither read nor write.	App. IV
			The various recreational athletic competitions organised have been somewhat frought by persistent inclement weather.	
			R. Gwesson Gower Brig! General Commanding 107th Infantry Brigade	

(A9175) Wt W2353/P360 600,000 12/17 D. D. & L. Sch 52a. Forms/C2118/15

21

Army Form C. 2118.

WAR DIARY

Instructions regarding War Diaries and Intelligence Summaries are contained in F. S. Regs., Part II, and the Staff Manual respectively. Title pages will be prepared in manuscript. Headquarters 107th Inf Brigade (*Erase heading not required.*) January 1919.

VR 39

Place	Date	Hour	Summary of Events and Information	Remarks and references to Appendices
MOUSCRON.	1/1/19		Units Education, Physical Training Inspections and Games.	
"	2/1/19.		-do-	
"	3/1/19.		-do-	
"	4/1/19.		-do-	
"	5/1/19.		Church Parades.	
"	6/1/19.		Units Training Rugby Match 107 Bde v 109 Bde. Result 109Bde 6 pts, 107 Bde 3 pts.	
"	7/1/19.		-do-	
"	8/1/19.		-do-	
"	9/1/19.		-do-	
"	10/1/19.		Route Marches carried out under Unit arrangements.	
"	11/1/19.		Units. Training. 9th R.Insk.Fus. beat 1st R.I.R. in Tug-of-War Competition.	
"	12/1/19.		Church Parades.	
"	13/1/19.		Units. Education, P.T.,Inspections , Games.	
"	14/1/19.		-do-	
"	15/1/19.		-do- Rugby Match 36th Div Team v Australians. Result, Div Team 13 pts Australians 3 pts.	

(A9175) Wt W2358/P360 600,000 12/17 D. D. & L. Sch 52a. Forms/C2118/15

Army Form C. 2118.

WAR DIARY
or
~~INTELLIGENCE SUMMARY~~

Instructions regarding War Diaries and Intelligence Summaries are contained in F. S. Regs., Part II. and the Staff Manual respectively. Title pages will be prepared in manuscript.

Headquarters 107th Inf Bde. (*Erase heading not required.*) January 1919.

Place	Date	Hour	Summary of Events and Information	Remarks and references to Appendices
MOUSCRON	16/1/19.		Units. Education, P.T. Inspections, Games. Final Bde Cross Country Competition. Result:-	App I
			First, 15th R.I.Rifles.-Second, 1st Bn.R.I.Rifles - Third, 107th Inf Bde H.Q and L.M.Battery.	
			Fourth, 2nd Bn. R.I.Rifles.	
"	17/1/19.		Units	
"	18/1/19.		-do- Final Div. Cross Country Competition. 15th R.I.Rif (Bde rep. team) were Second.	
"	19/1/19.		Church Parades.	
"	20/1/19.		Units Training. Basket Ball Demonstration by two teams United States Army.	
"	21/1/19.		Units Education and Training.	
"	22/1/19.		-do-	
"	23/1/19.		-do-	
"	24/1/19.		-do-	
"	25/1/19.		-do-	
"	26/1/19.		Church Parades.	
"	27/1/19.		Units Education and P.T.	
"	28/1/19.		-do- Capt.C.C.TITCHMARSH, Staff Captain proceeded for Temporary duty in	
			Q.M.Gs office G.H.Q.	

Army Form C. 2118.

WAR DIARY
or
INTELLIGENCE SUMMARY.
(Erase heading not required.)

Instructions regarding War Diaries and Intelligence Summaries are contained in F. S. Regs., Part II, and the Staff Manual respectively. Title pages will be prepared in manuscript. Headquarters 107th Inf. Brigade

January 1919.

Place	Date	Hour	Summary of Events and Information	Remarks and references to Appendices
MOUSCRON.	29/1/19.		Units Training.	
"	30/1/19.		-do-	
"	31/1/19.		-do- H.R.H. The Prince of Wales staying a few days at Divl. H.Q., visited 1st and 15th R.I.Rifles. He mixed freely with the men: his visit being much appreciated by all ranks.	
			GENERAL	
			Education Classes have been continued satisfactorily during the month. A return is attached showing in detail the classes held and numbers attending. The 'training' programme prescribed for one hours P.T. and inspection a day for all ranks from 9 till 10 am.	App II
			Voluntary Education classes from 10 - 12.30.am. Those who did not attend voluntary education, specialized in branches of Military Training e.g. Class for Young N.C.Os, Lewis Gunners, Signallers, etc. and one hour compulsory 'Education'; taking the form of an interesting article on book such as "The Primer of English Citizenship". being read to the men	
			Severe frost and snow in the last fortnight of the month greatly interfered with out-door games.	

R. Withycombe [signature] Brig-General,
Commanding 107th Infantry Brigade.

(A9475) Wt W2358/P360 600,000 12/17 D. D. & L. Sch 52a. Forms/C2118/15

Army Form C. 2118.

WAR DIARY

or

~~INTELLIGENCE SUMMARY~~

Instructions regarding War Diaries and Intelligence Summaries are contained in F. S. Regs., Part II. and the Staff Manual respectively. Title pages will be prepared in manuscript.

Headquarters 107th Infantry Brigade. (Erase heading not required.) February 1919.

Vol 40

Place	Date	Hour	Summary of Events and Information	Remarks and references to Appendices
MOUSCRON.	1-2-19.		Units Education, Physical Training, Inspections and Games. H.R.H. The Prince of Wales visited 2nd Bn. Royal Irish Rifles. Severe frost and heavy snowfall.	
	2-2-19.		Church Parades.	
	3-2-19.		Units Education, Physical Training, Inspections and Games.	
	4-2-19.		Inspection of 1st Bn. Royal Irish Rifles by Brigadier-General Commanding.	
	5-2-19.		Units Education, Physical Training, Inspections and Games.	
	6-2-19.		Inspection of 15th Bn. Royal Irish Rifles by Brigadier-General Commanding.	
	7-2-19.		Units Education and Physical Training. Severe frost interferes with carrying on of outdoor games.	
	8-2-19.		-do-	
	9-2-19.		Church Parades.	
	10-2-19.		Units Education and Physical Training.	
	11-2-19.		Brig-General P. Leveson-Gower. C.M.G., D.S.O., departed on leave to U.K. Lt. Col. J.P. Hunt. D.S.O., D.C.M., taking over command of Brigade.	
	12-2-19.		Units Education, Physical Training and Games. Frost continues to interfere with outdoor games.	
	13-2-19.		-do-	
	14-2-19.		-do- Regt. Dancing classes instituted as part of P.T. very successful.	
	15-2-19.		-do-	
	16-2-19.		Instructions received re formation of Army of Occupation. 107th Infantry Brigade being selected as Headquarters to administer cadre groups of Division. 12th R.I.Rifles, 108th Brigade being made up from 107th Infantry Brigade to join 2nd Division Army of Occupation. RHINE.	
	17-2-19.		Units Education, Physical Training and Games.	
	18-2-19.		Units Bathing. M. ST. IVES who has been Brigade Interpreter for two years, demobilized.	
	19-2-19.		Units Education, Physical Training and Games.	
	20-2-19.		-do-	
	21-2-19.		Lt. Col. C.M.L. Becher. D.S.O., returns from leave and takes over command of the Brigade.	

D. D. & L., London, E.C.
(10540) Wt W5300/P713 750,000 3/18 E 2688 Forms/C2118/15.

Army Form C. 2118.

WAR DIARY
or
~~INTELLIGENCE SUMMARY~~.
(Erase heading not required.)

Instructions regarding War Diaries and Intelligence Summaries are contained in F. S. Regs., Part II. and the Staff Manual respectively. Title pages will be prepared in manuscript.

Place	Date	Hour	Summary of Events and Information	Remarks and references to Appendices
MOUSCRON.	22-2-19.		Personnel (130 and 150 O.R's respectively) of 1st and 2nd Bns. Royal Irish Rifles for Army of Occupation, transferred to 12th Bn. Royal Irish Rifles.	
	23-2-19.		Personnel (100 O.R's) of 15th Bn. Royal Irish Rifles for Army of Occupation transferred to 12th Bn. Royal Irish Rifles.	
	24-2-19.		Units very weak numerically. No Parades.	
	25-2-19.		-do-	
	26-2-19.		-do-	
	27-2-19.		Brig-General P. Leveson-Gower. C.M.G., D.S.O., returns from leave and takes over Command of the Brigade.	
	28-2-19.		No Parades. - Battalions almost reduced to Cadre 'A' strength. A few still to be demobilized, a few for Army of Occupation retained to look after horses and to provide guards (which are gradually being disposed of)	

P. Leveson Gower

Brig-General,
Commanding 107th Infantry Brigade.

D. D. & L., London, E.C.
(10340) Wt W5300/P713 750,000 3/18 E 2688 Forms/C2118/10.

Army Form C. 2118.

WAR DIARY
or
~~INTELLIGENCE SUMMARY.~~

Instructions regarding War Diaries and Intelligence Summaries are contained in F. S. Regs., Part II. and the Staff Manual respectively. Title pages will be prepared in manuscript.

Headquarters 107th Infantry Brigade (Erase heading not required.) March 1919.

Place	Date	Hour	Summary of Events and Information	Remarks and references to Appendices
Mouscron.	1/3/1919		Nothing to report.	
	2/3/1919		-do-	
	3/3/1919		-do-	
	4/3/1919		-do-	
	5/3/1919		-do-	
	6/3/1919		Capt. H.D.C. CRAIG. Brigade Major proceeded on leave to PARIS.	
	7/3/1919		Nothing to report.	
	8/3/1919		-do-	
	9/3/1919		-do-	
	10/3/1919		-do-	
	11/3/1919		-do-	
	12/3/1919		Capt. H.D.C. CRAIG. Brigade Major returned from leave to PARIS.	
	13/3/1919		Nothing to report.	
	14/3/1919		-do-	
	15/3/1919		Orders received that 2nd Bn. Royal Irish Rifles were to proceed as Cadre to U.K.	
	16/3/1919		Nothing to report.	
	17/3/1919		2nd Bn. Royal Irish Rifles entrained for DUNKERQUE. en route to United Kingdom.	

D. D. & L., London, E.C.
(10340) Wt W5300/P713 750,000 3/18 E 2688 Forms/C2118/16.

9/8/41

Army Form C. 2118.

Instructions regarding War Diaries and Intelligence Summaries are contained in F. S. Regs., Part II. and the Staff Manual respectively. Title pages will be prepared in manuscript.

WAR DIARY

or

INTELLIGENCE SUMMARY

(Erase heading not required.)

Headquarters 107th Infantry Brigade. March 1919.

Place	Date	Hour	Summary of Events and Information	Remarks and references to Appendices
Mouscron.	18/3/1919.		Nothing to report.	
	19/3/1919.		-do-	
	20/3/1919.		Capt. W. SOMERS. M.C., Brigade Intelligence Officer proceeded on Leave to United Kingdom.	
	21/3/1919.		Nothing to report.	
	22/3/1919.		-do-	
	23/3/1919.		-do-	
	24/3/1919.		107th Infantry Brigade Office moved to No. 51 Rue des BERSEAUX., MOUSCRON and amalgamated with Headquarters 36th Division.	
	25/3/1919.		Nothing to report.	
	26/3/1919.		-do-	
	27/3/1919.		Capt. H.D.C. CRAIG. proceeded on Leave to United Kingdom.	
	28/3/1919.		Nothing to report.	
	29/3/1919.		-do-	
	30/3/1919.		-do-	
	31/3/1919.		-do-	

H.D.C. Craig Capt.
Brigade Major
for B.G.C.
107 I.B.

D. D. & L., London, E.C.
(10340) Wt W5300/P713 750,000 3/18 E 2688 Forms/C2118/16.

www.ingramcontent.com/pod-product-compliance
Lightning Source LLC
Chambersburg PA
CBHW080920230426
43668CB00014B/2162
9781474517744